THE STANLEY CUP

A HUNDRED YEARS OF HOCKEY AT ITS BEST

D1104590

D'ARCY JENISH

The Stanley Cup

The Stanley Cup

A Hundred Years of Hockey at Its Best

D'Arcy Jenish

M&S

CANADIAN CATALOGUING IN PUBLICATION DATA

Jenish, D'Arcy, 1952–
The Stanley Cup: a hundred years of hockey at its best

Includes index.
ISBN 0-7710-4406-2

1. Stanley Cup (Hockey) – History. I. Title.

GV847.7.J36 1992   796.962´648   C92-094378-0

The publishers acknowledge the support of the Canada Council and
the Ontario Arts Council for their publishing program.

Typesetting by M&S, Toronto
Printed and bound in Canada.
The paper used in this book is acid-free.

McClelland & Stewart Inc.
The Canadian Publishers
481 University Avenue
Toronto, Ontario
M5G 2E9

To Hélène, Jesse, and Isabel.
Your support made this possible.

Contents

1

THIS CUP IS OURS!

1893-1903

Professional hockey's ultimate spectacle occurs in late May every year when a single player, surrounded by jubilant teammates, stands at centre-ice in a packed and tumultuous arena, and hoists the Stanley Cup toward the heavens. This ritual, deeply engrained in the Canadian psyche, has become one of the most concise, compelling, and powerful images of victory in all of sport. Baseball has its mayhem on the pitcher's mound after the final out of the World Series. Football has its masked and armoured behemoths hooting and backslapping as they leave the field after the Super Bowl. The International Olympics Committee puts its champions on staid victory podiums. But for Canadians, none of these compares with the sight of a Mario Lemieux or a Wayne Gretzky, a Denis Potvin or a Guy Lafleur, a Bobby Clarke or a Bobby Orr holding the Stanley Cup aloft, its silver flanks glittering under the television lights while thunderous applause cascades down from all directions.

This gesture is ancient in origin and primitive in nature. Every player who holds the Cup above his head is responding to the same impulse that has seized the conquering warrior from time immemorial. It is the urge to stand on the hilltop or the rooftop to trumpet victory and show tangible proof of triumph. Yet this gesture is the perfect image for the television age, an era in which visual information has more power than the written or spoken word, and quick and simple acts, concise and dramatic pictures, capture events that are protracted, convoluted, complex, and sometimes tedious.

The simple but heartfelt act of hoisting the Stanley Cup aloft marks the end of a long season, a campaign that begins when training camps open in September, before the first frost or the first hint of colour in the leaves; a season that includes hundreds of games and thousands of goals; a season that lasts until the snow is long gone and summer is just around the corner. The Stanley Cup aloft is an image that blends the ancient and the modern, that represents joy and victory, that encapsules the hopes and aspirations of young players everywhere. It is an image that keeps the pros motivated and the fans interested. It has transformed a mere trophy, once worshipped for a night and forgotten the following morning, into a hallowed object, a gleaming icon.

The Stanley Cup, the object of all this adulation, stands a stately three feet tall and weighs a hefty thirty-two pounds. Today, at the age of 100, it is one of the oldest surviving sports trophies in the world, and is by far the oldest team trophy in North America. It has been around longer than the World Series or the Grey Cup and is old enough to be the grandaddy of the Super Bowl. Engraved on its silver flanks are the names of nearly 875 players, coaches and hockey executives. Of all the thousands, perhaps millions, of people who have ever played or coached the game, these are the fortunate few who have managed to reach hockey's summit, to experience the rapture of winning the Stanley Cup.

A century ago, the Stanley Cup was a simple silver bowl, a squat little trophy that stood seven-and-a-half inches high and measured eleven-and-a-half inches across, and possessed all the grace and stature of a soup tureen. It was created by a British silversmith but conceived by Frederick Arthur Stanley, one of those phantoms of Canadian public life who have perpetually hovered over the national stage. Stanley was a governor general of the post-Confederation era, a man with theoretically broad powers but little practical influence.

The son of a British prime minister, and a former parliamentarian himself, Stanley was a middle-aged aristocrat with an undistinguished record of public service in his native England when he was dispatched to Canada in 1888. Like most of his predecessors, he reached our shores by ship and our capital by rail, and five years later he returned to England by the same modes of transportation, unlamented and barely noticed, having caused scarcely a ripple in the public life of Canada, or a dent in our history.

Lord Stanley's assignment had been to preside as head of state over a geopolitical oddity stranded somewhere between colony and nation. A man of tact and good judgement, he avoided meddling in the political affairs of the young dominion except when it was absolutely unavoidable. In June 1891, he was called upon to appoint a successor to the venerable Sir John A. Macdonald, Canada's first prime minister, who had died while in office. Lord Stanley selected Sir John Abbott, who reluctantly accepted, only to become ill a year later. Abbott resigned, which forced the reluctant governor general to appoint yet another prime minister, this time the Nova Scotian Sir John Thompson.

The quiet British aristocrat would have slipped into obscurity, would have become just another nondescript name among the long list of men who have served as governor general, were it not for the fact that during his stay in Canada he developed a fondness for hockey, the winter game played by bundled and padded dervishes who swooped and swirled on the frozen ponds and sloughs and rivers of a snowbound country.

Every winter, Lord Stanley had his staff build an outdoor rink on the grounds of Rideau Hall, the governor general's residence in Ottawa, and he sponsored a team known as the Rideau Rebels, who wore bright red jerseys. Stanley's sons, Algernon and Arthur, were both members of the team, which primarily played exhibition games against other Ottawa clubs. But in February 1890 the Rebels travelled to Toronto for a series of three matches, and in late March that year they played a game against a team composed of senators and members of Parliament.

As his interest in the game grew, the governor general concluded that what hockey needed, if it were to grow and develop, was an annual champion. So on March 18, 1892, he asked Lord Kilcoursie, one of his aides and a member of the Rebels, to deliver a personal message during a banquet in honour of Ottawa's top hockey clubs. "I have for some time been thinking," the governor general wrote, "that it would be a good thing if there were a challenge cup, which would be held from year to year by the leading hockey club in Canada. There does not appear to be any outward sign of the championship at present, and considering the interest that hockey matches now elicit, I am willing to give a cup that shall be held annually by the winning club."

His offer accepted, Lord Stanley spent $48.67 of his own money to purchase a silver trophy, which he named the Dominion Hockey Challenge Cup. It was a gesture that saved the British aristocrat's name from obscurity, because from the beginning the trophy was known, not by its formal name, but simply as the Stanley Cup.

The Cup was awarded for the first time in the fall of 1893 to the Montreal Amateur Athletic Association (AAA) without any kind of formal tournament or playoff, because the Montrealers had finished first the previous winter in the Amateur Hockey Association of Canada, which was regarded as the country's premier league at the time. For their efforts, members of the team also received gold rings from the association.

From 1893 onward, however, the little silver cup was eagerly and zealously pursued by men who wore handlebar moustaches and parted their hair down the middle, who played for teams called the Shamrocks and the Thistles, the Bulldogs and the Silver Seven, the Victorias and the Union Jacks.

The first Stanley Cup match, the original battle for hockey supremacy, took place in Montreal on March 22, 1894, between the AAAs and the Ottawa Generals. It happened to be Holy Thursday, and that morning's Ottawa *Citizen* advised its readers that they could catch the 4:15 p.m. train and still get to Montreal in plenty of time for the game. Lord Stanley was not in attendance, however. He had returned to England, where he would reside until his death in 1908.

A crowd of five thousand, reckoned by many local observers to be the largest turnout ever for a hockey game, lined the edges of the Victoria Rink to cheer the local AAAs and to heckle the visiting Generals. It was by all accounts a simple but spirited affair. "Never before in the history of the game was such a crowd present or such enthusiasm evident," declared the next day's Montreal *Gazette.* "Tin horns, strong lungs and a general rabble predominated." Some of the fans stood on platforms about twelve inches above ice level, others watched from balconies. The match was played on natural ice, in a handsome vaulted building decked out with banners and bunting for the occasion, and the referee, one H. Scott of Quebec City, wore street clothes and a bowler derby.

The players were smartly attired in colourful jerseys and matching stockings but they wore nothing resembling padding or protective equipment. There were neither boards nor glass around the ice, neither blue lines nor red lines on the ice, and there was nothing like today's nets. Just two sets of upright poles and two determined teams, who played with speed and spirit.

The seven-member Ottawa squad opened the scoring ten minutes into the first half of the game but the Montreal team, composed of seven players plus a spare, tied it before the first half was over. From then on, it was all downhill for Ottawa, according to the accounts provided by the journalists in attendance. The *Gazette* wrote that "The Montreal defence seemed impregnable while the forwards rushed that puck around in a way that made the Ottawa men nervous."

When it was over, the Montrealers had prevailed by a 3–1 margin. Ottawa's Weldy Young had fainted from exhaustion, and Montreal's Billy Barlow had become a hero. He had scored twice for the AAAs, and the fans charged onto the ice and hoisted him to their shoulders to celebrate the first Stanley Cup victory the world had ever seen. Later, the athletic association honoured the players by purchasing gold watches for them at a total cost of $190.

Hockey had a champion, but precious little else. In those days, the sport was as raw and undeveloped as the land itself. A few thousand young men were playing the game in Quebec City, Montreal and Ottawa, in Kingston, Toronto and Winnipeg, and in scores of smaller, isolated communities in between. There were dozens of teams and a few leagues. But no one had a clear idea how the hockey champion of the dominion was to be determined each year. Lord Stanley had contributed the last piece of the puzzle, the prize that went to the champion. The rest remained to be invented.

Stanley had set the broadest possible terms of reference, stipulating only that his trophy was "to be held from year to year by the champion hockey club of the Dominion." In the formative early years, all Stanley Cup challenges were sent to John Sweetland, an Ottawa sheriff, and Philip D. Ross, editor of the *Ottawa Evening Journal,* the two trustees appointed by Lord Stanley to safeguard the Cup. They determined who could challenge the champion of the day, and when the games would be played. Sweetland and Ross sometimes accepted several challenges during a single year and scheduled Stanley Cup games at the beginning, in the middle, or at the end of the season. Occasionally, more than one team captured the Cup in the same year. Without precedents or protocols or anything resembling agreed-upon rules to guide them, the trustees proceeded by trial and error.

There were frequent conflicts and there was occasional confusion. Yet the pursuit of the Cup quickly took hold of the country and became a national passion.

For when it came to hockey, the rough and unpolished Dominion of Canada possessed an abundance of energy, enthusiasm, ambition and enterprise. As Canada developed, so did hockey. Teams and leagues were formed as fast as new regions of the country were opened and new wealth was created. No fewer than sixteen leagues produced champions who challenged for the Stanley Cup, although most of them quickly disappeared.

Challengers came from every corner of the country, from Sydney, Nova Scotia, from Victoria, B.C., from Dawson City in the Yukon. There were fifty-seven in all between 1893 and 1927, when the National Hockey League finally established its superiority over all rival leagues, and with that became the sole owner of the Stanley Cup.

During the first decade of competition, three Montreal senior teams, the AAAs, the Shamrocks, and the Victorias, practically owned the Cup, winning it a total of eight times. These teams were sponsored by social and athletic clubs whose members were of English, Irish, or Scottish descent. The players themselves were almost all anglophone.

Between 1890 and 1900 only three French Canadians played for senior teams in Montreal, according to Quebec sports historian Michel Vigneault. He adds that it was not until 1906 that a French Canadian player, H. Menard, was a member of a Stanley Cup winning team. Menard, whose first name was never reported in the English-language press, was a goalie for the Montreal Wanderers, whose players originally were predominantly of Irish background.

Several challengers attempted to wrest the Cup from the teams of English Montreal: students from Queen's University tried in 1895 and again in 1899, the Ottawa Capitals tried in 1897, and the Halifax Crescents in 1899. But the only serious threat and successful challenge during those first ten years came from the Victoria Hockey Club of Winnipeg. Formed in 1890 by a group of leading Winnipeg businessmen and grain merchants, the Victorias completely dominated the Manitoba and Northwestern Association, which included other teams from Winnipeg, as well as Brandon, Portage La Prairie, and Kenora, or Rat Portage as it was then known.

The Winnipeg Vics, as they were called, played for the trophy on eight occasions, winning twice, successfully defending their title once, and losing five times. By the time of the final Montreal-Winnipeg showdown in January 1903, a sharp but gentlemanly rivalry existed between the two cities, and the top players were well known to fans in both cities. Furthermore, the Winnipeggers always received loud, vocal support from a large contingent of Montreal fans when they were playing in the East. In those days, all three Montreal senior teams had their own loyal fans, and many of them would cheer for the westerners rather than a crosstown rival.

The Vics introduced themselves to the hockey establishment of Eastern Canada in the winter of 1895 by playing a series of exhibition games against senior teams in Toronto, Ottawa, Montreal, and Quebec. The westerners, who wore bright scarlet uniforms with gold trim and a small gold silhouette of a loping buffalo on their chests, outscored their eastern opponents by a total of 33 to 12.

Inspired by their triumphant eastern tour, the Winnipeg Vics issued their first challenge for the Stanley Cup in early 1896. Trustees Ross and Sweetland quickly scheduled a game for February 14 in Montreal against the defending champion Montreal Victorias. For the citizens of Winnipeg, all thirty-five thousand of them, this was a battle between the hinterland and the metropolis, between a David and a Goliath. "Out from the West go seven of the Prairie capital's most stalwart sons," declared the *Manitoba Free Press* on the eve of the match, "to do battle with the representatives of the three hundred thousand people who make up the population of Canada's greatest city."

Every seat in Montreal's Victoria Rink was occupied and the standing-room sections were jammed when the local Victorias skated on to the ice at 8:50 p.m. February 14. The Montrealers normally wore maroon uniforms with a large white V on the front of their sweaters, but they had switched to solid white tops to avoid confusion with their opponents. Five minutes after the home team appeared, the Winnipeg Vics took to the ice in their brilliant scarlet jerseys and received a hearty round of applause.

Back in Winnipeg, hundreds of hockey fans had gathered at three of the city's most prominent hotels, the Manitoba, the Queen's, and the Clarendon. They were kept informed of developments in the game through telegraph reports sent over the Canadian Pacific Railway wires from Montreal. Other fans stayed home and relied on the latest technological wonder, the telephone, to keep them abreast of the plays. The *Free Press* later reported that its single telephone "was never idle, nor the bell weary of ringing in response to the requests of anxious inquirers from the suburbs."

What the Montreal fans witnessed, according to one reporter in attendance, was "a magnificent, fast game." Winnipeg opened the scoring ten minutes into the match after defenceman Magnus Flett had lofted the puck from his own end of the rink back to the Montreal end, the standard play for defencemen in those days. Montreal captain and point man Mike Grant, one of the leading players at the time, then fiddled with the puck rather than lofting it back to the Winnipeg end. "The visitors' forwards got over the ice like ghosts and before Grant had time to recollect himself the puck was by him," the *Gazette* reported. "Dan Bain got the puck and a second later J. C. Armytage had scored." The Winnipeggers dominated the remainder of the half and led 2–0 after thirty minutes of play.

The second half was a completely different game. The Montreal Victorias overpowered the visitors but were stopped cold by George Merritt, the tall, slender Winnipeg goaltender who wore a huge moustache and white cricket pads to protect his legs. He was reportedly the first goaltender to wear such padding, and the idea immediately caught on with other goalies. "Merritt was a phenom," the *Gazette* declared. "There were 20 times in this half when under ordinary circumstances the Victorias would have scored. It was all due to the great work of Merritt." Winnipeg's two goals were enough to win the game and the Stanley Cup. The Vics had become the first team from Western Canada, and the first from outside Montreal, to win the Cup.

After the game, the two teams and a few invited guests enjoyed a cordial dinner together. The few Winnipeggers who had accompanied the team east had their own reasons for celebrating. They reportedly won a total of $2,000 betting on their Vics. Back at the three Winnipeg hotels, the first telegraph reports of the outcome arrived shortly before 10:00 p.m. local time. "Then cheer after cheer went up from the crowd," the *Free Press* reported. "Everybody wanted to shake hands with everybody else and, for several minutes, old enmities were forgotten in the magnificent victory."

In Montreal, there was dismay and disbelief. "That the victory of the visitors was a surprise to everybody but themselves goes without saying," the next day's *Gazette* concluded. Eager to recover the Cup, the Montreal Victorias asked for a rematch the following December. On Christmas morning 1896, a party of nine players and six supporters left Montreal's Windsor Station aboard a CPR passenger train destined for the Manitoba capital. Among those accompanying the team was a businessman named A. Shearer, the first manufacturer of hockey sticks in Canada, and club secretary Paul deSterneck, who later told the *Free Press* that he had come along "to look after the Stanley Cup on the return journey."

The Montrealers arrived in Winnipeg on the evening of December 27, and received a warm welcome at the train station from a large crowd of local residents, as well as from officers of the Victoria Hockey Club. "Carriages in waiting conveyed the party to the Manitoba Hotel," reported the next day's *Free Press.* "Before the rigs left the depot, the crowd gave vent to their good feelings by cheering."

The Montreal team held two practices on December 29, the day before the big game, and several hundred Winnipeggers attended both sessions. Captain Mike Grant refused to reveal the names of his starting seven before game time, but told the *Free Press*: "Our men are as fit as possible. We are prepared for the effort of our lives." Winnipeg captain Jack Armytage added: "We have done all in our power to put ourselves in proper shape to successfully defend the Stanley Cup."

With both sides ready, and excitement building in Winnipeg, scalpers were getting twelve dollars for a reserved seat in the city's McIntyre Rink. The 250 tickets for reserved seats had gone on sale December 24 at two dollars apiece and were all purchased in half an hour, the *Gazette* reported. On the day of the game, one Winnipegger exchanged two-and-a-half tons of coal for a ticket, and a Calgarian who had travelled to the Manitoba capital just to see the game paid fifteen dollars for a reserved seat. By 5:30 p.m., fans hoping for standing-room tickets were lined up outside, even though the temperature was minus four Fahrenheit. "Old and young, high and low jostled and froze for 2½ hours in order to be among the chosen few that could find standing room," observed a *Free Press* reporter.

For those without tickets, all was not lost. The management of the Manitoba Hotel had made arrangements to have a telegraph report of the game read in its spacious rotunda. "A special wire will be run from the rink to the hotel and every move of the puck will be announced," the *Free Press* told its readers on game day. The accounts of the game were also sent to Montreal and to communities in between where there were telegraph offices. As well, that night's operas at the Grand and the Bijou theatres were interrupted periodically for progress reports on the game.

Like the original showdown between the two teams, the rematch was cleanly played and very fast. The Winnipeg Vics quickly ran up a 3–0 lead, at which point the Montrealers lodged a protest against the work of the goal judge behind the Winnipeg net, and he was promptly replaced. The Montreal team scored the next two goals, but the Winnipeggers added another to lead 4–2 at half time.

In the second half, the Montrealers scored three straight goals to go ahead 5–4. When the game was interrupted because of a broken goalpost, this time the Winnipeg Vics complained about the goal judge behind the Montreal net, and he was replaced. Late in the game the home team tied the score. "The scene that followed was indescribable," declared a *Free Press* correspondent. "The crowd was beside itself with joy, and hats, handkerchiefs and muffs were frantically waved. Then did the play become fast and furious. The crowd kept time to every movement of the puck by the most vociferous yells."

Finally, Montreal forward Graham Drinkwater made a dashing rush up the ice and passed to teammate Ernie McLea, who fired the puck by Merritt for the winning goal. In a post-game interview Montreal captain Mike Grant told the press: "We never had a harder game. We had to work for everything we got." Over in the Winnipeg dressing room, forward C. J. "Toat" Campbell revealed that he had suffered a broken rib in the first half but ignored the advice of the team doctor and played the remainder of the game. At 11:00 p.m. both teams, along with forty invited guests, gathered for dinner in a private room at the Manitoba Hotel. When it was over, Hugh John Macdonald, son of Sir John A. Macdonald and a future Conservative premier of Manitoba, presented the Stanley Cup to Mike Grant.

In the wake of the rematch, the Montreal-Winnipeg rivalry subsided for a couple of years, and the Montreal Victorias easily retained possession of the Stanley Cup in 1897 and 1898. But the Cup matches of 1896, a mere two games, one played in Montreal, the other in Winnipeg, had laid the foundations for an enduring Canadian cultural phenomenon known as the hockey broadcast. During those two games, played long before there was such a thing as radio, or a voice such as Foster Hewitt's, or a phrase such as "He shoots, he scores," a few anonymous men invented the play-by-play account of a hockey game, and began creating the spare but spirited language used by television and radio broadcasters today.

These men were sportswriters and telegraph operators. From 1896 until the late 1920s, when live radio broadcasts displaced them, telegraph operators sat at rinkside or up in the press box, sometimes with a sportswriter or a couple of knowledgeable hockey fans feeding them information. Sometimes the telegraphers called the game themselves. They sat hunched over their little machines translating rushes and checks, shots and goals, and all the unpredictable action of a hockey game into morse code, which would be transcribed into English by an operator at the receiving end and then broadcast vocally or via bulletin boards to the loyal and anxious hometown fans.

In those days, long before Canadians huddled around the kitchen table listening to Foster Hewitt, hockey fans gathered in arenas, in hotel ballrooms, in theatres, and in the streets outside newspaper offices to catch the accounts provided by the telegraphers. These were the first hockey broadcasts and their existence, not to mention their cultural significance, has long been overlooked. Here was sport and technology – hockey and the telegraph – combining to link the disparate regions of a huge and underpopulated country.

The names of the early telegraphers and writers rarely appeared in print, but their play-by-play accounts of dozens of early Stanley Cup games have been preserved. The newspapers invariably ran a story about each game by one of their reporters, followed by the telegrapher's complete account. In some cases, the papers printed two telegraph accounts, one from the CPR and the other from the Great North Western Telegraph company. Here is a sample from a Stanley Cup game in mid-February 1900 between the hometown Montreal Shamrocks and the visiting Winnipeg Vics:

> Merritt has not been called upon to stop many shots. Defence working well now, most of the play around Winnipeg goal; soft ice telling on the Winnipegs. Tansey and Bain had a mixup behind the Shamrock's goal and Tansey got the worst of it. In the fall he hurt his stomach and the game was stopped. Game started again. Tansey resuming play. Half time called; weather mild. It is raining, and with an immense crowd inside the ice is getting very soft and sloppy.
>
> [Second] half started at 9:32 with a rush toward Winnipeg goal. Some end to end lifts that kept both defences on the alert. Shamrocks now on the defence almost entirely: puck not been near Winnipeg goal for five minutes. Fourth goal for Winnipeg. The tremendous cheering when Winnipeg scored showed that the Buffalos [a nickname for the Vics] have many fans here. Play now very fast and furious. Excitement all over the rink. The puck is now travelling faster than I can handle the telegraph key.

After a two-year hiatus, the Winnipeg-Montreal rivalry resumed in February 1899 when the western Victorias again challenged their eastern counterparts for the Stanley Cup. This time, the teams agreed to play a best-of-three series, rather than a single match. For the first time, the teams themselves were to receive a share of the gate, a sign of the sport's increasing prosperity, and the first hint of the professionalism to come. Under an agreement negotiated with the management of the newly opened Mount Royal Arena in Montreal, the teams would get one-third of the gross receipts from the first two games, or $633 each if the games sold out.

According to every newspaper account, the first game was one of the fastest ever played up to that time, and one of the most exciting. Winnipeg's Tony Gingras scored ten minutes into the first half, and that solitary goal stood as the game's only point until the fifty-ninth minute. "Two minutes before time was up no one would have given a cent for the chances of the home team," the *Free Press*'s correspondent wrote.

Back in Winnipeg, at the city's newly opened Auditorium, hundreds of children skated while the adults sat in the stands and packed the waiting rooms to catch the telegraph reports coming over the Canadian Pacific and Great North Western wires. Towards the end of the game, another *Free Press* reporter wrote, "Dispatches fairly rained in from the two instruments, and those standing around the machines produced their watches and began counting anxiously the minutes."

But the Montrealers were far from dead. With forty-five seconds left, Shirley Davidson darted down the ice and, ten feet from the Winnipeg net, passed to teammate Bob MacDougall, who unleashed a shot at George Merritt. The Winnipeg goalie made the initial save but was unable to clear the rebound, and MacDougall knocked it in. "Four thousand people were on their feet yelling till the walls shook," the *Gazette* reported. When play resumed, Montreal's Graham Drinkwater found an opening, dashed toward the Winnipeg goal, and scored the winning goal with just seconds left.

This breathtaking finish to the first game created enormous interest in the second match, slated for a couple of nights later. "Such an overflow of hockey enthusiasm never swept the city as is the case at the present time," the *Gazette* observed. "Everybody seems to have got the fever." When the two sides lined up to start the second game, all four thousand seats were filled, another three thousand fans were standing and fifteen hundred had been turned away. For the first fifty minutes, the game was every bit as fast and exciting as the first, according to all accounts.

Then, with Montreal clinging to a 3–2 lead, an outburst of

violence brought the game to an unexpected end. After being knocked off the puck by a Winnipeg player, Montreal's Bob Mac-Dougall raised his stick above his shoulders and felled Winnipeg's star forward Tony Gingras with a vicious two-handed slash across the knees. Although Gingras had to be carried off the ice, referee J. A. Findley only called a two-minute penalty. This infuriated the Winnipeggers, who demanded that MacDougall be thrown out of the game. They argued that both teams, as well as Findley himself, had agreed before the series started that a deliberate intent to injure would result in expulsion. In the heat of the argument, one of the Winnipeg players insulted Findley, who promptly skated off the ice and left the building.

At that point the Winnipeg players retreated to their dressing room and began changing. A few minutes later, MacDougall came by and apologized for losing his temper. He also offered to sit out the rest of the game, but team captain Drinkwater rejected that idea. Meanwhile the fans were becoming restless. "The stamping got louder and louder, and 7,000 people can make a lot of noise," wrote a *Gazette* reporter, who captured perfectly the uncertainty that suddenly took hold of everyone: "Nobody knew what to do after Findley left. Who was going to award the game? Who was going to order the teams to play? How would the match be decided? Who had jurisdiction?"

Fortunately, someone had pursued Findley and persuaded him to return after an absence of twenty minutes. He promptly marched into the Winnipeg dressing room and gave the visitors fifteen minutes to return to the ice. When they refused to do so, he awarded Montreal the game, and with it the Cup. Naturally, each city blamed the other for the incident. "The behaviour of the Winnipeg men is not a matter of congratulation," snapped the next day's *Gazette*. "They will return whence they came with diminished laurels." According to the *Manitoba Free Press*, the incident had left "a dark stain on the reputation of Montreal as a sporting city. The whole matter was a disgrace."

Despite that sour ending, the Winnipeg Vics made another run at the Stanley Cup in mid-February 1900. Their challenge went out to the Montreal Shamrocks, who had stripped the Montreal Victorias of the Cup by finishing first overall in the Canadian Amateur Hockey League (CAHL) in 1899. A best-of-three series was arranged and everyone involved was determined to concentrate on playing fair hockey. From the time the Winnipeggers arrived in Montreal until the final gong sounded to end the series, a sense of camaraderie and goodwill prevailed amongst the players. One jaded newsman, seemingly put off by it all, wrote that it was almost as though the lions had decided to lie with the lambs.

This series revealed the ways in which hockey was evolving as a business and a sport. Under a new revenue-sharing arrangement, each team received one-quarter of the gate, up from one-sixth the year before. Changes were also occurring on the ice. The goals now had a crossbar and netting strung between the posts, a change introduced a mere six weeks earlier during a CAHL game between the Montreal Shamrocks and Montreal Victorias. And the growing sophistication of the game was apparent in the competing styles of hockey played by the Winnipeggers and the Montrealers.

In the 1900 series, the westerners stuck to basic hockey as it was played at the time. Their point men would loft the puck from their own end of the rink to the Montreal end, in a manner resembling a punt in football. The Winnipeg forwards would race down the ice after the puck, hoping to outskate the Montreal forwards and put enough pressure on the Montreal defenders to create a scoring chance. Although it was a simple strategy, it worked well when executed properly.

The Shamrocks, who wore grey uniforms with green trim, played a more innovative game that relied on stickhandling and passing. The four forwards attempted to move the puck up the ice by passing it back and forth, which was called a combination play. The two defenders usually carried the puck themselves or passed it along the ice to one of the forwards, although they occasionally resorted to lifting.

The innovative Shamrocks prevailed by the narrowest of margins. The series went three games, and all three were decided by one goal. Winnipeg won the opening match 4–3 in Montreal's Mount Royal Arena before a sellout crowd of seven thousand, which one observer described as "people piled tier upon tier, four human walls." When it was over, the Winnipeg supporters erupted with emotion. The scene was described this way in the next day's *Gazette*: "Borne high above a struggling, frenzied humanity, surging upon the ice as one irresistible avalanche, the seven heroes of one of the most desperately fought contests in the annals of Canadian hockey were triumphantly carried to their dressing rooms."

Game two was every bit as tight, tense, and exciting. Scalpers were getting six dollars for a fifty-cent ticket and, for those who were betting on the game, nobody was giving odds. The game attracted a number of outside visitors, including Jimmy Havelin, a sportswriter with the *New York World,* Frank Stephens, president of the Wanderers Hockey Club of Halifax, and a twenty-member delegation from the Quebec Hockey Club. The Victorias were leading 2–1 with less than seven minutes left when the Shamrocks' captain, Harry Trihey, scored. Then with half a minute left, Trihey scored the winner on a solo rush. "At the finish, the spectators arose as one," said the *Gazette*'s observer. "From the boxes and upper benches rolled forth one great volume of sound. Both teams were carried off the ice."

The third game, another cliffhanger, was interrupted for the arrival of the governor general. "His Excellency Lord Minto and staff entered the vice-regal box on the east side, attracting as much attention as would a Japanese junk at a British naval demonstration," declared the *Gazette*. Montreal led 3–2 at the half, then went up by two early in the second. Then, the Vics scored consecutive goals to set up the dramatic conclusion.

Seated at ice level, one of the telegraphers provided this account of the final minutes: "Every man doing his utmost; crowd frantic, nearly everyone standing and screaming as one or other side has possession of the puck. Players so excited that off-sides are frequent. More shots on Shamrock goal that make the crowd scream. Play rough and reckless." With thirty seconds left, and the game tied at four apiece, Trihey scored the winning goal from a face-off in front of the Winnipeg goal. Shamrocks supporters immediately poured over the boards, on to the ice, and carried their heroes to their dressing room.

The Winnipeg Vics immediately announced that they were determined to try again for the Cup. They returned to Manitoba and won the provincial championship, which gave them the right to issue a challenge the following winter. As soon as the cold weather arrived in December 1900 and ice had formed in the Winnipeg Auditorium, the Vics embarked on "a conscientious system of training," as the *Free Press* called it.

By late January 1901, the team was ready to depart for Montreal for its second showdown against the Shamrocks, who had retained the Cup by winning the CAHL championship. A Winnipeg jeweller, T. J. Porte, gave each player a rabbit foot in a silver case as a good luck charm, and the *Free Press* told its readers: "No sporting event in Canada attracts more interest each year than the annual battle between the eastern and western giants for the world's hockey championship."

The truth of that bold declaration was borne out on January 30, the day that the best-of-three series opened. The game was easily the most popular topic of conversation on the streets of Montreal and Winnipeg, according to the newspapers in both cities. As game time approached, huge crowds began arriving at Winnipeg's rinks, hotels, theatres and other places where the play-by-plays provided by the telegraphers would be broadcast. Outside Montreal's Mount Royal Arena, a mob of fans with general admission tickets eagerly awaited the opening of the doors. "There was a great crush at the fifty-cent end of the rink," the *Free*

Press reported, "and more than one man had the buttons torn off his clothes in the frantic efforts to be one of the first through the doorway."

The game that night proved to be as tense and dramatic as almost every previous Stanley Cup match between the Vics and their Montreal rivals. With less than a minute to go, the score was tied 3–3. The Winnipeggers had control of the puck in the Shamrock end, and they swarmed around the net. Amid the frenzy and confusion, Burke Wood, a new member of the Vics, was left unguarded for a second. "When Wood got a nice pass from Gingras, he landed the puck between the posts," according to the *Free Press*. And that was the game.

Two nights later, the teams waged an even tighter battle. The Shamrocks, encouraged by fans waving green flags, tried to play their slick stickhandling and passing game. The Vics, who were determined to disrupt Montreal's sophisticated attack, hit hard and checked ferociously. At the end of regulation time, the score stood at 1–1. The Shamrocks suggested a fifteen-minute break before playing overtime, but the Vics refused and the game went on.

Seven minutes later, Dan Bain scored for Winnipeg. "The outburst which greeted Bain's goal is beyond the power of the pen to describe," a *Free Press* correspondent wrote. "Half the people in the rink sat motionless with the word disappointment written all over their faces. The other half rose as one and broke into frantic cheers. Scores of them poured over the sides of the rink and carried the boys to their dressing room."

After the defeats of 1896, 1899, and 1900, the Vics had finally won their second Stanley Cup, and their fans in Winnipeg were ecstatic. "When news of the victory was at last communicated, the crowds threw off all restraint," a *Free Press* journalist reported. "They began to celebrate with a vengeance. It is a fact that wines of foreign vintage were in demand last night. From the triumphant yells heard on the streets at an early hour this morning there are grounds for supposing that the celebration is still being carried on." The next morning, the *Free Press* itself seemed to be caught in a victory swoon. "THIS CUP IS OURS!" the paper shouted in letters an inch high at the top of the front page. Beneath the headline, the paper ran a sketch of the Cup. And the story of the game began with this short, jubilant exclamation: "Hurrah for the West!"

As the reigning champions, the Vics were entitled to receive challenges, rather than issue them, and they were entitled to meet their opponents at home in Winnipeg. In mid-January 1902 the Toronto Wellingtons, who were champions of the Ontario Hockey Association (OHA), boarded a train at the city's Union Station and left for the West in pursuit of the Cup. The Wellingtons, who wore white uniforms with red trim and were also known as the Iron Dukes, were the first challengers from Toronto. They were a youthful group of players, half of whom had barely reached the age of majority, which was then twenty-one. Because of their age and inexperience, they were viewed with a great deal of scepticism in Winnipeg and Montreal.

Shortly before the series began, a well-known Winnipeg stockbroker named W. G. Bell made a business trip to Toronto and was asked by a reporter how he rated the Wellingtons. His response was that they had "about as much chance as a snowball in a Turkish bath." Meanwhile, a Montreal *Herald* writer noted that the Iron Dukes were bolstering their line-up with players from other teams, and added sarcastically: "This match is not the Wellingtons versus the Winnipeg Victorias. It is Ontario versus the Vics."

The Stanley Cup was at stake, and the city of Winnipeg was humming with excitement as the series opened. The Cup was on display in the window of a Main Street jewellery store. Tickets for reserved seats went on sale almost a week before the best-of-three playoff began and sold out in a day. The opening game at the Winnipeg Auditorium drew a crowd of three thousand, well above the building's official capacity of two thousand, and dozens of fans watched from the rafters.

For the first thirty minutes, the Wellingtons put up a fight that surprised their opponents, the pundits, and the fans. They jumped to a quick 2–0 lead before the Vics scored, and they forced the Winnipeg players to do some serious soul-searching between the halves. "There was evidently some heart to heart talks in the dressing room during the resting period," the *Free Press* wrote. "When play resumed the champions performed like an entirely different team."

The Vics relied on their stamina, aggressiveness, and experience to strip the Wellingtons of their composure and to neutralize their offence. With the exception of a few harmless rushes toward the Winnipeg goal, the youthful Torontonians spent most of the second half trapped in their own end of the rink. Nevertheless, they kept the score respectable, losing 5–3.

Back home in Toronto, an OHA executive named John Ross Robertson waited nervously in the *Globe*'s newsroom for word of the outcome. "On receiving the news, he rushed to the telephone and gave the word for the blowing of the street railway whistle, which by three shrieks gave the news of the defeat to hockeyists all over the city," the *Free Press* reported.

In the next day's papers, Toronto sportswriters argued that the Wellingtons had performed nobly, and had demonstrated the high quality of Ontario hockey. "The false prophets of Ottawa, Montreal, Kingston and even Toronto have not a bit of consolation left," the *Evening Telegram* declared. "Winnipeg and a few other spots in this big Dominion must now acknowledge that the OHA produces just as good hockey material as the associations of Quebec and the West, where the weather conditions are much more advantageous."

Two nights later, a record crowd of four thousand jammed the Auditorium for the second game. One newspaper reported that a fan had paid an unprecedented sixteen dollars for a reserved seat, which had originally fetched two. Three young men spent $200 each travelling from "upper Saskatchewan" to see the game. And a party of twenty from Minnesota, none of whom had ever seen a hockey game, arrived to find all the tickets long gone. To ensure that they didn't go home disappointed, the arena management seated them in the ladies' waiting room, where they watched the game through a window.

The game itself was "replete with the most exciting incidents, spectacular rushes, brilliant stickhandling and close checking." The Wellingtons were badly outplayed but managed to put up enough of a fight to earn the respect of their opponents and the admiration of the fans. According to the *Free Press*, the Vics had possession of the puck for three-quarters of the game, and had an estimated twelve shots-on-goal for every one by the Dukes. Nevertheless, the Vics won only by a score of 5–3.

Following the game, the Vics honoured their adversaries with a banquet at the Queen's Hotel, where the Stanley Cup was prominently displayed at the centre of the room. Former players Merritt and Armytage commended both teams, and the Victoria club patron, Hugh John Macdonald, delivered a speech laced with lavish praise for the players.

With the series over, the Wellingtons headed back to Toronto. The Vics turned their attention to regular season play in the Manitoba league, and won their seventh straight league championship. In early March 1902 a more formidable opponent, the Montreal AAA, issued a challenge for the Stanley Cup. Trustees Sweetland and Ross approved the challenge and decided that the Vics should defend their title for a second time that season. It turned out to be one of the most memorable of the early battles for the Cup. When it was over, the Montreal players had been dubbed "The Little Men of Iron."

The Montrealers left Windsor Station for Winnipeg on March 9 amid a heavy snowstorm and with a rousing cheer from four hundred supporters echoing in their ears. "As the train disappeared into the mantle of falling snow," a local journalist wrote, "the club rallying cry 'Montreal, Montreal, sis, boom bah, Montreal, Montreal rah, rah, rah' resounded through the great station."

Upon their arrival, the Montreal team received a warm welcome from a crowd of eight hundred Winnipeggers. The players immediately boarded horse-drawn carriages for the ride to the Clarendon Hotel. Once again, the Winnipeg capital was full of anticipation over the upcoming series. Scalpers were getting from five to twelve dollars for reserved seats that were originally purchased for one to two dollars, and a resident of St. Paul, Minnesota, paid fifty dollars for a pair of seats. Both the CPR and the Great North Western Telegraph company had arranged to have operators at rinkside to send play-by-plays back to Montreal.

The first game drew a crowd of four thousand, and two thousand others had to be turned away. A group of former Montreal residents filled a section at the north end of the rink and did their best to compete with the wildly partisan Winnipeggers by yelling the AAA cheer and waving the association's blue and white colours. In Montreal, about five hundred AAA members gathered in the club gymnasium to catch the play by play, while thousands of other city residents congregated in the streets outside the *Montreal Star* offices to read the incoming bulletins.

For all the excitement and anticipation, the game turned out to be a dud. Tony Gingras scored for Winnipeg at the twelve-minute mark of the first half and that was the only goal of the night. The big problem was the weather. The temperature in Winnipeg had soared to forty-five degrees Fahrenheit and ruined the ice surface in the auditorium. "It is no easy matter to play on ice covered with an inch of water," the *Free Press* reported. A *Montreal Star* reporter added that "It was a common thing to see four men at one time sliding on their stomachs for a distance of 15 yards over the water-covered ice."

Two days later, a Friday, the temperature plummeted and a vicious storm howled across the prairies, paralysing trade and travel, and almost shutting the railways. "The White Ghost of the North," as a *Free Press* headline writer called it, blew from Friday evening till Sunday afternoon. Nevertheless, the Winnipeg

Auditorium was packed again for the second game, which was played on a perfect sheet of ice. The only distraction, the *Free Press* reported, was "snow drifting in through the openings in the roof and accumulating at the south end of the rink."

The Montrealers scored once in the first half and four times in the second half to bury the Vics 5–0. According to the *Free Press,* the lighter, quicker, more agile eastern players were superior in almost every respect to the bigger, stronger, more rugged Vics. "It was an inspiring sight to see the blue and white forward line sweep down the ice, the puck travelling from man to man with the precision of a machine," the *Free Press* reported.

In downtown Montreal, the AAA backers were ecstatic over the outcome. Hundreds of club members had again packed the association's gymnasium. "When it was announced that the score stood 3–0 in favour of Montreal, bedlam broke loose," one paper reported. "When the game was over, the frenzied Montrealers hugged one another with delight." Outside the *Star* offices, a huge crowd, larger than any gathering since the one that had assembled at the news of the assassination of American president William McKinley seven months earlier, blocked the street for several hours while the telegraph bulletins were coming in. Afterward, horse-drawn cabs roamed the streets carrying revellers shouting "What's the matter with Montreal, rah, rah, rah!"

The third game of the series was, by all accounts, one of the most dramatic that Winnipeggers had ever seen. Montreal's rookie rover Archie Hooper had scored twice by the seven-minute mark of the first. Gingras cut Montreal's margin to one with a goal ten minutes into the second half.

Although the Vics had a wildly excited crowd of four thousand behind them, they could not tie the score. "For the balance of the half, the Vics kept the puck almost constantly in the territory of the enemy, and shot after shot was poured in but all in vain," the *Free Press* reported. "Goalie Billy Nicholson stopped dozens of shots, and played one of the finest games ever seen here." The Montrealers withstood a ferocious siege, prompting a telegraph operator named Peter Spanjaardt to declare that they had held on to their lead "like little men of iron."

The next day's *Free Press* devoted an entire page to the outcome of the series, beneath the large banner headline: "AU REVOIR! SWEET STANLEY CUP!" The paper also carried a lengthy editorial praising the team's accomplishments. "Though defeated, the people are justified in regarding their Victorias as the greatest hockey team which has yet been produced. It is now seven years since the team made a name for itself in defeating the best eastern teams in a series of exhibition games. Since that date, it has held continuously the championship of Manitoba, and has thrice won the championship of Canada. It is a record that no other team, east or west, can parallel."

Meanwhile, the victorious AAAs returned to Montreal to a gigantic and tumultuous welcome. An estimated thirty thousand people jammed the streets around Windsor Station, and cheered the players "with lungs of leather and throats of brass," according to one report. The club had hired carriages for the players and had them waiting at the station, the plan being to use them in a Stanley Cup victory parade. But the players never got close to the carriages. The moment they walked out of the station, they were hoisted on to the shoulders of enthusiastic fans and carried to the club headquarters a couple of blocks away.

The final battle in the Stanley Cup war between the Winnipeg Vics and their Montreal adversaries occurred in late January and early February 1903. The Vics came east to meet the AAAs in a best-of-three series, but they ended up playing the equivalent of four and a half games before the matter was settled. The AAAs pasted the Vics 8–1 in the opening game. Two nights later, a Saturday evening, the teams were tied 2–2 at the end of regulation time. They played twenty-seven minutes of scoreless overtime, by which time it was midnight. The mayor of Westmount declared that a game begun on Saturday night could not be concluded on the Sabbath and sent everyone home.

Trustees Sweetland and Ross later ruled that it would be wiser to replay the game in its entirety rather than sell tickets for a match that might end within minutes, or even seconds. Winnipeg prevailed in the next encounter by a score of 4–2, setting up a decisive third game which the AAAs won 4–1. The 1903 series marked the end of the Montreal-Winnipeg rivalry that had dominated the first decade of Stanley Cup competition.

In the space of ten short years, the Cup had become the most hotly pursued prize in hockey. From the shores of the St. Lawrence to the heart of the prairies, players, promoters, and fans dreamed of winning it. For a country with a shaky identity, with language, religion, and geography to divide it, and little in the way of shared legends, heroes, or values to unify it, Lord Stanley's simple silver cup had aroused common passions among ordinary Canadians, and made heroes of ordinary men. It had created a rivalry between Montreal and Winnipeg where none existed in politics, business, or the arts. It had become a legitimate and potent unifying force.

But after the 1903 series, the Montreal and Winnipeg teams were swept aside as hockey powerhouses by the emergence of the game's first legitimate repeat winner. For the next three winters, the trail of the Stanley Cup would lead to Canada's capital, home of the Ottawa Hockey Club, the reigning world champions. In the press, they were known as the Ottawas or the Senators. In the street, they were called the barber poles, after their red, white and black knit turtleneck sweaters. In the lore and legends of the game, they have survived as the feared, revered, and nearly unbeatable Ottawa Silver Seven.

2

GAME TO THE CORE
1903-06

Frank McGee was a sparkling young Ottawa hockey player when the Boer War broke out between Britain and the Afrikaners of South Africa in late 1899. While thousands of young Canadians enlisted and marched off to defend the interests of the Empire on the battlefield, the twenty-year-old McGee stayed in Ottawa and mesmerized local hockey fans with his deft playmaking, his daring rushes, and his unwavering tenacity. In the winter of 1900, he led the Ottawa Aberdeens to the Quebec intermediate hockey championship and guided the Ottawa CPR team to first place in the Canadian Railway Hockey Union. But even though McGee never set foot on the battlefield in Africa, the Boer War cost him his sight in his left eye. Later in his career, he would earn lasting fame as the one-eyed sharpshooter of the Ottawa Silver Seven.

On the evening of Wednesday, March 21, 1900, the Ottawa CPR team travelled to Hawkesbury, a town on the Ottawa River sixty kilometres east of the nation's capital, for an exhibition game against a local squad. A group of prominent Hawkesbury residents had arranged the game to raise money for the Canadian Patriotic Fund, a grass-roots campaign set up to help pay

36

for the country's war effort. The event raised $120 after expenses were covered and was deemed a big success. Following the game, several civic dignitaries, including H. J. Cloran, the local MPP, delivered patriotic speeches to their fellow citizens. Before departing for home, the Ottawa players were treated to a banquet.

The next day's Ottawa *Citizen* ran a brief account of the game on the front page only because it was connected with the war effort. The CPR team had lost 10–4 thanks to dismal playing conditions. "The Ottawa boys were up against a snag as the rink was very small and the point man of the home team scored several goals from that position on lifts," the paper reported. "The lighting of the rink was effected by three coal-oil lamps and it was pretty hard to see the puck." Almost as an afterthought, and without further explanation, the paper added: "Frank McGee of the CPR got hurt by being cut over the eye."

The paper provided no detail on the nature of McGee's injury until six weeks later. On May 5, the *Citizen* noted that "Frank McGee, the well-known athlete who received a severe injury to his eye at Hawkesbury near the close of last season, is almost recovered but it is doubtful if the sight of the injured eye will ever be perfect." At the age of twenty, McGee appeared to be finished as a hockey player. In mid-January 1901, as his Aberdeen teammates were about to begin another season, the paper told Ottawa sports fans: "The team will be short one glistening star in the person of Frank McGee, whose hockey ability was known and admired by everyone who saw him play."

McGee sat out the 1901 and 1902 seasons because of his injury, although he regularly served as a referee. Early in 1903, however, he was coaxed out of retirement and jumped straight into senior hockey, the highest calibre and most competitive brand of hockey played in Canada at the time. McGee joined the Ottawa Senators and played his first game on January 17, 1903. The opposition that night was the Montreal AAA, the reigning Stanley Cup champions. Ottawa thrashed the cup holders 7–1, and

McGee scored twice. According to the next day's *Citizen*, he had proved that "he is qualified to stay with the best in the land."

Over the next four winters, McGee established himself as the best player of his day, despite his disability, and the Ottawa Senators emerged as one of the best teams in the first fifty years of Stanley Cup competition. They held the Cup at the end of the 1903, 1904, and 1905 seasons, and came within a whisker of holding on for a fourth consecutive season. During their reign, the Silver Seven, as the Senators came to be known, beat nine straight challengers. They played twenty-three Stanley Cup games and won eighteen, lost three, and tied two. They intimidated opponents with their speed, their toughness, their clever passing plays, and their awesome ability to put the puck in the net.

The Senators rose to prominence at a time when hockey was being played and watched as never before. Around the turn of the century, hockey as an organized sport exploded in popularity. There were leagues of every sort, and the sports pages of the country's newspapers were filled with the results of games and seasons and playoffs. There were leagues for merchants and manufacturers, bankers and civil servants, schoolboys and railwaymen. For the vast majority of players, hockey was a pleasurable pastime, a mere recreational activity. The most they could aspire to was a neighbourhood or local championship.

But, for a tiny minority of players, those good enough to compete at the senior level, hockey was a fast, intense, serious, and sometimes violent game. For these players, the ultimate prize was the Stanley Cup. These were the players whom the Canadian public filled arenas to watch, whom they bought newspapers to read about, whom they talked about and argued about. Amid this feverish growth, the Ottawa Senators rose to dominate the game like no team before them, and like no team after them until the late 1940s when the Toronto Maple Leafs won three Cups in a row. The Montreal Wanderers also held the Cup three years running, from 1906 through 1909, but their reign was interrupted by a loss to the Kenora Thistles, and they faced far fewer challenges than the Senators.

A total of about twenty men played with the Ottawa Hockey Club during the championship years, but a core group of half a dozen players carried the team. Goaltender Bouse Hutton, who joined the team in 1899, minded the nets through the the first two Stanley Cup seasons. Harvey Pulford and Art Moore played defence together almost without interruption from start to finish. McGee played centre in all but one of twenty-three Stanley Cup games. The key forwards were Harry Westwick, Billy Gilmour, and Alf Smith. All these players, with the exception of Art Moore, are now members of the Hockey Hall of Fame.

They were outstanding athletes in other sports as well. Hutton was a member of national champion hockey, lacrosse, and football teams, all in one year. Moore and Smith both played on Ottawa teams that won national championships in lacrosse and football. Westwick was regarded as one of the best lacrosse players in Canada in his day, and Pulford was one of the best all-round athletes in the country. He was the amateur heavyweight boxing champion of Eastern Canada from 1896 to 1898. At the same time he played for several Ottawa football and lacrosse teams that captured national championships. From 1905 to 1912, he was a member of the Ottawa Rowing Club, which won four Canadian championships, a U.S. national title, and made it to the semi-finals of the English Henley Regatta in 1911.

But when it came to hockey, Frank McGee stood out even among this group of champions. In twenty-two Stanley Cup games, he scored sixty-three goals. In twenty-three regular season games, he scored seventy-one goals, or better than three a game. Statistics alone come nowhere close to capturing the talent of Frank McGee. Here is how Frank Patrick, one of hockey's greatest innovators, described McGee: "He had everything, speed, stickhandling, scoring ability and he was a punishing checker. He was strongly built but beautifully proportioned and he had an almost animal rhythm. When he walked around the dressing room you could see his muscles ripple. They weren't blacksmith's muscles, either. They were the long muscles of a great athlete. You don't see many like him."

The Senators earned their first crack at the Stanley Cup in March 1903. Ottawa and the Montreal Victorias had finished the CAHL season in a first-place tie with identical records of six wins and two losses. The league executive decided that a playoff should be held to determine the league champion. The winner would also take the Cup, since the AAAs had automatically relinquished it by slipping to third place in the league.

After a considerable amount of bickering over the format, the teams settled on a two-game, total-goal series opening in Montreal March 7 and concluding in Ottawa March 10. The first game, played before forty-five hundred fans at the Mount Royal Arena, was described by the Ottawa *Citizen* as "a test of pluck and endurance rather than speed and skill." The temperature that day had risen to thirty-four degrees Fahrenheit, rain and sleet had pelted Montreal, and the arena ice surface was slushy and sluggish. Delays were frequent because the players kept breaking skate laces and blades.

With high quality hockey impossible because of the ice conditions, the teams played a rough, chippy game that ended in a 1–1 tie. According to the next day's Ottawa *Citizen*, Montreal centre Bert Strachan twice struck Frank McGee on the head with his stick and also clubbed Suddie Gilmour, whose brothers Billy and Davie also played on the team. Strachan attacked rover Harry Westwick three times, and on the third occasion broke a bone in the Ottawa player's right leg with a vicious slash. "Westwick skated off the ice and walked to the dressing room with the bone protruding through the skin," the *Citizen* reported. There was a doctor in the rink that night and, rather than go to a hospital, Westwick insisted that the doctor put the leg in a splint so that he could watch the rest of the game from the press box.

Three nights later, the teams lined up again and Governor General Lord Minto laid the puck on the ice between the sticks of centres Strachan and McGee to start the game. A crowd of three thousand fans, including a few dozen who watched from the rafters, packed Dey's Arena in Ottawa. Again the ice conditions were deplorable. In some places water lay two to three inches deep on the playing surface. But it scarcely bothered the Senators. "When Ottawa scored the first goal the din was deafening," wrote the *Citizen*'s observer. "When they kept scoring, and it was obvious that the Stanley Cup was theirs, the crowd's enthusiasm was unparallelled in Ottawa hockey history."

McGee scored three times for Ottawa while his linemates Suddie, Davie, and Billy Gilmour pumped in a total of five goals to complete an 8–0 rout of the Victorias. "It was a catastrophe," the Montreal *Gazette* reported. "The Victorias were over-matched and overpowered. No forward line in the CAHL can compare with Ottawa's." McGee was said to be skating as hard at the end of sixty minutes as he was at the start. The *Gazette* added that Ottawa point man Harvey Pulford "was merciless with his body, and anyone who came within his territory suffered severely."

Ottawa had won its first Stanley Cup, and a day later a member of the Victorias' executive brought the trophy to Ottawa by train and presented it to P. M. Butler, president of the Ottawa Hockey Club. However, the Senators scarcely had time to enjoy their triumph. Two nights after defeating the Victorias they were back on the ice to defend the Cup against the Rat Portage Thistles, the new champions of the Manitoba and Northwestern Association. The trustees had accepted the Thistles as legitimate challengers, and the teams decided to play the series immediately, rather than put it off until the start of the following season.

The Thistles were the pride of Rat Portage, a small but booming logging, mining, and flour-milling town in northwestern Ontario, which in May 1905 adopted its current name of Kenora. The Thistles, who wore solid white sweaters with a green thistle crest on their chests, eventually issued three Stanley Cup challenges before becoming the only team from a small town ever to win the coveted trophy. In the process, the Thistles also became one of the most celebrated and admired of the early challengers.

The team was formed in 1894, according to Lakehead University sports historian Ronald Lappage, and a contest was held to find a name. The club executive settled on the Thistles, the entry submitted by a carpenter of Scottish descent named Bill Dunsmore. The seven-member team was comprised almost entirely of local players, and the nucleus of the Thistles had been together since 1896. They had a loyal and ardent following in their hometown, which was evident when they left for Ottawa.

"A big crowd was on hand at the station to witness the departure of the team," declared a wire service dispatch that appeared in the eastern papers. "The platform was jammed from end to end as the train pulled out of the depot, and the boys, who were on the platform of their sleeper car, were given a most enthusiastic send off." The CPR had provided a special car for the players, and they had tied large streamers on both sides announcing "The Thistle Hockey Club, Rat Portage."

But when they skated on to the ice at Dey's Arena in Ottawa, a long way from home, from their supportive fans and their familiar opponents, a nervous group of Thistles stumbled and embarrassed themselves. "Stage fright was the explanation, and stage fright it evidently was," the next day's *Citizen* concluded, "for in the first half the visitors were badly rattled and the Ottawas scored six goals." McGee and the Gilmour bothers took care of all the Ottawa scoring.

The Thistles regained their composure in the second half and completely dominated the play. They scored twice but could not overcome the damage done in the first thirty minutes. For the powerful Ottawa team, it was a routine victory, except for the following curious incident, which was mentioned in passing at the end of the *Citizen*'s account of the game: "A new puck had to be secured in the second half as the one in play rolled into a hole in the ice and could not be resurrected."

Two nights later, the Senators beat their western opponents

by a score of 4–2 to take the two-game, total-goal series by a margin of 10–4. The *Citizen* noted that the Thistle forwards possessed dazzling speed but did not pass the puck as freely and skilfully as Ottawa's forward line. And the Rat Portage defencemen used a stick check to take the puck from opposing forwards, while the Ottawa defencemen always played the man, which subsequently became the accepted way of playing defence in hockey.

The Thistles returned to Rat Portage a little wiser for their trip to Ottawa, having learned a few lessons about how the top team in the land played the game, but they also went home poorer. The games had attracted small crowds of fifteen hundred and a thousand because they were played on poor ice, at the end of the season, and they coincided with the opening of a new session of Parliament. As a result, the Thistles lost $800 on the trip.

At the end of December 1903, just as a new hockey season was about to begin in Eastern Canada, another western team arrived in Ottawa determined to strip the Senators of the Stanley Cup. The trustees had accepted a challenge from the Winnipeg Rowing Club, champions of the Western Canada Hockey League the previous winter. However, the other clubs in the CAHL complained bitterly that the Ottawa-Winnipeg series would disrupt the start of their season. "The matches for the Cup have simply paralyzed the game here," charged the Montreal Victorias' president, Fred McRobie. "Unless the Cup matches are put on a proper system, like the footballers play, the sooner the Cup leaves here never to come back the better."

The dispute over the Winnipeg challenge arose because in those days there was no agreed-upon format for scheduling Stanley Cup series. In this case, trustees Sweetland and Ross decided the Winnipeggers were the reigning champions of a legitimate league. So they accepted the challenge and ordered the Senators to defend their crown.

But the citizens of the competing cities warmly embraced the series. Hundreds of Winnipeggers, including former members of the powerful Victorias club of the 1890s, packed the city train station to see the players off. In Ottawa, the day before the series opened, the *Citizen* reported: "The match is the one topic of conversation in sporting circles."

For all the anticipation, however, the first game was a disappointing rout. Ottawa thrashed the Oarsmen 9–1. McGee scored four goals and Westwick, who had recovered from the compound fracture suffered in March 1903, added three. Afterwards, the Winnipeggers complained bitterly over Ottawa's rough play. Captain Billy Breen told the *Citizen*: "All I have to say is that it was the dirtiest game I ever played in."

The *Ottawa Evening Journal* carried this graphic account of one particularly vicious incident: "A thoroughly dirty and cowardly thing was done by Alf Smith of the Ottawas which escaped the attention of the referee and most of the audience, owing to its taking place a long way from the puck. Smith, in a rush up the ice, was bodychecked by Joe Hall and lost the puck. The puck travelled back to the Ottawa end. Smith and Hall were travelling in the rear of the play when Smith turned and deliberately cracked Hall on the head with his stick, knocking him down and out." Hall required five stitches to close the wound on his head but managed to whack Smith and cut him for four stitches.

By the end of the game, five of the nine Winnipeg players were hurt, and the Ottawa fans were thoroughly disgusted with their own team's tactics. In the second game, they vented their displeasure by cheering for the challengers from start to finish. The Senators, in a rare display of overconfidence, lost 6–2 to a fired-up Winnipeg team that possessed "speed, combination play, stamina and aggressive tactics," according to the *Citizen*.

In the third and deciding game, the players put on a blazing display for the twenty-five hundred fans even though it was minus twenty Fahrenheit and bitterly cold in Dey's Arena. "Both sevens fought with the desperation of despair," the *Citizen* reported. "For 40 minutes they battled and their efforts elicited the wildest applause from the spectators. Then McGee scored and pandemonium broke loose. It was spectacular hockey; hockey that thrilled and that kept the crowd on its feet."

The Senators won by a score of 2–0, and retained the Stanley Cup. In the opinion of the local newspapers, the series had proved to the sceptics the value of Cup competitions. "Ottawa has been enriched by a second series of Stanley Cup games," the *Citizen* declared. "The carping critics who allege that the silverware is a drawback rather than an encouragement to hockey should go back to the forest primeval. The Stanley Cup matches keep the east and west in touch in hockey matters and keep the games on a standard basis. Both sides learn and improve."

Winnipeg fans also showed that they had lost none of their ardour for Stanley Cup games. Huge crowds gathered at half a dozen locations in the city where telegraph returns of the games were posted or broadcast by megaphone. Although it was a chilly fifteen degrees Fahrenheit on the evening of the deciding match, several thousand fans stood outside the *Free Press* offices while the game was in progress to catch the telegraph reports. The bulletins were projected on to the wall of the building using a device called a stereopticon, which was similar to a modern overhead projector. The *Free Press* also had two illustrators sketching the action described in the telegraph reports. "In the three hours of play, about four hundred slides were thrown on the screen," the newspaper boasted the next day.

With their reign intact, the Senators turned to regular season play in the CAHL. In early February, however, they dropped out of the league after a dispute over an unfinished game. Ottawa had arrived ninety minutes late for a match January 30 against the Montreal Victorias and had a 4–1 lead when the game was called at midnight. The league executive, composed of officers from the other teams, ordered the teams to replay the entire game the following day. Ottawa refused and walked out. The remaining CAHL members argued that Ottawa should relinquish the Cup. But trustee Ross overruled them and said that the

Senators would retain the right to defend the Cup until the end of the season.

The dust from that dispute had barely settled when Ross had to decide which of two Ontario challengers would be allowed to meet Ottawa. The Berlin Union Jacks, champions of the Western Ontario Hockey Association, and the Toronto Marlboros, winners of the Ontario Hockey Association, both wanted a shot at the Cup. To the disappointment of Berlin, a community renamed Kitchener during World War I, Ross selected the Marlboros.

Both games were played in Ottawa and the Senators skated to an easy 6–3 win in the first game. Two nights later, Ottawa romped to an 11–2 win. McGee scored eight of Ottawa's seventeen goals, including five in the second game, a record in Stanley Cup play at the time. In its coverage of the final match, the *Citizen* lamented the poor quality of the opposition. "The Ottawas for the full hour made the work of the OHA representatives look like that of a bunch of schoolboys," the newspaper sniped.

From the perspective of the Toronto papers, the series looked considerably different. Ottawa won the first game, according to the *Telegram*, on the strength of rough, physical play that at times bordered on brutality. The *Telegram*'s reporter complained that while the Marlboros had stuck to "clean Ontario hockey," their opponents had consistently "played the man to the utter disregard of the puck." On the day of game two, the *Telegram* candidly told its readers: "There is no one on the Marlboros or among their followers who hopes for a victory tonight. Players and officials even considered forfeiting the game rather than being hacked to death again."

After the second game, even the *Telegram*'s bitterly partisan observer was full of praise for the Senators. "A team picked from all Ontario could not beat the Ottawas as at present constituted," he wrote. "Their defence is colossal. The forward line knows every wrinkle in hockey and they are fast and clever. They rush in fine combination and double back fast to cut in on counter rushes. They are adept body checkers and, though not particularly heavy, know how to use every ounce they have to the best advantage. It is the man who is the object of the check. Absolutely no attention is paid to the puck."

While Ottawa was disposing the Marlboros, the Queen's University team that had won the Intercollegiate Hockey Union championship issued a challenge. Trustee Ross accepted it and set the dates for a series. But the Queen's students had to back out because the games would have conflicted with the university's medical exams. The vacancy was quickly filled by the Montreal Wanderers, champions of the four-team Federal Amateur Hockey League, which had just completed its first season of competition. Ross scheduled a two-game, total-goal series, and Ottawa agreed to play the first game in Montreal.

The match was played March 2, on soft, slushy ice, before a rowdy crowd of six thousand. From the tone of the press reports, both fans and reporters may well have witnessed a war rather than a hockey game. "The number of penalties imposed was appalling," the *Citizen*'s staffer wrote. Every player on the ice, except the goalies, was sent off at least once, and some players were penalized half a dozen times. Each side blamed the other for the carnage. "The Ottawas were chopped and slashed every time a man got the rubber," the *Citizen* stated. "In sheer desperation the cup holders had to give it back and play the Wanderers at their own game. They showed the Montreal people that they were game to the core, not a man lying down under the gruelling attack."

Afterward, the Senators' dressing room resembled a hospital ward. "It was positively pitiful to see McGee's legs," declared the *Citizen*. "They were chopped until they were discoloured and swollen in an awful manner from the knees down. Alf Smith's head was split and his left eye blackened, while Jim McGee's head required the application of a bandage."

The game had started at 8:40 p.m. and, thanks to delays caused by scuffles, skirmishes, and penalties, it was still not complete four hours later. The score was tied 5–5 at the end of regulation time, but the Wanderers would not agree to play overtime. Over the next couple of days, executive members of the two clubs argued furiously over how to complete the series. When they couldn't reach an agreement, the two clubs decided to abandon the series, although the Wanderers protested bitterly that they were not to blame.

In any event, another challenger was *en route* to Ottawa and determined to dethrone the Senators. The Brandon Wheat Kings had earned their shot at the Cup by defeating the Thistles to win the championship of the Manitoba and Northwestern Association. They left Brandon aboard a special CPR sleeper called The Ashcroft, and the players attached a large streamer to one side of the car announcing that the "Wheat City Hockey Club" was on board.

The Wheat Kings arrived in Ottawa on the five o'clock train March 6. With three days before the opening game, they had time to tune up on the ice and to tour the nation's capital as the guests of Clifford Sifton, the Liberal member for Brandon and the minister of the interior. They also became embroiled in a strenuous debate with the Senators over who would referee the matches. The Wheat Kings proposed thirteen different men, but the Senators rejected them all because they were from Montreal. The teams finally settled on Fred Chittick of Ottawa. For all the debate which occurred, Chittick was never once accused of favouritism and had an easy time maintaining order since both teams stuck to hockey, rather than hooliganism, throughout the two-game series.

The Senators defeated the Wheat Kings in the same efficient, convincing manner with which they had subdued almost every opponent they had faced since their reign began a year earlier. They won the first game 6–3 and the second 9–3. Brandon opened the scoring in the first game, and that was the only time they were ahead in the series. McGee himself outscored the entire Brandon team, notching eight goals, including five goals in the opening match. The *Citizen* described one of McGee's goals this way: "Frank made the most sensational play of the whole game when he hurdled from centre through almost the entire Brandon team and scored unaided."

Only two members of the Wheat Kings played well enough catch the attention of the Ottawa crowds. One was coverpoint Lorne Hanna. The other was Lester Patrick, a twenty-year-old point man playing in his first Stanley Cup series. He was destined to become one of the most influential and innovative people to be associated with the game, and even then demonstrated a flair for playing the game his way. "Patrick at point was another good one," the *Citizen* noted, "when he wasn't up doing the forward act in an attempt to score."

Apart from Hanna and Patrick, the Wheat Kings were outplayed and overpowered by a team that was now recognized as peerless. "Victorious over Brandon, Ottawa wound up its season with a record unsurpassed for brilliance in the history of hockey," the *Manitoba Free Press* declared. "They have defended the Cup against the champions of four leagues and demonstrated that they are without equals in the hockey world. It is hard to see an all-star team from across Canada beating them."

Ottawa had played thirteen games in the winter of 1904, including eight games in defence of the Stanley Cup, far more than any other champion had ever been required to play in a single season. The Senators lost only once, to the Winnipeg Rowing Club, and they outscored their opposition 100–39. McGee was the big gun for Ottawa, scoring twenty-one goals in the eight Stanley Cup games; teammate Alf Smith was second with thirteen goals. Yet the team rarely played before a sellout crowd in Ottawa. At one point during that winter a *Citizen* writer lamented the fact only two thousand to twenty-five hundred fans were attending the games when the building could hold twice as many people. "Ottawans do not appreciate the fact that in the Stanley Cup games they have an opportunity of witnessing exhibitions of hockey that can not be excelled anywhere the game is played," said the paper's writer.

But the success of the Senators seemed to attract rather than deter potential challengers. On March 4 that year, the Amherst Ramblers, champions of the Nova Scotia Amateur Hockey League, had issued a challenge for the Stanley Cup, but trustee Ross and the Senators decided that it was too late in the season to stage another series. "This will be the last match of the season," the *Citizen* told its readers during the Brandon series. "The executive of the club has decided it is about time to hang up the hockey sticks and think about golf."

Before the final bell sounded to end the 1904 season, Ross used the pages of his paper, the *Ottawa Evening Journal,* to chastise the men who ran the teams, and the men who played the game, for what he viewed as excessive and unnecessary violence. "The finest game in this world to watch, hockey as our leading Canadian teams play it, is being made a byword and a disgrace by the manner in which matches are conducted and foul play tolerated," lamented Ross. "Unless a radical change occurs at once in the conduct of hockey matches, the noble winter sport of Canada must, at least in this part of the country, sink in the public estimation to the level of pugilism." Like numerous commentators since then, Ross recommended stiffer penalties, and urged club executives to control their players in order to reduce the amount of violence in the game. Like almost every similar commentator since then, he was ignored.

Having established themselves as the unconquered and unquestioned kings of hockey, the Senators squared off the following winter against the weakest and strangest opponent they would face during their three-year reign. In December 1904 a motley group of men called the Dawson City Klondikers issued a Stanley Cup challenge. In a departure from his normal policy, Ross accepted the Dawson City challenge even though the team was not the champion of a recognized senior league.

The players, in fact, had next to no hockey credentials at all. Perhaps the most notable member of the Dawson City contingent was the team's promoter and general manager, Joe Boyle, a Toronto-born adventurer and entrepreneur. Boyle had been lured to the Yukon by the gold rush of 1898 and, in a few short years, had become known around Dawson City as the King of the Klondike. Backed by the Rothschilds, he made his millions by dredging for gold in the Klondike River valley, by supplying the town with lumber for sidewalks, wharves, and buildings, and by erecting power plants that supplied Dawson City with electricity. Before his death in England in 1923, Boyle had battled the Bolsheviks during the Russian Revolution, he had been one of the last people to see Czar Nicholas alive, and he had promoted one of the biggest fiascos in Stanley Cup history.

The Yukoners set out for Ottawa on December 19 and, according to the *Citizen,* the players themselves had put up $3,000 to cover the cost of the expedition. They hoped to recoup the money through their share of the gate receipts from the games they played in Eastern Canada. Throughout their gruelling three-week, four thousand-mile odyssey, the Ottawa papers carried periodic dispatches on the team's progress. In one early report, which appeared in the *Citizen,* an unnamed player wrote: "The Dawson team leaves with little other than their courage, pluck and confidence and very little more substantial support than the good wishes of their intimate friends."

The Klondikers walked the first 320 miles to Whitehorse, averaging between twenty-three and forty miles per day and staying at police detachments. They had to sit out a storm in Whitehorse for two days before boarding a train to Skagway, Alaska. They arrived in Skagway only to learn that the ship to Seattle, Washington, had left two hours earlier, although the captain had waited a day for the team to arrive. The Klondikers spent five days in Skagway waiting for the next ship. On January 9, the *Citizen* carried this item about the next leg of the team's trek: "The trip down the coast was extremely rough and all the boys were in such condition they cared not whether the ship sunk or not."

After a cross-country train trip, the challengers finally arrived in the capital of the Dominion a day before the opening match and checked into the Russell Hotel. The players had to buy equipment and uniforms at a local store since they had brought only their skates with them. They also found that they had won instant renown among the citizens of Ottawa. Hundreds of fans strolled through the lobby and rotunda of the Russell Hotel before the series started, hoping to catch a glimpse of the players who had completed an epic voyage in search of the Cup.

"The matches are creating the greatest interest of any Stanley Cup contests yet played in Ottawa," the *Citizen* reported. In anticipation of larger than usual crowds, the management of Dey's Arena pleaded with the public to refrain from smoking while the games were in progress. "It is almost always the case that so much weed is consumed during the progress of a match that along about half-time the air is full of dense smoke and even the lights are dimmed by the clouds," an arena employee complained.

On the evening of January 13, before a crowd of twenty-two hundred that included the Governor General Lord Grey, his wife, and a vice-regal party from government house, the Klondikers finally lined up to play hockey. But the daring and determination that no doubt served these men so well on the outer edge of the civilized world deserted them on the ice in Ottawa. In two games against the Senators, the Klondikers lost 9–2 and 23–2. In the second game, McGee scored fourteen goals, including four in the space of 140 seconds, a feat unmatched to this day. "There is only one verdict left after last night," the *Citizen* wrote following the second game. "The Klondikers are scarcely above city league class."

From Ottawa, promoter Boyle and his band of Klondikers embarked on an exhibition tour that took them to Montreal, the Maritimes and across southern Ontario. By early March, they had arrived in Toronto to play the Marlboros. Meanwhile, the Senators were preparing to defend their Stanley Cup title against the Thistles of Rat Portage, who were now recognized as one of the best teams in the country.

When they issued their first Cup challenge in March 1903, the Thistles were hardly taken seriously by the sporting world of Eastern Canada. But the following season they were again one of the top teams in Western Canada, losing narrowly to Brandon in the Manitoba and Northwestern Association final. In the winter of 1905, the Thistles dominated the Manitoba league once more and the eastern papers kept their readers informed of the team's accomplishments. Moreover, Rat Portage centre Tom Phillips was widely regarded as one of the two top players in Canada at the time. The other was Ottawa's Frank McGee.

"Who is the best hockey player in Canada?" the Montreal *Herald* asked its readers. "Nine out of 10 people will reply that either Frank McGee or Tom Phillips is. These two players are undoubtedly in a class by themselves. Phillips is the speedier, but he has nothing on McGee in the matter of stickhandling and has not the same generalship. Where each shines is in pulling doubtful games out of the fires of uncertainty."

Game one of the best-of-three Stanley Cup final belonged to Phillips and his Thistles. The Rat Portage captain scored five times and led his team to a 9–3 rout of Ottawa. McGee, a right-handed shot, was on the sidelines with a broken right wrist while forward Billy Gilmour, another Ottawa stalwart, wasn't playing because he was attending university in Montreal. Their positions were filled by a couple of players called up from a local junior team.

As three thousand dejected Ottawa fans filed out of Dey's Arena in Ottawa that night, hardly believing that the champions had been beaten so badly, there was joy and jubilation elsewhere in Canada. Hundreds of Montreal fans gathered outside one of the newspaper offices on Peel Street, completely blocking the thoroughfare and cheering wildly every time Rat Portage scored.

Similar scenes occurred in Winnipeg. "Citizens of all classes, creeds and ages, men, women and children, jammed every place where telegraph reports of the game were available," according to a dispatch that appeared in the Ottawa *Citizen*. And nowhere were the fans happier than in Rat Portage. "The result simply set the town wild," one press report stated. "Processions of cheering citizens paraded the streets till late at night."

With the Senators' reign as Stanley Cup champions in peril, Ottawa fans rallied around their team as never before. A record crowd of thirty-five hundred showed up two nights later for the second game. Up in the press box there were reporters from the Ottawa papers, the Montreal *Gazette, Montreal Star, Manitoba Free Press,* Winnipeg *Tribune,* the Rat Portage *Miner and News,* and one of the Toronto dailies. The Thistles appeared on the ice at 8:25 p.m., and twenty minutes later the Senators skated on. To everyone's surprise, McGee and Gilmour were back in the lineup. The *Citizen* reported that at the sight of the two star forwards "the spectators went into a frenzy of delight."

After a considerable amount of persuasion, the Ottawa club executive had coaxed Gilmour back into uniform. As for McGee, he simply responded to the call of duty. A doctor encased his broken right wrist in a light steel cast for protection. He then wrapped both wrists heavily with bandages so that the Thistles would not be able to tell which wrist was broken and put him out of the game with a well-placed slash. Although McGee was held scoreless, winger Alf Smith scored three times, and Gilmour added one as Ottawa beat Rat Portage 4–2.

Two nights later, a crowd of four thousand jammed Dey's Arena, clinging to "girders, posts, rafters and every available spot from which a glimpse could be obtained," according to the *Citizen,* and a thousand were turned away. Another huge crowd, estimated at four thousand, gathered in the streets of downtown Montreal to catch the telegraph bulletins as they were received at the offices of the *Star,* the city's leading English-language newspaper at the time. The crowd was so large that the paper had to have someone announce the game, and the cheering at critical points could be heard for blocks.

With the championship of the Dominion riding on the outcome, the two top teams in the land and the two best players in the game staged an exhilarating display of hockey. Phillips opened the scoring ten minutes into the first half, but McGee tied it six minutes later. Phillips scored again to give Rat Portage a 2–1 lead at half time. Eight minutes into the second half Ottawa's Alf Smith tied the game, then Tom Hooper put the Thistles ahead 3–2. McGee got that one back, and Harry Westwick added another to give Ottawa the lead for the first time in the game. But Phillips notched his third of the game to tie the score 4–4 and set up a dramatic conclusion. Here is how one of the telegraphers called the final minutes:

> Ottawa takes desperate chances to score now. Pulford is up on the firing line. The line Smith, Westwick, McGee, Gilmour, Pulford continue the bombardment. It is all Ottawa now with the Thistles defence fighting desperately to hold them off. Phillips and McGimsie work down as far as centre but Pulford makes another of his rushes. He and McGee close on the nets. Frank gets the puck. Brown comes at him but McGee sidesteps and drives the puck into the nets between the legs of Giroux. The rink had been in a furore but it bursts into a veritable Niagara of sound now. Young and old weep with joy. Only 90 seconds to play.

With a 5–4 win, and a 2–1 series victory, the Senators had retained the Stanley Cup for a third straight season, and again stood at the pinnacle of Canada's great winter game, as hockey was known in those days. As for the Thistles, they had taken a pounding. "Silas Griffis' knee is swollen to twice its normal size, and he and Billie McGimsie were hardly able to stand on their skates toward the end," the *Montreal Star* reported. "Every man was badly cut around the face, except Brown and Giroux. Phillips had no fewer than seven cuts on his face."

While the Thistles were understandably disappointed, they had made a lasting contribution to the game. The Rat Portage defencemen introduced a new way of playing defence, which was immediately copied by the Senators. The Thistle defencemen lined up side by side, rather than one in front of the other. They rushed with the puck rather than merely lifting it down the ice. As well, they moved up the ice with the forward line instead of staying back to defend the goal. Moreover, the Thistles played so well that they left the nation's capital with their reputation enhanced. "If the Cup had to go, there's no team I'd sooner give it to than the Thistles," said Ottawa's Alf Smith. "I take my hat off to Rat Portage and its hockey team. Long may they flourish."

Two weeks after the Rat Portage series, the Ottawa Hockey Club honoured the victors with a banquet at the Russell Hotel. It was an intimate affair in which the officers of the team and the players, about twenty-seven people in all, sat at one large round table, according to the *Ottawa Free Press*. There were speeches by practically everyone, and the team colours were everywhere.

Red, white, and black streamers had been strung across the ceiling. A sign saying "Our boys," decorated in red, white, and black carnations, had been hung above table. Hanging vertically from the sign were two hockey sticks, also covered in carnations, and between the sticks dangled the word Ottawa. The team colours were also worked into the menu. "Around the oysters were diamond-shaped pieces of tissue paper in red, white and black," the *Free Press* reported. "The soup contained tiny vegetable stars in the club colours while the fish was moulded to represent a hockey shoe and stick. The detail did not stop there. The ice cream was red, white and black with a diminutive pennant planted on top."

In the winter of 1905-06, the Senators and the Thistles were once again two of the premier teams in the country. But the Montreal Wanderers, who wore white sweaters with a broad red band and a large W emblazoned on their chests, had also emerged as a powerhouse. Ottawa and Montreal were both competing in the newly formed Eastern Canada Hockey Association (ECHA). As the ten-game season progressed, the two teams compiled identical records and quickly became involved in a tense race. For Ottawa, the stakes grew as the season progressed. One bad game, one unexpected loss, would cost the team first place and the Stanley Cup. And in late February and early March, the Senators also had to meet two outside challengers, the Queen's University team, which had won the intercollegiate title, and the Smiths Falls team that had captured the Federal Amateur Hockey League championship.

Queen's proved to be more a distraction than a legitimate challenge to Ottawa. The Senators clobbered the students 16–7 in the first game and 12–7 the following night. The only noteworthy aspect of the series was that the Ottawa press for the first time referred to its team as the Silver Seven, and then only in passing. "In the last half of last night's game," the *Citizen* reported, "the silver seven had a practise rather than a match."

Smiths Falls managed at least to throw a scare into the potent Ottawa squad during the first game of the two-game series. The Silver Seven scratched out a narrow 5–4 win in the first game, which piqued the interest of Ottawa fans. A record forty-five hundred people showed up for the second game only to see Ottawa thrash Smiths Falls 8–2.

Two days later, on March 10, 1906, Ottawa travelled to Quebec City for its final game of the ECHA season, while the Wanderers were playing their last match against the woeful Montreal Shamrocks. Both teams won that night to finish the season with identical 9–1 records. They agreed to play a two-game, total-goal series for the league championship, and the Stanley Cup. Meanwhile, the Thistles had also won their league again and submitted another challenge for the Cup. But because it was already mid-March, the Thistles agreed to play the winner of the Ottawa-Montreal showdown the following January.

The prospect of a playoff between the Silver Seven and the Wanderers created enormous excitement in both Montreal and

Ottawa. At 7:30 a.m. on March 14, the day of the opening game, several hundred people were lined up outside the Montreal's Mount Royal Arena to buy tickets. By the time the tickets went on sale at 9:00 a.m., the line up stretched several blocks and within half an hour they were sold out. Throughout the day, scalpers were getting up to five dollars for a one-dollar ticket.

That night a crowd of seven thousand fans packed the arena, several hundred of whom had travelled from Ottawa on a special train put on by the Grand Trunk Railway. Thousands more Ottawa fans stood outside the *Citizen* building on Sparks Street in Ottawa to read the telegraphed bulletins. Inside, the phones rang all night. "Till after midnight, all the telephones in the *Citizen* were constantly busy without so much as a minute's let up, the enquiries including many from all the towns of the Ottawa valley."

But for all the excitement, the evening was a dreadful disaster for Ottawa. The Silver Seven lost 9–1, and almost everyone was baffled by the dismal showing of the champions. "What came over the Silver Seven in that game no one knows," the *Ottawa Free Press* observed. "Not a single member of the team appeared anything like his form."

Although the next game appeared to be a mere formality, five hundred Montrealers took the Grand Trunk to Ottawa, and another four hundred came by the CPR. The Wanderers were among the travellers on the Grand Trunk, and had to dress for the game on the train because it arrived at 7:15 p.m., a little more than an hour before the opening face off. Contingents of fans came from Smiths Falls and Cornwall, and arrangements were made to send telegraph reports of the game to towns up and down the Ottawa Valley. A crowd of six thousand, including hundreds who sat in the aisles, packed Dey's Arena. Shortly before game time, the president of the Ottawa Hockey Club, George Murphy, led Governor General Earl Grey and his wife across the ice to the vice-regal box.

What occurred that night in Ottawa still ranks as one of the grittiest performances and greatest comebacks in Stanley Cup history. The teams played scoreless hockey for twelve and a half minutes until the Wanderers' captain, Lester Patrick, gave Montreal a 1–0 lead in the game, and a 10–1 lead in the series. The Montrealers in the crowd leapt to their feet, cheering wildly and waving hats, megaphones and team flags.

Then Ottawa erupted. The *Montreal Star* estimated that the Silver Seven bombarded the Wanderers' goalie, who was identified only as H. Menard, with close to two hundred shots, while the *Citizen* reported that for three-quarters of the game the Wanderers never got the puck past centre-ice. Ottawa scored nine straight goals, including five by Harry Smith and two by McGee. With less than two minutes remaining, the series was tied 10–10.

"This was the feat that was supposed to be superhuman but it was accomplished, and then it was that the crowd of six thousand went literally wild," the Montreal *Herald* reported. "Hats and overcoats were thrown recklessly in the air, vocal organs were strained to the utmost, and embraces given and returned boisterously by utter strangers. Pandemonium reigned for ten minutes." Even the governor general was on his feet waving his hat and cheering wildly.

The crowd's joy was shortlived. Ottawa immediately launched another desperate attack, with every man up, furiously swarming around the Montreal net. But in a moment of recklessness, Ottawa lost the puck, Patrick pounced on it, and raced down the ice to score on Percy LeSueur in the Ottawa net. That made the total score 11–10 Montreal. Refusing to quit, the Silver Seven threw every man into the attack and left their own end undefended except for LeSueur. And again Patrick came through for the Wanderers, scoring on what was described as "a wild, slap-dash rush."

The Wanderers had a two-goal lead, time was running out, the Silver Seven's glorious reign was coming to an end. Here was the play-by-play of the final frantic moments as it went out over the telegraph wires and appeared in the next day's papers:

The Ottawas, stung by the prospect of defeat after such a great battle, plunged headlong at the visitors' nets. The men charged and shot and fell, within a few feet of victory, and the great crowd behaved like inmates in a vast asylum. The noise, deafening at all times, grew into a fearful uproar. It was all in vain, however, and as the bell sounded a great wave of groans swept out from the stands, drowned, however, in a moment by the exultant roar of the Wanderers' supporters as they ran on the ice to carry off their team.

So ended the reign of hockey's first dynasty. The Silver Seven, as they have come to be known, had earned a hallowed place in the history of the game based on their formidable defence of the Stanley Cup from March 1903 through March 1906. The following winter McGee retired from hockey and Gilmour also quit. Harvey Pulford, Harry Westwick, Art Moore, and Alf Smith, the other key players, stayed in the game. The Ottawa Hockey Club remained competitive, finishing second to the Wanderers in 1907, but the team was no longer a powerhouse.

Pulford went on to win acclaim as a rower, and as late as 1924 won the Ottawa city squash championship. Alf Smith went on to coach senior lacrosse, and Bouse Hutton came out of retirement in 1906 to play lacrosse for the Ottawa Capitals team that won the national senior championship. When their playing days finally ended, most of the Silver Seven spent the rest of their adults lives in Ottawa, living quietly and enjoying their status as hockey legends. A notable exception was Frank McGee, who had led them to their greatest accomplishments.

McGee worked in the Interior Department of the federal government until the outbreak of World War I in 1914. He was thirty-five years old at the time but nevertheless volunteered for service overseas and was accepted, despite his disability. In December 1915, McGee was wounded while fighting in France, and spent nine months recovering in England. On September 4, 1916, shortly before he was due to return to action, he wrote a letter to his brother, D'Arcy McGee, a prominent Ottawa lawyer. In it he said that he had been offered a posting in Le Havre, a French coastal town well behind the front. Instead, he insisted upon returning to combat duty. Twelve days after writing that letter he was killed in action at Courcellette, France.

Frank McGee's obituary appeared in the Ottawa *Citizen* on September 25, 1916, nine days after his death. It was awkwardly placed between a business story about the price of potatoes and an advertisement for women's dresses. But that took nothing away the anonymous author's obvious admiration and respect for the late Lieutenant McGee. And brief as it was, the obituary managed to capture the spirit of a man who had recovered from a devastating eye injury to become the greatest hockey player of his day, and the heart of one of the best teams ever assembled.

"Canadians who knew the sterling stuff of which Frank McGee was made, and they were not confined to Ottawa alone, were not surprised when he donned another and now more popular uniform and jumped into the greater and grimmer game of war," the *Citizen*'s reporter wrote. "And just as in his sporting career he was always to be found in the thickest of the fray, there is no doubt that on the field of battle Lieut. McGee knew no fear nor shunned any danger in the performance of his duty."

3

ROUGH AND TUMBLE

1907-17

Tall, bearded, and imperious looking, Michael John O'Brien was a backwoods, turn-of-the-century tycoon and a millionaire several times over. In 1916, on one of the few occasions when his income was a matter of public record, he earned $1.6 million after tax. Born in Nova Scotia in 1851, he settled in Renfrew, Ontario, ninety kilometres west of Ottawa, with his wife and seven children. But O'Brien was rarely home. The man known as M. J. to financiers and labourers alike spent most of his time roaming Eastern Canada and managing his empire. He built railways, owned one of the world's richest silver mines, harvested timber, and operated sawmills, woollen mills, and munitions factories.

Although he once travelled from Renfrew to New Orleans to see a prize fight, M. J. O'Brien was never known as a sportsman. Not until late 1909, that is, when in a fit of pique he financed the creation of the National Hockey Association (NHA), forerunner of the National Hockey League. He also put up the money to launch the Montreal Canadiens, and he bankrolled a colossal bidding war for professional hockey players that became the talk of the country, all because he was determined to see the Renfrew

Creamery Kings win the Stanley Cup. Once the new league was established, O'Brien put his eldest son, Ambrose, then just twenty-five, in charge of day-to-day operations. In fact, the restless tycoon may never have seen his Creamery Kings play, and there is nothing to suggest that he was a fan of the game.

O'Brien's quixotic venture occurred amid a decade of turbulence and upheaval caused primarily by the advent of professional hockey. In those years, from 1907 until the formation of the NHL in 1917, there were almost no rules or conventions to govern the signing of players or to restrict their movements. One team could raid another's roster, and the players were free to sell their services to the highest bidder. Star players could move from team to team, from city to city, from league to league, sometimes in a single season.

It was a chaotic, free market that ideally suited the temperament of the wealthy and energetic O'Brien and the small circle of affluent Renfrew residents who ran the Creamery Kings as a pastime. "We want the very best team money can buy, the best team in the world, in fact," declared George Martel, a member of the team's executive committee. "And we don't care where the players come from."

Shortly after that bold declaration appeared in the Renfrew *Journal*, O'Brien and his fellow marauders stunned the hockey establishment of eastern Canada by signing two of the biggest stars in the game, Lester and Frank Patrick. At the time, the Patrick brothers were working for their father, who ran a lumber business in Nelson, B.C. Lester Patrick had already signed a contract with the Edmonton Eskimos and was due to play in an upcoming Stanley Cup challenge series against the defending champion Ottawa Senators. Despite that commitment, Lester Patrick and his brother received twenty-six telegrams over a two-week period from six different eastern clubs, who wanted to sign them. In a single day in December 1909, Lester Patrick received offers of $1,200 from the Montreal Wanderers, $1,500 from the Ottawa Senators and $3,000 from the Creamery Kings.

Patrick accepted Renfrew's offer only after the Creamery Kings offered his brother, Frank, $2,000 for the season.

Although the salaries offered the Patrick brothers would consume half the team's gate receipts for the 1910 season, the Creamery Kings had only begun. On December 28, 1909, Renfrew scored its biggest coup by signing Fred "Cyclone" Taylor, star defenceman of the Ottawa Senators and one of the most sensational players in the game. Taylor signed for $5,250, and the entire sum was deposited in his Ottawa bank account. The previous year he had earned a total of $2,800 playing hockey and working full-time as a clerk in the federal Immigration Department. His clerking job paid about thirty-five dollars a month. "When the contract was signed, Taylor became the highest-paid athlete in Canada and, on a per-game basis, in the world," wrote Frank Cosentino in his 1990 book, *The Renfrew Millionaires.* "He was being paid $5,250 for a 12-game season over two months. Ty Cobb, the great American baseball player, had recently signed for $6,500. That was over seven months and 154 games."

In their frantic bid to bring the Stanley Cup to Renfrew, O'Brien and his fellow raiders signed several other talented but lesser-known players to lucrative contracts. They snatched Herb Jordan, a high-scoring centre, from the Quebec Bulldogs. They signed forwards Fred Whitcroft and Hay Miller while they were in the East as members of the Eskimo team that was challenging the Senators for the Stanley Cup in January 1910. And in mid-February, with the season half over, they pried centre Newsy Lalonde from the Montreal Canadiens. Renfrew's star-studded line-up had a payroll of $16,000, and the Creamery Kings quickly became known as the Millionaires.

O'Brien's spending spree was triggered by his belief that trustees P. D. Ross and William Foran, as well as the directors of the Ottawa Hockey Club, had unfairly denied Renfrew a shot at the Stanley Cup. The Creamery Kings had issued challenges for the Cup in the spring of 1907 and again in the spring of 1909. On both occasions, Ross and Foran had turned them down, at least partly because there were a number of outstanding challenges from other parts of the country. Prior to the 1909 season, Renfrew applied for a franchise in the powerful Eastern Canada Hockey Association but the town's bid was rejected, largely because of objections raised by the men who ran the Ottawa Hockey Club. Stymied by the trustees, and snubbed by the hockey barons of the nation's capital, the directors of the Creamery Kings finally turned to the town's wealthiest and most powerful citizen, M. J. O'Brien, in late 1909.

O'Brien and his cronies pursued the Cup with a rare combination of zeal and audacity, but their aspirations were anything but extraordinary. After the reign of the Silver Seven ended, a remarkable number of small towns and budding Canadian cities attempted to win the coveted Cup. The challengers came from New Glasgow, Sydney, and Moncton in the Maritimes, from Galt, Berlin, and Port Arthur in Ontario, and Edmonton in the West. They had names like the Cubs and the Bearcats, the Miners and the Eskimos, the Union Jacks and the Victorias.

In most cases, the leading citizens of these communities – doctors, lawyers, and businessmen – organized and ran the teams. They were successful men in young and growing communities. Hockey quickly became more than a pastime and a private passion once they saw that the game could be used to promote their towns. A championship team provided a tremendous boost for the civic ego. And winning the Stanley Cup would be better than any amount of advertising. A Renfrew or a Sydney, a Galt or a Berlin, could achieve instant renown from one end of the Dominion to the other. However, only one such community, Rat Portage, Ontario, now called Kenora, succeeded in winning the Cup, and Kenora's Thistles held on to it only briefly. The rest of the challengers from small-town Canada proved to be woefully weak and provided no competition at all for the powerful clubs like the Ottawa Senators and Montreal Wanderers.

As for the Renfrew Millionaires, they came no closer to winning the Stanley Cup than the other small-town teams, despite the money and the might of M. J. O'Brien. In 1910, they finished third in the NHA with a record of eight wins, three losses, and one default. The following season, the Millionaires finished third again. By then, however, M. J. O'Brien and his fellow backers had decided that professional hockey would never be a paying proposition in Renfrew and the franchise was shifted to Toronto for the 1912 season.

In 1912 and 1913, Moncton and Sydney made their futile bids to win the Stanley Cup. They were the last challengers from small-town Canada. From that point on, the pursuit of the Cup ceased to be an egalitarian free-for-all, open to big and small communities, to amateur and professional teams alike. Instead, it became a trophy pursued exclusively by professional teams based in big cities. By 1914, the Stanley Cup playoff series had been transformed into an annual showdown between East and West, much like today's Grey Cup. It was a duel between the two professional leagues in Canada at the time, the NHA in the East and the Pacific Coast Hockey Association (PCHA) in the West.

The decade from 1907 to 1917 was also an era of firsts. Quebec City won the Stanley Cup for the first time. Vancouver became the first city west of Winnipeg to capture the Cup. Toronto finally produced a Cup winner, twenty-one years after Lord Stanley donated his trophy. The Portland Rosebuds became the first American-based team to compete for the Cup, the Seattle Metropolitans became the first American-based team to win it, and the Montreal Canadiens won the first of their twenty-three Cups.

At the start of this decade of sweeping change, the Montreal Wanderers were the unquestioned kings of hockey. They had dethroned hockey's first dynasty, the Ottawa Silver Seven, in March 1906, and went on to hold the Cup three years running. The Wanderers began their defence of the Cup in late December 1906 when a team called the Cubs from New Glasgow, Nova Scotia, arrived in Montreal for a two-game series.

The Cubs were an unknown, unheralded bunch, and the

Montreal sporting establishment had no idea what to expect of them. "There is not a great deal to go by relative to the strangers," the Montreal *Gazette* reported. "Not much attention has been paid in Montreal to eastern hockey. The fact that this is but the second challenge from that section of the country seems to indicate that the Maritime players have not had a great deal of confidence in their prowess." In fact, the Cubs were no match for the Wanderers, and they surrendered by scores of 10–3 and 7–3. The matches attracted far thinner crowds than an important regular season senior game.

The Cubs had barely left Montreal when a representative of the next challenger arrived to set the dates for a series that was destined to capture the attention of hockey fans everywhere. J. F. MacGillivray, a lawyer and secretary-treasurer of the Kenora Thistles Hockey Club told the Montreal sports press that the team was considered better than ever. The Thistles had won the Manitoba and Northwestern Association title the previous winter, but their Cup challenge had been set over to 1907 because the series between the Wanderers and the Silver Seven had not been completed until late March 1906.

The Thistles arrived in Montreal in mid-January 1907 for the two-game, total-goal series with essentially the same team that had come so close to upsetting the Silver Seven in March 1905. Eddie Giroux was in goal, Silas Griffis at coverpoint, Tom Hooper at rover, Roxy Beaudro at right wing, Billie McGimsie at centre, and the great Tom Phillips at left wing. The Thistles had bolstered their team by picking up point man and Montreal native Art Ross from the Brandon Wheat Kings.

The series generated enormous interest across the country. The Kenora *Miner and News* reported that newspapers from Nova Scotia to British Columbia posted telegraph reports of the games in progress and added: "All across Canada the struggle for the coveted Cup is being watched with the biggest interest." The *Manitoba Free Press* reported that "Winnipeg people have come to look upon the Kenora boys with almost as much pride and affection as they did the champion Victorias." Sportswriters flocked to Montreal from various parts of the country, as well as from Pittsburgh and Buffalo. And there were six thousand fans, including several hundred from Kenora, packed into the Mount Royal Arena for the opening game.

The Thistles were known for their speed and they did not disappoint the hockey world that night in Montreal. According to the *Gazette,* the visitors played a nearly faultless game that was fast and clean. The paper added that the challengers were skating as hard in the final moments as they were at the opening face off. "It was a ripping fast match," the *Gazette* reported. "The visitors were simply great on skates. They move along beautifully. The term poetry on ice has meaning when an enthusiast watches the Thistle players." Kenora's forwards also checked Montreal's potent forward line of Ernie Russell, Lester Patrick, Pud Glass, and Ernie Johnson into submission and skated off with a 4–2 win. The star of the night was unquestionably Tom Phillips, who scored all four Kenora goals.

On the night of the second game, January 21, 1907, it is doubtful whether the emotions at ice level were any higher than they were in Kenora, the isolated lumber and mining town in northwestern Ontario, whose principal links to the rest of the world were the railway and the telegraph. The railway had brought the town's beloved Thistles to Montreal, and the telegraph brought back up-to-the minute reports of their exploits on the ice. The following account of that evening, written years later by an anonymous resident of Kenora, is now in the archives of the town's Lake of the Woods Museum:

> Thru the good graces of Principal Roberts, we high school kids had no homework that night and all sports minded townsfolk gathered at the Victoria rink to hear the first hand reports of the game. This was long before any radio was available. A telegraph receiver was installed in the band room and a running report of the game was read by Mr. Joseph Johnson,

one of the team executives. The first 30 minutes of the game was all Kenora and our team led 5 to 2. Our hopes were high, especially when we scored the first goal on resumption of play, making it 6–2. Then the roof fell in. Montreal scored the next four goals, 6–3, 6–4, 6–5, 6–6 with two minutes to play. With each bulletin Mr. Johnson's face was getting longer and longer and it looked like it was all over. The next telegram came in and Joe came bounding out yelling and waving the wire over his head. Bedlam broke loose but it was sometime before we knew the score as in the excitement Joe lost his voice and there were too many goals to show them on his fingers. Finally things quieted down and we were able to learn that with time running out Kenora scored two quick goals to win 8 to 6 and to be the only small town in Canada ever to win the Stanley Cup.

The Thistles received a tumultuous welcome when they returned home and later attended a more orderly and sedate reception at the Kenora opera hall. The team's triumph inspired some grandiose civic dreams. The town fathers declared that they would build the biggest arena in the West, a 4,000-seat masterpiece, to replace the decrepit Victoria rink that was known for its small playing surface and gloomy lighting. However, the Thistles' reign as Stanley Cup champions proved to be short and turbulent.

The Wanderers swept through the Eastern Canada Hockey Association (ECHA) season in 1907 with a perfect 10–0 record and promptly issued a Stanley Cup challenge. They asked William Foran, who was filling in as trustee on behalf of P. D. Ross, to order that the games be moved from Kenora to Winnipeg, which had a suitable arena. The Wanderers also asked Foran to prohibit Kenora from using outside reinforcements for their defence of the Cup.

Foran ruled that the games should be played in Kenora, provided the Thistles won their league championship, because their fans deserved to see them defend the Cup, but he sided with the Wanderers on the issue of outside players. Kenora had recruited Harry Westwick and Alf Smith from Ottawa late in the season, and Foran ruled them ineligible for Cup play. He also scheduled a two-game, total-goal series for March 20 and 22.

In mid-March 1907, the Montrealers left for Winnipeg to await the outcome of a playoff between Kenora and Brandon for the western championship. The Thistles, meanwhile, were arguing vociferously with Foran over the eligibility of Westwick and Smith, as well as over the dates for the series. Dozens of telegrams flew back and forth, and the newspapers carried long, detailed accounts of the dispute. Foran insisted that he would simply order Kenora to forfeit the Cup and return it to him if Westwick and Smith played. Kenora stipulated that it would not play without the pair.

The Thistles never did settle their dispute with the trustee. Instead, the teams themselves reached a compromise that allowed the series to go ahead. Kenora agreed to play the series in Winnipeg, and the Wanderers agreed to let Westwick and Smith play. This infuriated Foran, who insisted that he would declare the series null and void. But the teams simply ignored the trustee's ultimatum and lined up to play hockey on evening of March 23, a Saturday. The Winnipeg rink was jammed, and hundreds of fans were turned away. A telegraph operator, sitting at rink side, reported that the crowd cheered wildly when the Thistles appeared. He also had this to say: "There is betting all over the rink. Big bets were made in the dressing rooms before the game."

The game was played on soft, water-covered ice, a distinct disadvantage for the speedy Thistles, and the defending champs were simply no match for the hungry Wanderers. "[The Wanderers] came West with the determination to prove to the hockey world that they are the best team on skates," the *Gazette* reported. "When at last the order to advance was given they fell on the enemy with a vigor and impetuosity that carried everything with it." The Wanderers routed the Thistles 7–2, meaning that they had a five-goal lead going into the second game and had virtually won the Cup.

Nevertheless, the second game proved to be a thrilling exhibition of hockey, played on hard, fast ice before a crowd of six thousand. Three times the game was tied before Kenora's Fred Whitcroft finally scored with minutes remaining to make it 6–5 for the Thistles. "As an exhibition of lightning fast, scientific hockey, the game was without doubt the finest ever seen on Winnipeg ice," the Montreal *Star* reported. "Each and every man showed himself a marvel of strength and endurance. The vast throng that filled the rink was on its feet soon after the game started, and all through the contest stood up and cheered."

Having recovered the coveted Cup that they had lost two months earlier, the Wanderers received a thunderous welcome upon arriving in Montreal on March 30. A few enthusiastic fans went out to Vaudreuil, forty-eight kilometres west of the city, in order to greet the team. Thousands more gathered outside Bonaventure Station in downtown Montreal. "The surrounding streets were packed by a mass of swaying humanity," the *Gazette* reported. When the team finally arrived around 6:00 p.m., the players climbed aboard two large horse-drawn wagons for a parade through St. James, Peel, Ste-Catherine, and Victoria streets, ending at the Savoy Hotel. The fans boisterously followed the players through the streets in automobiles, buses, and on foot.

Outside the hotel, a crowd gathered and demanded speeches from some of the players. Lester Patrick spoke, and point man Hod Stuart concluded by saying: "We won the Cup in the most gentlemanly manner we could and I am glad to see that Montrealers appreciate it." With that, the team retired to the Savoy for a private dinner and the huge crowds began to disperse.

The 1908 hockey season opened with two Stanley Cup challenges held over from the previous season. The Ottawa Victorias, the capital city's second senior team and the winners of the

Federal Amateur Hockey League, wanted a crack at the Wanderers and so did the Renfrew Creamery Kings, the reigning champions of the Upper Ottawa Valley League. Trustees Foran and Ross ruled that the two teams should hold a preliminary playoff for the right to meet the Wanderers. Ottawa proved to be the superior team, but the Victorias were no match for the powerful Wanderers, and lost by scores of 9–3 and 13–1.

The most exciting game of the 1908 season, in which the Stanley Cup was at stake, occurred February 28 when the Ottawa Senators and Montreal Wanderers squared off for first place in the ECAHA. For the Wanderers, finishing first meant that they would retain the Stanley Cup. The Senators, on the other hand, could wrest the Cup from Montreal with a first-place finish.

Close to a thousand Ottawa residents travelled to Montreal on the day of the game, and the Senators' red, white, and black colours were evident throughout the downtown area all afternoon. Back in the capital, huge crowds gathered at the Grand Union Hotel and the Ottawa Amateur Athletic Club to catch the telegraph bulletins provided by the *Ottawa Free Press*.

At the Mount Royal Arena, meanwhile, bedlam reigned. The unreserved sections of the rink were packed solid by 7:30 p.m., an hour before game time, and there were still six thousand people lined up outside the west door hoping to get in. When the arena management decided to cut off ticket sales, the unruly crowd began pushing against the door. Arena employees, aided by police, finally succeeded in closing and barricading the door.

Several dozen men then scaled the walls and scrambled over a web of electric wires, causing the lights in the arena sign to explode like artillery shells. Nevertheless, most of these gatecrashers managed to slip into the building through openings in the roof. "Finally at 8:45 the east door was opened and those in the swaying mass at that side were sucked in by the human current," the *Otawa Free Press* reported. "Windows, doors and bric-a-brac were smashed and the arena company probably suffered a $400 or $500 loss." Nevertheless, the game got underway.

Ottawa held a slender 1–0 lead at half time, prompting a bold Senator fan to rise amid a group of Wanderers supporters and offer 4–1 odds on the final outcome. The *Free Press* told the story: "One prominent Ottawa professional man stood up in a heavily populated Wanderer section and with a handful of $20 and $50 bills shouted 'I will lay $400 to $100 Ottawa wins.'" The Montrealers yelled at the man to sit down, but he repeated his offer before stuffing his money back in his pocket and muttering: "You are weak hearted supporters." Despite such optimism on the part of the Senator supporters, the Wanderers roared back with four goals in the second half, and won the game 4–2.

With that win, the Wanderers went on to capture the ECHA crown and automatically retained the Stanley Cup. They then faced two challengers, the Winnipeg Maple Leafs, champions of the Manitoba Hockey League, and the Toronto Maple Leafs, winners of the newly created Ontario Professional Hockey League. The Winnipeggers were a pushover for the Wanderers, losing 11–5 and 9–3. Expecting that the Torontonians would be the weakest of the challengers they faced that winter, the Wanderers insisted upon playing a one-game, sudden-death playoff with the Toronto Maple Leafs.

It almost proved to be a costly mistake. The Toronto roster included two future stars, winger Bruce Ridpath and centre Newsy Lalonde. The game was played on dreadful ice that was soft, slushy, and covered with water. As a result, it was a dull, ragged, penalty-filled exhibition. "The players with their water-soaked boots and uniforms were in anything but an angelic mood and it took little to provoke retaliation," the *Gazette* noted.

Furthermore, the Wanderers were guilty of some astonishing lapses. Late in the second half, with Montreal leading 4–3, Ridpath was hurt on a play in the Wanderers' end, which caused a long delay. "When the rubber was faced off, the Wanderer defence players, including goalie Riley Hern, were talking with a friend at the side," the *Gazette* reported. "Lalonde, seeing the long opening before him, lifted the disc dead on the Wanderer net. Hern was yards away when the umpire's hand went up giving Toronto the goal which made it 4–4." That seemed to wake up the Wanderers because they promptly scored twice and hung on to win 6–4. They finished the 1908 season as Stanley Cup champions for the third consecutive year. They had equalled the feat achieved by the Silver Seven, although there was a blemish on the Wanderers' record – their loss to the Thistles in January 1907.

Prior to the 1909 season, the Wanderers again had to defend their title. The Edmonton Eskimos, champions of the Alberta Hockey League, had issued a challenge at the end of the 1908 season that was carried over because the trustees had given priority to the Winnipeg and Toronto challenges. However, the Eskimo team that arrived in Montreal to play the Wanderers was not the same team that had won the Alberta championship the previous winter. The executive of the Edmonton Hockey Club decided to take advantage of the professionalism that was sweeping through the game and simply buy the best players available. Trustees Ross and Foran placed only one restraint on the club's activity; they said that Edmonton could not sign anyone who had played in a Stanley Cup series the previous winter.

In the fall of 1908, Eskimo player-manager Fred Whitcroft went shopping for talent in the East. He returned in late November having signed Renfrew goalie Bert Lindsay, father of future NHL star Ted Lindsay, Portage La Prairie defenceman Hugh Ross, Montreal Shamrock defenceman Didier Pitre, Renfrew forward Steve Vair, and former Thistle star Tom Phillips. Whitcroft completed his recruiting drive by signing Lester Patrick to play defence. The only local players on the team were forwards Jack Miller and Harold Deeton.

After practising for nearly a month, and playing three exhibition games against a local team, the Eskimos left for the East on December 16. Several hundred fans showed up at the train station to see the team off and the players had attached a streamer to their car, which read: "Edmonton Hockey Club after the championship of the world." Phillips and Patrick, meanwhile, met their new teammates in Winnipeg, and actually never set foot in the Alberta capital.

Newspapers across the country criticized Edmonton's attempts to buy a Stanley Cup win and called for changes in the rules to prohibit such signing sprees. The Toronto *Telegram* snidely commented that "The only thing on the team that belongs to Edmonton are the sticks and uniforms, and they were imported too." The Vancouver *Province,* noting that Phillips was being paid $600 for two games, added sarcastically: "That makes his time on the ice worth just $5 a minute." And the *Manitoba Free Press* added this lament: "It is no longer a question of local pride and ambition but a matter of the club that has the most money. The conditions certainly are rotten and the historic old Cup now really represents nothing."

The first game of the two-game, total-goal series drew six thousand fans and the Eskimos led 3–2 at the half. But they collapsed in the last thirty minutes and lost 7–3. The Eskimos looked like they had a chance of upsetting the Wanderers when they ran up a 4–1 lead in the second game. However, when the final whistle sounded, Edmonton had scratched out a narrow 7–6 win. Ironically, the two best Eskimo players turned out to be Deeton and Miller, the local boys who got into the game only after a couple of the high-priced imports were hurt.

The Wanderers finally lost the Cup in March 1909 to the Ottawa Senators, their most serious rival throughout the three years the Montrealers held the trophy. The Senators had a solid goaltender in Percy LeSueur, and a spectacular defenceman in Fred "Cyclone" Taylor. They also had the most potent offence in the Eastern Canada Hockey Association (ECHA) that year. Forwards Marty Walsh, Bruce Stuart and Albert Kerr finished first, third, and fifth in scoring while Billy Gilmour, the former Silver Seven player, contributed eleven goals in as many games.

The showdown between the Wanderers and the Senators occurred in Ottawa on March 3, 1909, toward the end of the twelve-game ECHA season. The winner was assured of first place, and with it the Stanley Cup. For Ottawa fans, the major issue in the days leading up to the game was whether or not Cyclone Taylor could recover from an injury suffered the previous week against the Montreal Shamrocks.

"Taylor was playing in magnificent form at the time and the crowd was roaring in appreciation of one of his spectacular plays," the *Gazette* reported. "Taylor had carried the puck from one end of the rink to the other and swerved at top speed around the Shamrock goal." At that point he crashed to the ice and slid into the boards. Play was stopped, and Taylor was carried to the dressing room. A doctor cut open his skate to find his sock soaked in blood and a ragged three-inch cut on the inside of his right foot. Taylor had been skating with such speed that his left skate blade had sliced through his right skate and into his foot.

The speedy defenceman spent a couple of days in bed then met with the Ottawa sporting press to announce that he would play against the Wanderers. "When the Stanley Cup is at stake," he told the eager Ottawa scribes, "I can stand any amount of pain." Taylor disclosed that he would wear a steel plate and some padding to protect the wound. Although he was still limping, Taylor had enough confidence in his team's chances to participate in the pre-game wagering. The Ottawa players bet nearly a thousand dollars on the game. "The money was left in the safe at the Russell Hotel, and is to be covered at 3–2, Ottawa being the favourites," the *Gazette* told its readers. "Bruce Stuart, Marty Walsh and Fred Taylor also put up $500 against a Montreal traveller's $400 that they would win."

A noisy crowd of sixty-five hundred attended, including five hundred Montrealers, and they witnessed a superb exhibition of hockey. "The teams went at one another fiercely," said the *Gazette.* "There was no let up from the very start to the last minute, and no mercy was shown in the checking with body and stick." Taylor was said to have played with his usual brilliance until he was struck on the head by the puck early in the second half.

The score was tied 3–3 at the half, and as the minutes ticked by in the second half it became apparent that the next goal would probably decide the matter. Finally, ten minutes into the second half the Senators scored, and the crowd erupted. Hats and banners filled the air and, according to the *Citizen,* the cheering seemed to shake the building.

Fifteen minutes later they added an insurance goal. Then with the desperate Wanderers throwing every man into the attack, Ottawa pumped in three goals in the last three minutes to make it an 8–3 rout. When the gong sounded to end the game, half the fans in the arena clambered on to the ice to congratulate the players. They hoisted Walsh, Taylor, and Gilmour to their shoulders and carried them to the dressing room. For several hours after the game, Senator supporters roamed the streets of downtown Ottawa shouting jubilantly at the top of their lungs.

The 1909 season had ended on a triumphant note for the Senators and their fans, but the 1910 season began with turmoil and confusion. In December 1909, three challengers, Galt of the Ontario Professional Hockey League, the Winnipeg Shamrocks of the Manitoba Hockey League, and the Edmonton Eskimos of the Alberta Hockey League, all wanted a crack at the defending cupholders. Unfortunately for the challengers, the executive of the Ottawa Hockey Club was preoccupied in frantically trying to protect its championship team from the marauding Millionaires of Renfrew, who were determined to wreak havoc on the Senators by signing their best players.

Almost every day in December 1909, the Ottawa papers were filled with detailed accounts of the Renfrew raid. One story declared that Renfrew had offered Cyclone Taylor $2,000 to sign with the Creamery Kings, as well as a job paying $1,200 a year. A few days later, the papers reported that Albert Kerr had been offered $2,000, Marty Walsh had been offered $3,000, and both were offered $1,200 a-year-jobs. A day later, another story said Taylor and Fred Lake had both been offered $3,000, and jobs paying $1,200 a year. "Will Renfrew Never Let Up?" the Ottawa

Citizen asked in an anguished headline over one story, while the *Ottawa Evening Journal* declared: "All Canada is flushed with amazement at the fight for Ottawa players."

Amazed perhaps, but not overly sympathetic. In Edmonton, the Eskimos were pushing the Stanley Cup trustees to schedule their challenge series for late December. The Eskimos had signed Lester and Frank Patrick for the series but had agreed to release the brothers if the series was not played before New Year's. At the same time, the Senators and several other eastern clubs, including Renfrew, were wiring offers to the Patricks almost daily.

By mid-December, the Edmonton *Bulletin* had begun to accuse the trustees of discriminating against the Eskimos. The facts were clear, the *Bulletin* told its readers: Ross and Foran had deliberately refused to schedule an early series so that the Alberta champs would lose the Patrick brothers. The newspaper went on to accuse the trustees of acting at the behest of the Senators, declaring: "William Foran and P. D. Ross sit on a gilded hockey throne in Ottawa. There is a power behind that throne. That power is the Ottawa Hockey Club. No one doubts it."

In any event, after a tumultuous month, in which Taylor and the Patrick brothers all signed with Renfrew, the trustees finally scheduled the Stanley Cup challenge series. The Winnipeg Shamrocks dropped their challenge, so Ottawa lined up against Galt first, and Edmonton second. The Galt series was described by the newspapers as a farcical encounter. Ottawa, wearing new uniforms with vertical stripes, never seen before on a hockey sweater, won the first game 12–3 and the second 3–1. "The Ontario league champions played like a lot of schoolboys and seemed to be hardly out of intermediate class," one paper reported. "Fans shouted 'Shoot!' whenever a Galt player got as far as centre and the advice was usually taken."

The Eskimos arrived in Ottawa in mid-January 1910 a couple of days before their series opened and discovered that there was more talk of money than hockey in the nation's capital. "Renfrew has $5,000 in the bank to offer Jack Miller, Bert Boulton and Harold Deeton if we lose the Stanley Cup," the *Bulletin* reported. "This is authoritative."

A day later the newspaper was reporting that O'Brien had blank contracts worth a total of $10,000 for the same three players sitting in a safe in Ottawa. Although the Eskimos obviously had some talented players, they too were swept aside by the Senators by scores of 8–4 and 13–7. When the series was over, two of their players, Miller and Fred Whitcroft, stayed in the East to play for Renfrew.

The biggest Stanley Cup battle of 1910 again turned out to be a regular season game between the Wanderers and the Senators. This time the two old rivals belonged to the National Hockey Association (NHA), the league that M. J. O'Brien had bankrolled. The decisive battle occurred March 5 in Ottawa and tickets were sold out two weeks in advance. With a full house guaranteed, the owners of Dey's Arena warned local fans that smoking would be strictly prohibited at the game, and police officers would eject anyone caught lighting up. "It is not a bluff," the *Citizen* advised its readers. "It is a genuine crusade to stamp out the chief annoyance at hockey matches. At a number of big games this winter, the smoke toward the close became so dense that one could not tell the players apart from any distance."

The game was played on slushy ice covered with pools of water. By the end both sides were exhausted, but the Wanderers had prevailed by a 3–1 margin to win their fourth Stanley Cup in five years. A week later, the Montrealers successfully defended the Cup against the Berlin Union Jacks of the Ontario Professional Hockey League in a dull, one-sided match. With their latest victory, the Wanderers had established themselves as one of the greatest teams of hockey's formative era. But they faded after the 1910 season, and never recovered.

The Ottawa Senators stormed back to the top of the NHA in 1911 with a win-loss record of 11–3 and brought the Cup back to the nation's capital. Three days after the season ended, the Galt professionals, champions of the Ontario league, arrived in Ottawa and were thrashed 7–4 by the Senators. The game, played on slushy ice, was described as one of the poorest exhibitions of hockey seen in Ottawa that winter.

Fortunately, the weather turned cold in time for the next Stanley Cup game between the Senators and the Port Arthur Bearcats, champions of the New Ontario League. The Bearcats proved to be less capable than Galt, and suffered a 13–4 shellacking at the hands of Ottawa. Afterwards, the Ottawa *Citizen* boasted: "The challengers will take back to the wilds of northern Ontario nothing but sympathy and a remarkable respect for the abilities of the invincible Ottawas."

In 1912, the Senators and their fans expected that they would again waltz to the top of the NHA, which by this time had been reduced to four teams. Two of its teams, Haileybury and Cobalt, had folded after the 1910 season, and the Millionaires pulled out following the 1911 campaign. The surviving franchises adopted a couple of fundamental changes for the 1912 season, eliminating the rover and opting instead for six-man hockey. This season, for the first time, the players also began wearing numbered jerseys. Other leagues in Eastern Canada quickly adopted these changes, but seven-man hockey lasted in parts of Western Canada for another ten years. By the 1912 season, most leagues had also switched from two thirty-minute halves to three twenty-minute periods.

As the four surviving teams in the league approached the end of the eighteen-game season, the Ottawa Senators and the Quebec Bulldogs were locked in a tight race for first place. The crucial confrontation between the frontrunners happened on March 3 in Ottawa. The teams battled to a 5–5 tie after sixty minutes of play, in what the *Citizen* described as "easily the most sensational game in Ottawa since the 1905 series between the Silver Seven and Kenora."

The Senators and the Bulldogs fought on through twenty-three gruelling minutes of overtime, which left the players "staggering under the weight of their exhaustion." Finally, Quebec's Joe Hall picked up a loose puck, carried it out from behind the Ottawa net, and scored from a bad angle. "The signal that Quebec had scored came as such a blow that the Ottawa followers lapsed into silence," the *Citizen* wrote. "The gloom was punctuated only by the wild shrieks of the loyal bunch of Quebec rooters." The triumphant Bulldogs had won their first championship.

The Bulldogs were a talented and youthful team with the potential to become a powerhouse for several years. Centre Joe Malone, the star of the team, was twenty-one years old. His wingers, Eddie Oatman and Jack McDonald, were both twenty-two. Malone, Oatman, and Mcdonald had finished sixth, seventh, and eighth respectively in the NHA scoring race that year. The following season, Malone soared to the top with a remarkable forty-three goals in twenty games. Defenceman Goldie Prodgers, the youngest player on the team, was a mere twenty years old. The only veterans were thirty-two-year-old defenceman Joe Hall and the thirty-three-year-old goaltender Paddy Moran.

But prior to the 1913 season, the Bulldogs lost three of their top players, Prodgers, Oatman, and McDonald, to the Pacific Coast Hockey Association (PCHA), founded in December 1911 by Lester and Frank Patrick. The Patrick brothers played only one season in Renfrew before returning to the West and the family lumber business. They initially awarded PCHA franchises to Vancouver, Victoria, and New Westminster, and stocked the teams with twenty-three players recruited from the eastern leagues. By recruiting talented players such as Prodgers, Oatman, and McDonald, the Patricks quickly established their league as one of the best in the country.

Quebec filled the vacancies and, after a shaky start, won

eleven straight games, finishing atop the NHA with a win-loss record of 16–4, well ahead of the second-place Wanderers. Quebec's remarkable recovery was the most unexpected development of the 1913 season, and prompted this observation from the Montreal *Gazette*: "Few ever imagined after the raid of the Patricks that Quebec would again land the coveted honours as the team had practically to be rebuilt from unknown players."

As champions of the NHA, the Bulldogs retained the Stanley Cup, but had to defend it against the Sydney Miners of the Maritime Professional League. Before the Miners arrived, a former member of the Ottawa Silver Seven provided a harsh assessment of the Maritime league. Alf Smith had spent several weeks coaching an East Coast team that winter and returned to tell the Montreal *Gazette*: "I don't say they haven't got good men down there, but the good men are scattered two or three to a team and the rest are bush leaguers. The hockey would hardly compare with any of the NHA teams." Smith's remarks, as unflattering as they were, proved accurate.

The Bulldogs whipped their East Coast challengers 14–3 in the first game of the two-game, total-goal series. Malone, by then recognized as one of the best players in the game, led the attack with nine goals. He sat out the second game, and the Bulldogs prevailed by a more reasonable margin of 6–2. The Sydney Miners were to be the last team from the Maritimes to travel west in search of the Stanley Cup. The Halifax Crescents in 1900 were the first. The New Glasgow Cubs tried in 1906 and the Moncton Victorias in 1912. All had failed, leaving Atlantic Canada as the only region that has never produced a Stanley Cup champion.

As for the Bulldogs, they faltered in 1914 while the Montreal Canadiens and Toronto Blueshirts finished on top of the NHA with identical records of 13–7. The Blueshirts then won a two-game, total-goal playoff, and automatically took possession of the Stanley Cup. Toronto's first Cup-winning team then began to prepare for its next challenge: a best-of-five series against the

Victoria Aristocrats, champions of the Patricks' Pacific Coast league.

During the regular season, Emmett Quinn, president of the NHA, and Frank Patrick, his PCHA counterpart, had reached an agreement, with the tacit approval of the Cup's trustees, under which the champions of the two leagues would play off annually for the Cup. The series would be played in the East one year and the West the next. Because of the distance involved, Quinn and Patrick agreed on the best-of-five format so that the visiting team would be assured of three games and sufficient gate receipts to cover expenses. They also agreed that when the series was played in the East, NHA rules would apply in games one, three, and five, and PCHA rules would prevail in games two and four. The format would be reversed when the series was played on the coast.

When the Patricks founded the PCHA in 1912, they retained the position of rover, whereas the NHA had moved to six-man hockey that winter. However, the Patricks were ahead of the easterners in a couple of other areas. They painted two blue lines on the ice to create a centre ice-zone that was sixty-seven feet wide, and they allowed forward passing within the zone. In the NHA, with its undivided ice surfaces, a player receiving a forward pass was ruled offside and play was halted. The Patricks also adopted a penalty system under which a player was sent off for an infraction and his team played shorthanded for a specified time. In the NHA players were fined for an infraction, sometimes as little as two dollars, but stayed on the ice.

After winning the PCHA title in 1914, Lester Patrick and his Aristocrats boarded a train for Toronto, assuming that they only had to conform to the rules set out in the new agreement. As a result, they neglected to submit a formal challenge for the Stanley Cup. Trustees Ross and Foran responded by declaring that they would not recognize the Aristocrats as champions if they won the upcoming series. The press, the public, and the teams scorned this pedantry and ignored the trustees. The first East-West showdown was billed in the press as the Stanley Cup and world championship series. The Cup was on display at the Eaton's store on Yonge Street, and hundreds of hockey fans from small communities surrounding Toronto poured into the city for the big series.

"The interest in the Stanley Cup series is phenomenal," the *Toronto Star* reported, although the paper admitted that a recent Ontario Hockey Association senior final between two local teams had aroused even greater interest because both rosters were comprised largely of Toronto players. In any case, the first game drew a capacity crowd of sixty-five hundred to Toronto's Mutual Street Arena, the only rink in eastern Canada at the time which had artificial ice. The Blueshirts won by a margin of 5–2. A *Star* reporter described the game as "very slow and devoid of interest except for spots of five minutes duration in the second and third periods."

The dull opener apparently took some of the shine off the series. Only forty-four hundred fans attended game two, which was played under western rules, and scalpers were stuck with seven hundred tickets they couldn't sell. Yet the crowd witnessed a wonderful game. "It was hockey of a brand to make the blood run hot and red," the *Star* reported. The Blueshirts held a 3–2 lead after the first period but were down 5–3 going into the third. They tied the game with nine minutes remaining, but neither team could break the deadlock during regulation time.

Throughout the game, the Blueshirts were baffled by the PCHA's forward passing in the centre-ice zone. "It was heart-rending to see the way Victoria fooled the Blueshirts in that centre ice section," the *Star* said. "A Victoria man bottled up by Toronto players would back up, when suddenly a comrade would dash up the uncovered side of the rink, take a pass on the fly and shoot before the defence had a chance to move." With a decided advantage in the centre ice-zone, the Aristocrats completely dominated the overtime. But after eighteen minutes of play, the Blueshirts' Minnie McGiffen, his face bloodied by a butt end that left a gash above one eye, scored the winning goal.

Two nights later, the teams met again, this time under eastern rules. The Aristocrats played a gallant game from the beginning, displaying "speed, puck carrying ability, ginger and stamina," according to the *Star*. But in the dying minutes, with Toronto holding a 2–1 lead and Victoria's chances evaporating, a scuffle erupted that brought the game to an end.

Toronto's Al Davidson and Victoria's Bob Genge wrestled vigorously for a few minutes then "dropped their sticks and went at it with gloved fists." Other players rushed in to separate the combatants, then both sides retreated to their dressing rooms. "Police inspector Geddes went to the dressing rooms and personally warned the players that any more pugilistic exhibitions would be treated just as if they had occurred on the street and arrests would be made," the *Star* reported. It was anything but a dignified end to a championship series. Nevertheless, the Blueshirts had brought the Stanley Cup to Toronto for the first time in the trophy's twenty-one-year existence.

The reign of the Blueshirts was short-lived. In 1915, the team slipped to third place in the NHA behind the Senators and Wanderers, who finished in a tie for first. The two old rivals met in a two-game, total-goal playoff, and Ottawa won 4–1. The Ottawa papers immediately declared the Senators Stanley Cup champions, and the Cup itself went on display in the window of a Bank Street jewellery store. The Senators remained champions for only thirteen days, however, the time required to travel to Vancouver and to play three games against the Pacific Coast champions, the Vancouver Millionaires.

Frank Patrick's Millionaires had romped through the three-team coast league with a 13–4 record and, in order to appease the trustees, had submitted a proper challenge for the Cup. They then awaited the arrival of the Senators, who boarded a Grand Trunk Pullman late on the afternoon of March 15 to an enthusiastic send-off from several hundred loyal fans. The team arrived on a Saturday, attended a show at one of Vancouver's live theatres that night, and the following afternoon toured Stanley Park and Marine Drive by auto as guests of the Millionaires.

The western hospitality came to an abrupt end when the series opened Monday night at Vancouver's Georgia Street Arena, which was then the largest rink in Canada, with a seating capacity of ten thousand. A crowd of seven thousand was on hand, and watched a game that was close for about twenty minutes. The score was tied 1–1 when Frank Patrick broke the game open early in the second. "Patrick swept through the entire Ottawa team to score a sensational goal," the Vancouver *Sun* reported. The Senators never recovered, and were beaten by a score of 6–2. The *Sun*'s assessment of the game was simple: "The champions swept the Easterners off their feet with dashing speed and relentless backchecking."

The Senators sunk even further in games two and three. Cyclone Taylor, who had jumped to the Pacific Coast league after leaving the Renfrew Millionaires, led the Vancouver attack in the second game by scoring three goals, including a brilliant end-to-end rush in which he raced through the Senators single-handed. The final score was 8–3 Millionaires. Two nights later, Vancouver pummelled Ottawa 12–3. In summarizing the outcome, the *Sun* declared: "Vancouver clearly and cleanly fulfilled every claim to superiority over the Easterners."

The Ottawa-Vancouver series in 1915 was a one-sided rout, but the 1916 final proved to be a nailbiter with historic overtones. The Montreal Canadiens had earned their first crack at the Stanley Cup, and for the first time an American-based team was competing for the trophy. The Portland Rosebuds, who joined the PCHA in 1915, had a line-up laced with former eastern players. Defenceman Ernie Johnson had starred with the Wanderers in their glory years. Centre Tommy Dunderdale and right winger Eddie Oatman had bolted from the Bulldogs to play in the Pacific Coast league. The Canadiens' roster included two of the most famous players in team's history, Georges Vezina and Newsy Lalonde, as well as two stars of the early era, Jack Laviolette and Didier Pitre.

The Rosebuds arrived in Montreal a mere twenty-four hours before the opening faceoff and, with little rest and with no practice, upset the Canadiens 2–0 playing under eastern rules. The Montreal betting crowd favoured the Rosebuds in game two, because Coast league rules were in effect. And Portland's chances jumped another notch when the Canadiens announced shortly before game time that Lalonde was out with a severe cold and Laviolette with a badly broken nose. But the Canadiens defied the odds and scratched out a 2–1 win thanks to a solid defence and Vezina's great goaltending.

Game three was described as "one of the most brilliant exhibitions of hockey ever witnessed in the local arena," until a brawl erupted in the third period. Montreal was leading 4–3 when Portland's Johnson flattened Lalonde, who had returned to the lineup. Lalonde came up swinging, and Oatman jumped in to help Johnson. That brought the rest of the players, including the spares, into the melee. Referee Harvey Pulford and his assistant had lost control, but help arrived unexpectedly in the form of the police. "The fight was not brought to a finish until police chief Moffatt and his constables forced their way on to the ice and laid a warning hand on the combatants," the *Gazette* reported. The scrap deflated the Rosebuds, and the Canadiens sailed to a 6–3 win.

With the Rosebuds facing elimination, Ernie Johnson announced that he was sitting out the rest of the series. The problem was that Sam Lichtenhein, owner of the Wanderers, had obtained a court order granting him Johnson's share of the gate receipts. Lichtenhein had previously won a $2,000 judgement against Johnson after the player broke a contract and jumped to the Coast league in 1912. The court had ruled that Lichtenhein was entitled to Johnson's share of the gate as a partial payment of this judgement. The defenceman did not start game four but dressed for the start of the second period "after a lot of persuasion from friends and acquaintances at the rink," according to the *Gazette*. By then, the Rosebuds were comfortably in the lead, and they went on to win 6–5.

The deciding game was played before a small crowd, on a perfect sheet of ice, and with four minutes to go in the third was tied 1–1. Goldie Prodgers, a former Quebec Bulldog who had been a Montreal spare for most of the season, scored the winner on a gritty end-to-end rush. He outmuscled a couple of Portland forwards, skated into one Rosebud defenceman and knocked him down, then deked the last defender Johnson. "As the Portland goaltender came out to meet him, Prodgers skated around him and lobbed the puck into the net," said the *Gazette*. The significance of the Canadiens' victory was immediately apparent to hockey-mad Montrealers. As the next day's *Gazette* observed: "In winning this series, the Canadiens added to hockey history. They are the first French Canadian team ever to hold the coveted trophy."

There was nothing in the way of a parade, a reception or a celebration to acknowledge the occasion, however. The following day, the Canadiens left for Chicoutimi to play an annual exhibition game against a local team. Then they were off to Nwe York and Cleveland for a series of exhibition games against the Rosebuds.

After their Cleveland encounters, the Canadiens and the Rosebuds never met again. Portland tumbled to third place in the 1917 Coast league season, and by the following spring had dropped out of the league altogether. The Canadiens faded badly in the second half of the 1917 season but nevertheless earned the right to meet the Ottawa Senators in a two-game, total-goal playoff, and prevailed by a single goal. And on March 12, 1917, the Canadiens left Windsor Station aboard a CPR Pullman as two hundred enthusiastic supporters waved and cheered from the platform. Their destination was Seattle, Washington, where they were to meet the Metropolitans to decide the Stanley Cup and world championship.

The Patricks had set up the Metropolitans in 1916, assigned the team red, white, and green uniforms, and stacked the roster with former members of the 1914 Cup-winning Toronto Blueshirts. Goaltender Harry Holmes, right winger Jack Walker, left winger Frank Foyston, and spare Cully Wilson had all jumped from Toronto. After two seasons in the West, the ex-Blueshirts and their teammates were poised to bring the city of Seattle its first world championship in any sport.

Perhaps because the Canadiens were involved, and had already achieved renown as the Flying Frenchmen, the series generated considerable interest well beyond the Seattle city limits. "From over the northwest, hundreds of hockey enthusiasts have made preparations to attend the games," the Seattle *Times* reported before game one. "The largest delegation will come from Vancouver, but Portland and other cities will contribute their share of patrons. Outlying towns in Washington and several hamlets away back in the wilds of British Columbia will also be represented."

Montreal took the first game by a convincing margin of 8–4, largely on the strength of Didier Pitre's four-goal performance, and Vezina's work in net. "Pitre's bullet-like drives went past Holmes so fast that Holmes could not see them," said the *Times,* adding that "Vezina was peppered with five times as many shots as the Seattle goaltender but he fended the most difficult shots with ease."

After this auspicious start, the Canadiens' fortunes declined rapidly. They were beaten 6–1 in the second game, 4–1 in the third, and were thrashed 9–1 in the fourth. The Seattle *Times* described the final game as a dull, uninspired contest, but, dull game or not, the Seattle fans were thrilled. "The largest crowd that ever saw a hockey game in the arena stood and cheered until the iron girders of the roof rattled as the Seattle team left the ice with world's title safely won," the *Times* reported.

Nor did the dull final game dampen the enthusiasm of the *Times'* writer, for he cast the series as an epic struggle that would long be remembered. "Historians who write of the rise and fall of Les Canadiens dynasty will record how this dashing band of Flying Frenchmen travelled 3,000 miles to find an adversary worthy of its steel and discovered a foe that outclassed it in every department of the great ice game," he wrote. "By winning the fourth and deciding game, manager Pete Muldoon's puck chasers earned the distinction of being the first American team ever to win the supreme honours of the hockey world."

With Seattle's victory, a precedent-setting series and a tumultuous decade of change had ended. Professionals had established themselves as the game's premier players, so small-town challenges for the Stanley Cup became a thing of the past. Many of the game's contemporary features, such as twenty-minute periods, numbered sweaters, six-man hockey, and detailed scoring records, had been introduced.

The game also proved to be durable enough to survive the first great war of the twentieth century. By the summer of 1916, dozens of players had enlisted for military service and were destined to fight in the trenches of Western Europe. Some, like Goldie Prodgers and Eddie Oatman, were in their prime when they enlisted. Others, like Harry Broadbent, returned from the war and became star players. A military team, comprised of the members of the 228th Battalion, even joined the NHA and played the first half of the 1917 season before withdrawing to go overseas. Despite the exodus of players, the Stanley Cup was contested and awarded throughout World War I. Ironically, during a period of turmoil and instability, the men who ran hockey finally developed a regular format for the Stanley Cup playoffs; a yearly showdown between the best professional teams in the East and the West.

Over the next decade, however, the public's perception of these transcontinental series changed dramatically. They came to be seen as confrontations between regions, battles that threw the haughty, old East against the ambitious, young West. They also became tests of superiority: between the newly founded National Hockey League and the ever-precarious Pacific Coast league; and between the East's six-man and the West's seven-man game. As these perceptions took hold of a hockey-crazed populace, the Cup final was recast, reinvented, and rejuvenated. The crowds became as big and boisterous as ever, the rivalries as intense and heated as they had been, and the Stanley Cup final retained its place as Canada's premier sporting event.

4

SENATORS
AND LESSER MEN
1917-27

In his playing days, when he patrolled right wing for the Ottawa Senators and later the Toronto Maple Leafs, Frank Finnigan had thick, tousled hair, eyes that burned with determination, and the snarly demeanour of a young Jimmy Cagney. Small but aggressive, an average scorer but a tenacious checker, Finnigan was a player of moderate talent and exceedingly good fortune. He was in uniform and on the ice for the official openings of three arenas: the Ottawa Auditorium in the fall of 1923, Madison Square Garden in 1925, and Maple Leaf Gardens in 1931. He played beside men who had been his boyhood heroes, men like Frank Nighbor, Jack Darragh, and Eddie Gerard, and he competed against some of the biggest stars the game has ever produced, men like Howie Morenz, Aurèl Joliat, and Eddie Shore. And his name was inscribed on the Stanley Cup twice: he was a member of the 1926-27 Senators, the last Ottawa team to capture the Cup, and the 1931-32 Maple Leafs, first Leaf team to win it.

In December 1990, at the age of eighty-nine, Frank Finnigan was robust and amiable, and residing in his hometown of Shawville, Quebec, 100 kilometres miles north of Ottawa. He was the sole surviving member of the 1926-27 Senators and one of four survivors from the 1931-32 Leafs. Time had bleached and straightened his hair so that it stood stiff and thick as a paint brush dipped in white latex. His handshake was firm, his eyes sparkled, and his pride was still as sharp as the wristshot he used to score most of 121 big-league goals. The scars he acquired during fourteen NHL seasons and 558 games had faded with the passage of years. But after decades of wear, the ring he wore on the third finger of his left hand, a gold Stanley Cup ring with twelve small diamonds set in the shape of an O, a gift from the city of Ottawa, still glittered untarnished. He was given the ring in the spring of 1927 when the Senators were world champions.

Frank Finnigan launched his career in a primitive covered rink in his hometown, playing night games beneath smoky, oil-burning lamps strung above the ice and travelling three or four hours by horse-drawn sled to out-of-town games in villages like Qyon and Fort Coulogne, Quebec. In his prime, he and his Ottawa teammates travelled in private and comfortable Pullman cars. They had their own porter, Sammy "Horseshoes" Webber, and they stayed in the best hotels. They dined on filet mignon and strawberry shortcake, even when strawberries were out of season, and some of them made more money than the prime minister.

They lived like princes, and they played like hounds. From 1917 to 1927, the NHL's first decade, its Ottawa Senators were the best hockey team in the world. Of the thirty-six players who wore the red, white, and black of the Senators in that era, fifteen are now in the Hockey Hall of Fame. And, said Finnigan, who died in December 1991, they were a local team in a way that few professional hockey teams have ever been. Most of the players came from Ottawa or the surrounding area, and most graduated to the Senators after polishing their skills in the city's own highly competitive senior league.

Finnigan could still recite the names of his teammates from the 1927 Cup team, and their hometowns, as though he were reading from the previous night's program. "King Clancy was from Ottawa. Eddie Gorman was from Buckingham, that's twenty miles outside Ottawa. Alex Smith was from Ottawa. Alex Connell was from Ottawa. Cy Denneny was originally from Cornwall. George Boucher was from Ottawa. Milt Halliday was from Ottawa. Frank Nighbor was Pembroke. Hec Kilrea was from Ottawa. Jack Adams came from Toronto. Hooley Smith was from Toronto."

At the height of their power, the decade between 1917 and 1927, the Senators finished first in the NHL seven times and won four Stanley Cups, when no other team managed to win more than one. Two Montreal teams, the Canadiens and the Maroons, each won a Stanley Cup. The Arenas and the St. Pat's, who represented Toronto in the nascent NHL, both captured the Cup. The Victoria Cougars of the Pacific Coast Hockey Association won in 1925.

On one occasion tragedy intervened. The 1919 final between the Canadiens and the Seattle Metropolitans was played in Seattle. Each team had won two games and they had tied the fifth game when the series was cancelled. This was the year of the influenza epidemic that swept North America. Five members of the Canadiens had become ill, and one of them, defenceman "Bad" Joe Hall, died. In a century of play, it was the only time that the Cup was not awarded.

The Senators reigned during an era of ambitious expansion of professional hockey, a brief boom that would be unmatched until 1967. At the time, only two Canadian cities, Montreal and Toronto, had populations exceeding 500,000 people and only four, Winnipeg, Vancouver, Hamilton, and Ottawa, had more than 100,000 inhabitants. In 1918, Canada was providing the players, the fans, and the financial backing for six professional teams. Ten years later, ego and ambition had eclipsed prudence and common sense and hockey was cluttered with teams and leagues. At one point, three professional leagues, the National, the Pacific Coast, and the Western Canada, were operating simultaneously. At the height of the boom, there were sixteen professional hockey teams, nine based in Canada, and six in the United States.

The NHL began its existence with three solid franchises, Montreal, Ottawa, and Toronto, and a fourth that was alternately located in Quebec City and Hamilton. By the end of its first decade, the NHL had grown to ten teams, including six south of the border. The Pacific Coast Hockey Association had three teams in 1918, the Vancouver Millionaires, the Victoria Aristocrats, and the Seattle Metropolitans. Professional hockey sprang to life on the Canadian Prairies in 1921 with the creation of the Western Canada Hockey League, which had four teams: the Edmonton Eskimos, the Calgary Tigers, the Regina Capitals, and the Saskatoon Crescents. When the Seattle Metropolitans folded prior to the 1924-25 season, the Pacific Coast and Western Canada leagues merged to form the six-team, all-Canadian Western Hockey League.

The rise of the Western Canada league added a new wrinkle to the annual East-West battles for the Stanley Cup, which began in 1914. After one year of operation, the western league had established itself as a high-calibre organization, and its teams had demonstrated that they were capable of competing with the National and Pacific Coast clubs. As a result, the western league champion was allowed to participate in the Stanley Cup final. With the inclusion of a third league, the format of these springtime showdowns changed almost yearly. But the tempo, spirit, and intensity of the games hardly fluctuated at all. What was at stake, after all, was the world championship of hockey, as the Stanley Cup finals were called in those days.

For the public and the press, the games were more than a mere sporting event. The East-West showdowns began to reflect the regional rivalries that have always smouldered just beneath the surface of Canadian politics. The West's one win during this formative decade, the Victoria Cougars' 1925 Stanley Cup victory, unleashed a volley of western chest-thumping. "The easterners are learning how hockey should be played from western teams," declared the Victoria *Colonist* on its editorial page, while an emboldened editorial writer at the *Calgary Herald* went even further. To his eye, the era when "the effete East looked down upon the plainsman and the far westerner" appeared to be over.

But the optimism of the western papers was premature and unwarranted. As the historian John Thompson noted in his 1985 book about this era in Canada's past: "Western arrogance was to melt faster than natural ice in an unseasonable thaw. The Montreal Maroons took Lord Stanley's silverware back to central Canada in 1926, and it was not to return for 58 years." At the end of the 1926 season, professional hockey fizzled in the West, largely because WHL teams, based in small markets and playing in small arenas, could not compete for players with the financially stronger NHL. The western owners sold their best players to the NHL for a total of $258,000, and in 1927 the Stanley Cup became the exclusive property of the NHL, not by decree or edict, but by default.

However, the East-West showdowns had demonstrated the NHL's superiority over its western rivals. And no team did more to establish the supremacy of the NHL than the Ottawa Senators. The Toronto Arenas were the first NHL team to win the Stanley Cup, beating the Vancouver Millionaires three games to two in 1918. But the Senators became the first NHL team to win back-to-back Cups, and they went on to win three times in four years.

Immediately after Ottawa won its second straight Cup on the evening of April 4, 1921, the Millionaires' coach, Frank Patrick, pushed his way through a throng to reach the Senators' bench. He shook hands with Tommy Gorman, co-owner of the Senators and sports editor of the Ottawa *Citizen*, and exclaimed: "You have the greatest hockey team I ever saw. They are better than the Silver Seven, the Little Men of Iron or any other sextet I have ever watched."

The Stanley Cup finals that pitted East against West also

became battlefields for the different brands of hockey being played in Canada at the time, particularly the East's six-man game and West's seven-man game. By 1922, the East won the battle when the Pacific Coast league finally dropped the rover, as the seventh man was called.

When the Ottawa Senators began to assert themselves early in the NHL's first decade, the Stanley Cup final was still a hybrid blend of six- and seven-man hockey played under eastern rules one game and western rules the next. The Senators earned a berth in the Cup final in 1920, the NHL's third year of operation. The Seattle Metropolitans had won the Pacific Coast league for the second straight year and earned the right to represent the West. The entire final was scheduled to be played in Ottawa, giving that city's hockey fans their first taste of Stanley Cup play in almost a decade.

The Mets arrived in the Canadian capital aboard a CPR Pullman at 5:00 p.m. on March 21, the day before the final started. The players stepped off the train to find a city ablaze with excitement over the impending world championship of hockey. Even though it was a Sunday, a fact duly noted by the Ottawa *Citizen,* a crowd of over two thousand fans showed up to welcome the Mets. Team members were given rousing ovations as they walked into the station, and police officers had to hold the crowd back.

A few blocks from the train station, the Cup was on display in the window of the R. J. Devlin Company, a Sparks Street furrier. The display also included photos of all the previous Ottawa teams to win the coveted trophy, including the famous Silver Seven. The *Citizen* reported that every day thousands of Ottawa residents were dropping by for a look at "the celebrated piece of silverware which has caused so much strife, so much heartbreaking excitement and so much joy in all parts of Canada."

Tickets for the opening game of big series ranged in price from 55 cents to $2.20 apiece. They went on sale the morning of Friday, March 19, and were sold out almost immediately. The

Ottawa club had to turn down requests for tickets from members of Parliament and senators, and from fans from as far away as Toronto and Quebec City. According to the *Citizen,* reporters arrived in the capital from across the country.

Ottawa's Laurier Street Arena was suitably decorated for the series. The Union Jack and the Star Spangled Banner hung from the girders. At the north end of the building, a huge sign read "Welcome Western Champions." The band of the Governor General's Foot Guard had been hired to play the two anthems. Arena management had appealed to fans to avoid smoking during the games. And the city police were determined to discourage the disagreeable practice of ticket-scalping.

Despite these preparations, there was one thing the city could not control, and that was the weather. On the afternoon of the first game, the temperature soared to forty-three degrees Fahrenheit. By game time, the natural ice at the Laurier Street Arena was coated with a thin sheet of water. Although the players were soaked from head to foot by the time the game was over, they had staged "one of the most stubbornly contested matches in the history of hockey," said the Ottawa *Citizen.*

With ten minutes to go in the game, and the Metropolitans clinging to a 2–1 lead, Frank Nighbor stole the puck from Seattle's Jack Walker at centre-ice. Nighbor, the Pembroke insurance man who was a master of the poke check, turned and bolted toward the Seattle blue line. He eluded two defenders before slipping the puck by Mets goalie Harry Holmes. "For a moment there was a hush over the big crowd of 7,500," the *Citizen* reported. "Then pandemonium broke loose. Everywhere fans young and old threw hats in the air and waved their coats and pennants."

Six minutes later, Ottawa's Eddie Gerard led a rush with George Boucher on his left and Jack Darragh on his right. Gerard took a shot and Holmes stopped it. Darragh, who had headed for the net like a flash, arrived just in time to tap in the rebound and give Ottawa a 3–2 lead. The Senators, always known as a formidable checking team, then shut down the Mets until regulation time expired.

Despite the opening loss, the Seattle players were confident of victory in the second game because it was to be played under western rules, which allowed seven men on the ice and forward passing in the centre-ice zone. But Ottawa prevailed, this time by a score of 3–0, and the weather was again a factor. The temperature had soared to fifty-seven degrees and arena employees were scraping water off the ice all day. Because of the poor ice surface, the *Citizen* reported that "brilliant hockey was out of the question as it was almost impossible to carry the puck with high speed or do much stickhandling."

Anticipating a sweep of the series, the city of Ottawa scheduled a banquet and Stanley Cup presentation at the Château Laurier following the third game, which had to be postponed a day because of the weather. Although the game was played under the East's six-man rules, Seattle bounced back to win 3–1, and ruined Ottawa's victory bash. With ten minutes to go in the game, Nighbor and Darragh skated to the bench, too exhausted to continue, and collapsed. "There is a limit to human endurance," the *Citizen* remarked the next day, "and it had evidently been reached."

By this time, NHL president Frank Calder, a former schoolteacher and Montreal newspaperman, had grown weary of the sloppy playing conditions, and ordered the series completed at Toronto's Mutual Street Arena, still the only rink in Eastern Canada at the time with artificial ice. Playing on a perfect sheet of ice, under western rules, the Mets skated to an easy 5–2 win and led almost from the beginning. "Seattle bewildered Ottawa with their forward passes in no man's land," noted the *Citizen*.

The final game was played April 1 before five thousand enthusiastic fans. It rained heavily in Toronto that night, but the artificial ice surface at the Mutual Street Arena stayed hard. The game was tied 1–1 until early in the third period when, according to one newspaper report, "Jack Darragh slipped through the Seattle defence and, dodging around Jim Riley, scored the goal that cracked the hearts of the Seattle players." The Senators pumped in four more goals to win the game 6–1, and the series three games to two. Afterwards, each Ottawa player received a bonus of $390.97 and the Seattle players $328.48, which one observer described as "the richest world series melon the players have yet cut."

The following season, 1920-21, the Senators finished second during the NHL's twenty-four-game regular season, two points behind Toronto. But they won the ensuing playoffs and the right to defend their Stanley Cup title against the Pacific Coast champions, the Vancouver Millionaires. The Senators left the nation's capital for Vancouver shortly after midnight March 16 aboard a CPR Pullman called "The Azilda." It was decorated with fresh cut flowers and supplied with "sufficient smokes to last the boys throughout the trip," according to the *Citizen*. Forward Harry Broadbent had married Leda Fitzsimmons about twelve hours before the team departed and brought his new bride with him. Veteran player Jack Darragh made the trip only after Mayor Frank Plant had persuaded Darragh's employer, the Ottawa Dairy, to give him time off.

At each whistle-stop during the long transcontinental trip, at North Bay, Sudbury, and Chapleau in Northern Ontario, at Winnipeg, Moose Jaw, and Medicine Hat in the West, the Senators stepped off "The Azilda" to stretch their legs on the station platform. At each stop they received a warm reception from former Ottawa residents and ordinary fans who turned up to meet the reigning world champions.

On March 19, a Saturday, the Senators stopped in Calgary for an exhibition game against the WCHL's Tigers. Playing before a packed arena, the Senators won 2–0. A number of Ottawa natives attended the game, including one Jack Kerr, who had ridden a hundred miles on horseback to see the Senators play. After attending a dinner hosted by the Calgary Board of Trade, the team boarded the train again for the final leg of the trip and game one of the Stanley Cup final.

Despite their Calgary tune-up, and the advantage of the East's six-man rules for the first game, the Senators were no match for the fired-up Millionaires and a sellout crowd of ten thousand wildly enthusiastic fans. Vancouver skated to an easy 3–1 win in the opening game, in part because Millionaire goalie Hugh Lehman completely baffled the Senators by using a forward pass to move the puck up the ice to his teammates. A Canadian Press reporter wrote that Lehman repeatedly "shot the puck like lightning to awaiting forwards at centre ice, then Vancouver would attack before the Ottawas could regain their balance."

The Millionaires' impressive opening-game performance heightened local interest in the series. Tickets for the second game sold out in two hours, and the Vancouver *Sun* sports editor, Al Hardy, declared: "The city is seized by hockey fever. Even the government's liquor bill, which has afforded denizens of the vale ammunition for unfettered oratory during the last six weeks, is a dead issue for the time being." And for a while, it appeared as though the Senators were just as dead.

The Millionaires scored two goals in the first two minutes of the second game, while the Senators, in Al Hardy's words, "played like wooden Indians." However, Ottawa battled back, tying the game 3–3 midway through the second and winning it with a goal late in the third by the newlywed Broadbent.

Ottawa won the third game playing under western rules, and Vancouver took the fourth game, which was played by eastern rules. The fifth and deciding game was played April 4. The West's seven-man rules were in effect and a crowd of twelve thousand, well above the building's capacity, attended the game. There were still three thousand people lined up outside the rink when city police officers ordered the arena management to stop selling tickets.

With this huge crowd watching, and the world championship

at stake, the players performed like men possessed. For the first twenty minutes, the Millionaires controlled the play. "They harried the Ottawa forwards like a rat terrier landlord hounds his tenants," Hardy wrote. Alf Skinner scored late in the first period for Vancouver, but Ottawa's Jack Darragh scored two quick goals midway through the second. From that point on, Hardy reported, Ottawa's defence "held tighter than the warts on a golf ball."

With two minutes left in the game, and Vancouver's hopes evaporating, defenceman Lloyd Cook punched Senator captain Eddie Gerard in the mouth. Ottawa's Sprague Cleghorn flattened Cook with two punches and triggered a brawl that brought the police over the boards to separate the teams. When the final whistle blew, Ottawa goalie Clint Benedict leapt in the air, and his teammates danced with joy.

Six days later, the triumphant Senators arrived home to a Stanley Cup parade through the streets of downtown Ottawa. Thousands of people lined the route, and hundreds attended a reception at city hall. The celebration concluded with a banquet for the world champions at the Château Laurier. Five members of the fabled Ottawa Silver Seven attended, as did members of almost every amateur and professional athletic club in the city. "The whole populace paid homage to its hockey victors," declared the next day's *Citizen*, "as ancient Rome paid homage to its gladiators."

The Senators' reign as Stanley Cup and world champions was interrupted in the spring of 1922 by the Toronto St. Pats, who emerged as NHL champs and went on to defeat Vancouver in a five-game final. One year later, Ottawa again finished atop the NHL standings, won a post-season showdown against Montreal, and for the third time in four years represented the East in the Stanley Cup playoffs. A new wrinkle was added to the annual East-West confrontation by the inclusion of the WCHL champion Edmonton Eskimos. Under an agreement worked out by the Stanley Cup trustees, Ottawa met the Pacific Coast champion Vancouver Maroons in a best-of-five semi-final, and the winner advanced to a best-of-three final against the WCHL champs.

Apart from these changes, the 1923 playoffs were remarkable for the number of injuries suffered by the Senators, and the emergence of twenty-year-old Frank "King" Clancy as a star performer for Ottawa. The Senators were hurting from the moment they stepped on the ice to start the semi-final against Vancouver. Cy Denneny had suffered a bad cut and a slight fracture to his skull when he was clubbed by Montreal's Billy Couture during the NHL playoff. And Lionel Hitchman, a spare defenceman, had arrived with a broken nose.

Five minutes into game one, during a goalmouth scramble, Senator goalie Clint Benedict was knocked unconscious briefly and cut for several stitches by Alf Skinner's errant high stick. Nevertheless, Benedict shut out the Maroons 1–0 in a game characterized by "brilliant skating, flashy stickhandling, deadly shooting and relentless backchecking," according to the Vancouver *Sun*. Misfortune struck again early in game two when Vancouver's Mickey Mackay fired a shot that hit Benedict in the face and "split his lip, loosened his teeth, and knocked him on his back." After that, a rattled Benedict was unable to perform up to his capabilities, and the Senators lost 4–1.

Ottawa's woes continued when substitute Harry Helman was cut on the face by a teammate's skate during a practice. The injury was serious enough to keep Helman in hospital for several days. At that point, Senator secretary Tommy Gorman appealed to Pacific Coast president Lester Patrick for permission to use Billy Boucher, an Ottawa native and a member of the Canadiens, who had made the trip west with the Senators. But Patrick refused, and Stanley Cup trustee William Foran backed him.

Despite the injuries, the Senators won the third game by a score of 3–2, clinging to their slender lead for the final eighteen minutes "like a bulldog to the seat of a tramp's trousers," according to the Vancouver *Sun*. And they eliminated the Maroons with a 5–1 win three nights later. But captain Eddie Gerard dislocated his left shoulder, leaving Ottawa with a mere six players fit enough to line up against the team then reputed to be the fastest in pro hockey, the Edmonton Eskimos.

Well rested after the WCHL playoffs and perfectly healthy, the Edmonton players skated like whirlwinds in their white sweaters with green trim. "Bullet" Joe Simpson, regarded as hockey's fastest skater at the time, and Duke Keats, the slickest centre in the West, had plenty of room to move because the wounded Senators played a tight defensive game with three men back and two up front. Ottawa's strategy was simply to concede most of the ice surface to the healthier Eskimos while keeping them away from Benedict. Swift as they were, the Eskimos put the puck by the steadfast Benedict only once in the first game, settling for a 1–1 tie through sixty minutes, and losing 2–1 in overtime.

For the Senators it was another painful victory. Defenceman George Boucher bruised his foot so badly he could hardly skate by the end of the game. An hour and a half before the second game, he shot cocaine into the foot to kill the pain but still couldn't skate. Gerard, unable to raise his left arm any higher than his chin, bandaged his damaged shoulder and played. Only three members of Ottawa's eight-man roster were injury-free for the second game of the 1923 final. The Senators scored ten minutes into the game, then "for 50 minutes that lone tally was guarded as forcefully as the Royal Mint on Sussex Street," wrote Ed Barker in the *Citizen*.

With his teammates cut, bruised, and battered, the twenty-year-old King Clancy stepped into the breach and soared from substitute to star overnight. In the two-game final, he played both defensive positions and all three forward positions. He also took a turn in goal when Benedict was penalized in the second game, and stopped two shots. One of them was a long shot by Joe Simpson. Clancy dropped his stick, caught the puck baseball style with both hands and casually tossed it aside. "He's the greatest kid in the world," the veteran Gerard exclaimed after Ottawa's 1–0 victory. "He was the hero of the series," added Maroons coach Frank Patrick.

Five days later, the Senators arrived at Central Station in Ottawa to a tumultuous noon-hour welcome. Mayor Frank Plant and a delegation of civic dignitaries greeted the players. The forty-five-member Ottawa Silver City Band serenaded them with "Home Sweet Home" and forty police officers tried to keep the crowds back. The players, their wives, and the assembled dignitaries then paraded through downtown streets in thirty-three cars decorated with banners and bunting and signs identifying the players.

Mayhem accompanied the parade. School kids clambered aboard the cars, riding on the running boards, bumpers, and spare-tire racks. The huge crowds forced the band members to march single file, rather than four abreast as planned. The streets were so clogged with crowds and cars that the parade could hardly move. "Everyone in Ottawa who had a motor car seemed to head for the station or the Chateau Laurier," the *Citizen* reported. "At points there was a tremendous jam."

In the fall of 1923, the Senators moved from the Laurier Street Arena to the new Ottawa Auditorium, built at a cost of $355,000 and equipped to make artificial ice. Frank Finnigan jumped from the Ottawa senior league to the Senators that season, fulfilling a boyhood dream. "I knew by the time I was nine that I was going to be a professional hockey player," said Finnigan. "We didn't have radio or television then, of course, but I used to save my money and buy every newspaper from Ottawa that I could get my hands on. The train used to come into Shawville at six every evening, and as soon as I would hear that whistle blow I would head down to Joe Turner's confectionery or Doc Clock's drugstore and get my papers. I wasn't very good at school but I could certainly read the sports pages of the *Ottawa Journal* and the Ottawa *Citizen* at a very early age."

Finnigan joined a Senators team still stacked with the veterans who had brought the Stanley Cup to Ottawa three of the previous four seasons. In 1923-24, they placed first during the twenty-four-game regular season with thirty-two points. But the second-place Canadiens, who had finished six points back, beat the Senators in a two-game, total-goal playoff. The Canadiens were led by two budding superstars, two dynamic young players who were the epitome of speed and spirit, who would enjoy long, illustrious careers and earn lasting fame. Montreal's rookie centre Howie Morenz was immediately acclaimed for his exhilarating speed, while sophomore left winger Aurèl Joliat was renowned for his indomitable spirit.

"Morenz was the most terrific hockey player I ever saw, or will see," Finnigan said. "He was just like a bird. He broke out of his own end, and he'd come down the ice like lightning. Lots of times I'd give him a body check. It was the only way to stop him. You'd think you were finished with him, but he'd go back and say, 'Give me that puck.' And down he'd come again. He could do everything. Shoot. Score. And he had terrific speed. He really was terrific, all the time every game. He wouldn't play a good game today and bad game tomorrow. Nope, there's no Morenzes in there today."

The Joliats of this world are just as rare. He was known to hockey fans of the 1920s and 1930s as the Mighty Mite because he stood just five feet, six inches tall, and weighed a mere 136 pounds. "He was pale, drawn, anemic-looking at best," Montreal *Herald* sports editor Elmer Ferguson wrote in 1938 after Joliat had retired. "He had dead-white skin, almost unhealthy in its pallor. His ribs showed through. He was flat muscled, thin of hips, scrawny of legs. But somewhere in that pale sickly looking body there pulsed a mighty motor. Joliat did his work by guile, by sheer skill that at times rose to exhilarating heights. He was the ghost, the will o' the wisp of the ice, expressionless, flitting from point to point as if divining by instinct where plays would break."

After eliminating Ottawa in early March 1924, the Canadiens

awaited the outcome of the western playoffs and the start of the Stanley Cup showdown in Montreal. The Calgary Tigers had won the Western Canada Hockey League crown, while the Vancouver Maroons triumphed in the Pacific Coast league. The Tigers and Maroons then embarked on a best-of-three playoff. The winner, they decided, would be awarded a berth in the Stanley Cup final, while the loser would meet Montreal in the semifinal.

While the western playoff was in progress, Montreal general manager Leo Dandurand declared that his Canadiens would play either the Tigers or the Maroons for the Stanley Cup, but not both. Dandurand quickly backed down, however, after receiving an ultimatum from Lester Patrick, president of the coast league, and E. L. Richardson, his western league counterpart. Either both western leagues would compete, the westerners said, or the Stanley Cup could sit on the shelf and collect cobwebs.

On the morning of March 18, the Tigers and the Maroons arrived in Montreal aboard the same train. It was snowing heavily, the temperature was well below freezing, and the opening game of the semi-final between the Canadiens and the Maroons was just eleven hours away. Yet Dandurand, along with his star defenceman, Sprague Cleghorn, and several hundred fans, were standing on the platform to greet the westerners as they stepped off the train.

Frank Patrick's Maroons were making their fourth straight Stanley Cup appearance, but Vancouver's age and experience proved no match for Montreal's youth and speed. "Howie Morenz, Billy Boucher and Aurel Joliat are lightning fast," wrote *Calgary Herald* sports editor Howard Kelly, who had accompanied the teams east. "Morenz is a mercurial glider, there's no mistaking that fact. He is a hurricane." Montreal won the first game of the best-of-three semi-final 3–2 before a sellout crowd of six thousand at the Mount Royal Arena. Playing on slushy ice two nights later, the game was tied 1–1 midway through the third when Joliat scored the winner after a dazzling end-to-end rush. "Hughie Lehman sprawled to make the save but was unable to smother the rebound," Kelly wrote. "Joliat made a sensational dive and knocked the rubber in just as it lay in front of the goal line."

After watching the semi-final, the well-rested Tigers in their yellow and black stripes lined up against the Canadiens for the opening game of the best-of-three final. Calgary's confident coach, Lloyd Turner, declared: "It's a pretty safe bet that we shall pack the Stanley Cup back to the Prairie." Former Montreal great Newsy Lalonde, who was coaching the Saskatoon Sheiks at the time, added: "I warned the Canadiens not to underestimate the Tigers." Calgary's roster included three future hall-of-famers, defenceman Mervyn "Red" Dutton, who went on to play ten years in the NHL, Herb Gardiner, another defenceman who lasted three seasons in the NHL, and forward Harry Oliver, who played eleven seasons in the NHL. But the other seven were journeymen, who earned modest salaries and fleeting acclaim.

Upon the shoulders of these men of modest talent rode the hopes and aspirations of a proud, prairie city. The Tigers were the first Calgary team to compete for the Stanley Cup, and back home thousands of fans eagerly devoured up-to-the-minute reports from Montreal. The *Herald*'s Kelly provided play-by-play accounts of the game to a telegraph operator sitting beside him at the Mount Royal Arena, and the telegrapher instantly relayed the information to the newspaper's editorial offices. A *Herald* employee then used a megaphone to broadcast the play-by-play to the crowd in the street outside. The newspaper had ten telephone operators working a special switchboard to handle calls from fans. As well, the *Herald* told readers that its radio station, CFAC, would "send out the running story of the game and those with receiving sets are invited to tune in." For good measure, on the evening of the first game, the paper published a pink-coloured extra edition at 9:00 p.m. giving a complete account of the action.

A throng of three thousand fans, comparable to those that turned out to hear play-by-plays of World Series games, jammed the streets around the *Herald* building on the evening of March 22 to listen to an announcer with a megaphone bellow the plays. "The crowd was keyed up to the highest pitch of excitement," the newspaper reported. But the enthusiasm quickly evaporated. The man with the megaphone described three goals by Morenz and another by his linemate Boucher before Tiger defenceman Gardiner put one by Georges Vezina in the Montreal net. Before the night was over, Montreal scored two more goals. "As nearly every person was a Tiger booster, they did not get many thrills out of the continued Tiger reverses," the *Herald* remarked. "But when Herb Gardiner broke through to notch the only Tiger goal, the mightiest cheer of the evening rent the air."

Calgary's coach, Lloyd Turner, remained defiant in defeat. He blamed the deplorable condition of the natural ice at the Mount Royal Arena for his team's poor performance and demanded that the remainder of the series be played on the artificial ice at the Ottawa Auditorium. "We didn't have a hockey game at Montreal," he snapped. "It was an exhibition of water polo and the Tigers were completely at sea, while the Canadiens appeared to be right at home."

Three nights later at the Ottawa Auditorium, Calgary's Bernie Morris and Montreal's Howie Morenz lined up at centre-ice to start the second game before a crowd of eight thousand. Federal Opposition leader Arthur Meighen stood between the opposing centremen and dropped the puck in a ceremonial face-off. The governor general and his wife, Lord and Lady Byng, watched the game from their private box. When the evening was over, the scoreboard said Montreal 3, Calgary 0, and the Canadiens had won their second Stanley Cup.

Morenz scored the winning goal early in the first period, and left-winger Boucher added an insurance goal early in the third. "It was left to Joliat to finish off the evening with a sensational goal," the *Herald*'s Kelly told the fans back home. "He took possession at the Canadiens defence and, in a dazzling raid that glittered with spectacular stickwork, he ducked and dodged his way past Tiger checks, slipped around the left side of the net, circled like a swallow, and guided the cake into the yawning goal mouth."

Although they had been swept in two straight games, the Tigers had redeemed themselves with a ferocious second period attack in which they outshot the Canadiens 23–6. Only the unbeatable and fearless Vezina prevented Calgary from turning the game into a rout, according to Kelly, who rose above partisanship to find honour in defeat. "Calgary was beaten by a worthy team," he concluded. "After being ripped, battered and torn wide open by the Tigers in the second, the Frenchmen staged a wonderful closing stanza that was fine to behold."

The Canadiens again emerged as NHL champions in the 1924-25 season and in mid-March boarded a private Pullman for the transcontinental trip to the Stanley Cup final. This time around, however, they would be facing only one western adversary, Lester Patrick's Victoria Cougars. The Pacific Coast league had folded prior to the 1924-25 season because Seattle withdrew its franchise, leaving the PCHA with only two teams. But the surviving Cougars and Vancouver Maroons had been allowed to join the renamed Western Hockey League.

En route to Victoria, the relaxed and confident Canadiens played poker and bridge, and listened to jazz music. "As the train sped through the vast bush country of northern Ontario toward the plains," one newspaperman wrote, "the interior of their car resembled a cabaret more than the abode of a team of championship athletes. Perched on a table at one end of their car, a Victor phonograph jazzed away with Doo-Waka-Doo, Insufficient Sweetie and a hundred other racy melodies that were strangely incongruous to the wild scenery outside the train windows." The same observer added that the phonograph sat silent the day the train passed through the Rockies because the players were too absorbed by the spectacular scenery to be bothered with music.

Upon arriving in Victoria, on the day the best-of-five series was to begin, the Canadiens found the small and normally quiet town of Victoria rife with excitement over the impending play-off. It was the first, and only, Stanley Cup final ever played in Victoria, and the four thousand tickets available for the opening game had all been sold in three hours. Lester Patrick and the entire Cougar team greeted the Canadiens at the Empress Hotel.

Montreal coach Leo Dandurand then met the press and introduced his players. The forward line consisted of Morenz, Boucher, and Joliat, while Sprague Cleghorn and Billy Couture were on defence. Guarding the Canadiens' goal, he said, was thirty-six-year-old Georges Vezina. "He is a real French-Canadian who cannot speak English," the gregarious Dandurand added, "and is the father of twenty-two children, including three sets of triplets, and they were all born in the space of twelve years."

While the Montrealers were mostly young, and mostly French-Canadian, the Cougars, who wore blue uniforms with gold trim, were an aging group of players from various parts of the country. But they had plenty of Stanley Cup experience. Goaltender Harry "Happy" Holmes had appeared in six Cup finals, while forwards Jack Walker and Frank Foyston had been in five each. And they had a clever coach in Lester Patrick. In the 1925 final, Patrick changed forever the way hockey was played by demonstrating the effectiveness of regular line changes.

At the time, western rules allowed a team to make substitutions anytime during a game. Eastern teams, playing under NHL rules, could change players only after the referee had blown his whistle to stop the play. Regardless of which rules were in effect, Leo Dandurand's starting six were all sixty-minute men. In the 1924 playoffs, his regulars had set an endurance record by playing two games against Ottawa, two against Vancouver, and two against Calgary without a single substitution. In the 1925 final, Dandurand's sixty-minute men finally met their match.

Game one was played under western rules, allowing Patrick

to change his lines at will, and the Cougars skated to an easy 5–2 win. In the second game, with eastern rules prevailing, the Cougars forced numerous stoppages in play in order to switch lines. The effectiveness of Patrick's strategy was evident when Morenz was forced to take his first breather of the series halfway through the second game. By the third period, when Walker scored to give the Cougars a 3–1 lead, fatigue and frustration were getting the better of the Canadiens. "Walker's goal was followed by one of the crudest and most brutal assaults seen on the ice here," the Victoria *Daily Times* reported. "Boucher, the bad man of the NHL, jumped into Walker and smashed the veteran into the boards. Walker staggered for a second but collapsed unconscious."

With his team on the brink of elimination, Dandurand revived his players with a rousing pep talk prior to the third game. As the *Daily Times* reported: "He waved a raft of telegrams in front of their eyes, told them what the East was expecting of them, and if they didn't win there would be no joy around the breakfast tables in Montreal in the morning." The Canadiens won the third game 4–2, on the strength of a hattrick by Morenz, but they were no match for Cougars three nights later. They lost the game 6–1 and the series 3–1.

Victoria had won its first, and only, Stanley Cup, and years later Lester Patrick would reflect proudly on how he had changed hockey. "The Canadiens came west and those easterners who came with them in their hard derby hats bet their last dollar that an upstart team in Victoria couldn't stop them," he told a *Maclean's* magazine writer in 1950. "Who could stop Morenz and Joliat and Boucher? Who could score on the great Vezina? But I knew we'd win because our second line would just tire them out, and it did. From then on, with three, then four interchangeable lines spelling each other, the game speeded up and is immeasurably faster now than ever." The age of the sixty-minute man was over.

The Cougars won the Western Hockey League championship

again the following season and in late March made the long trek east to defend their Stanley Cup title against the NHL champion Montreal Maroons. But this time around, Lester Patrick had no novel tactics, no surprise strategies to use against his eastern adversaries, and the Maroons won handily by three games to one. Montreal goalie Clint Benedict, a former Senator, shut out the Cougars in all three Maroon wins and posted a goals-against average of 0.75. When time expired in the fourth game on the evening of April 6, 1926, and the triumphant Maroons and the dejected Cougars skated off the ice, a series, a season, and an era had come to an end.

There would be no more Stanley Cup showdowns between the best teams from Eastern Canada and Western Canada for decades. The West would not produce another Stanley Cup champion for fifty-eight years, not until the Edmonton Oilers defeated the New York Islanders in 1984. During the summer of 1926, the Western Hockey League folded, a victim of falling attendance, rising costs and the ambitious, aggressive expansion of the NHL into the United States. The NHL admitted the Boston Bruins in 1924 and expanded again in 1925 to include the Pittsburgh Pirates and New York Americans. And by the start of the 1926-27 season, the NHL had grown to ten teams with the addition of the Chicago Black Hawks and the Detroit Cougars.

Hungry for talent, the new NHL franchises raided the western league and snapped up its biggest stars. Edmonton's Bullet Joe Simpson, once the fastest skater in all of hockey, joined the New York Americans. Duke Keats, another former Eskimo and one of the West's smoothest centremen, jumped to Detroit. Lester Patrick joined the New York Rangers as coach and general manager. Mickey Mackay, who entertained Vancouver hockey fans for years, signed with the Black Hawks. Eddie Shore, who starred on defence for the Regina Capitals and Edmonton Eskimos, went to Boston. So began hockey's version of the diaspora, the great exodus of players from the hamlets and villages, the cities and towns of the Prairies and the West Coast, and their migration to the cities of the East, where they played before big crowds and earned big salaries. And so began the NHL's reign as hockey's premier professional circuit.

While this transformation was occurring, and professional hockey rotated on its axis, becoming a North-South spectacle rather than an East-West one, the stable, steadfast Senators, the team comprised almost entirely of local boys, managed to rise to the top one more time. They finished the 1926-27 regular season in first place overall, having led from opening night on. In the Stanley Cup semi-final, they blanked the Canadiens 4–0 in Montreal before a crowd of 13,500, the largest ever to witness a hockey game in Canada at the time, and won the two-game, total-goal playoff by a score of 5–1. Then the Senators travelled to Boston to meet the Bruins, winners of the NHL's new American division.

The Bruins could have sold thirty thousand tickets for the opening game, so strong was the demand, but their arena sat only nine thousand. Those who did get in witnessed a dull, drab, conservative game. Neither team scored through sixty minutes of regulation time, nor could they put one in during two ten-minute overtime periods. By that point, the ice was in such poor shape that the game was called. Ottawa won the second game, which was described as "fast and thrilling" in a Canadian Press report, by a score of 3–1.

The series then shifted to Ottawa. Several hundred Boston fans accompanied the Bruins, and Senator fans began lining up at 4:00 a.m. to buy tickets for game three. The Ottawa Auditorium maintenance men "devoted the whole day to making a perfect sheet of ice," the *Citizen* reported, and would not allow anyone on the playing surface until game time. The Bruins and Senators played to a 1–1 tie in regulation time that night. Despite the best efforts of the maintenance crew, the game was called because of rough ice when neither team had scored after two ten-minute overtime periods.

The Senators wrapped up the series with a 3–1 win in the

fourth game. The turning point was Frank Finnigan's second-period goal, which broke up a scoreless tie. Ottawa's veteran centre, Frank Nighbor, playing in his sixth Stanley Cup final, raced down left wing and fired a shot at the Boston net. Bruin goaltender Hal Winkler made the save but gave up a fat rebound. "Finnigan was on the puck like a hawk after a hen, and circled for a close up shot," according to the *Citizen*. "His aim was accurate as the disc flew into the upper corner. Finnigan's goal rattled the Bruins and less than three minutes later Denneny scored." Denneny completed the Ottawa scoring in the third, while Harry Oliver, the former Calgary Tiger, scored Boston's only goal.

After the game, several members of the Bruins vented their frustration on an innocent referee. Angered by the officiating in the third period, Bruin coach Art Ross, defenceman Billy Couture and a couple of others assaulted referee Jerry Laflamme, a Toronto doctor, as he headed for his change room. "It was a disgraceful ending," the next day's *Citizen* declared. "The game itself was a thriller, undoubtedly the fastest and most cleanly contested match of the season." League president Frank Calder apparently agreed with the newspaper's assessment. Within forty-eight hours, he had suspended Couture for life, and handed out several fines.

As for the Senators, they had won the O'Brien Cup, the NHL championship trophy, and they were automatically awarded the Stanley Cup. The demise of the Western Hockey League meant that there were no teams anywhere who considered themselves strong enough to challenge an NHL champion. The Cup belonged to the Senators in the spring of 1927. Henceforth it would be the exclusive property of the NHL.

"The Ottawas are once more the undisputed champions of the world," the *Citizen* declared proudly. But the bulk of the population accepted the city's ninth Stanley Cup in thirty-four years with a nonchalance that bordered on indifference. A local sportswriter reported that the just completed hockey season had been the longest on record, beginning November 16 and ending

April 13, "three days short of five months, entirely too long, according to many fans." There was no victory parade for the Senators, no spontaneous outpouring of appreciation. Nevertheless, the city council decided that a civic banquet would be held to honour the Senators, and struck a committee to plan the event. On April 22, 1927, nine days after the series ended, coach Dave Gill took a train to Montreal to pick up the O'Brien Cup and the Stanley Cup.

The banquet was finally held May 5 at the Château Laurier and attracted some three hundred of Ottawa's leading citizens. The Senators were led into the ballroom by a piper, and welcomed with hearty applause. In most respects, it was a typical civic dinner. Mayor J. P. Balharrie and a few dignitaries delivered speeches laced with local pride, praise, and boosterism.

It was also an evening in which Ottawa's glorious hockey history was proudly displayed. Philip Ross stood at the head table to present the Stanley Cup and told his audience how honoured he had been that day in 1893 when Lord Stanley had summoned him to the governor general's residence. The British aristocrat, he recalled, had personally asked him to serve as trustee of a hockey trophy he was donating to the young Dominion of Canada.

At a nearby table sat some turn-of-the-century players who were revered in Ottawa as living legends: Alf Smith, Harvey Pulford, Harry Westwick, Horace Merrill, Bouse Hutton, and Bill Hague. They had played for the Silver Seven, Ottawa's first great hockey team. They were yesterday's heroes come to pay homage to the city's newest champions and to present gold Stanley Cup rings to the regulars, the substitutes, the trainer, the mascot, and the Senators' porter, Sammy Webber. A more recent group of heroes, Clint Benedict, Eddie Gerard, Harry Broadbent, Harry Helman, and Morley Bruce, former Senators whose names were all engraved on the Stanley Cup, sat at another table.

But an evening spent in the glow of victory, in the soothing nostalgia about past triumphs, an evening that should have been reserved for reminiscence and revelry, was disrupted by doubts and anxieties about the future of the Senators. The glorious past collided with the uncertain future when Mayor Balharrie read a telegram from Frank Ahearne, son of a prominent Ottawa businessman and principal owner of the Senators. Ahearne was in New York that night but told the gathering that he intended to sell his interest in the club, which had been losing money for several years.

Ahearne's father, Thomas, said that he knew nothing of his son's plan and tried to calm the anxiety raised by the telegram. So did NHL president Frank Calder, who said: "If such a calamity should happen that Mr. Frank Ahearne should want to dispose of his interests, the NHL will not permit the Senators to leave Ottawa, and the American teams would be the first to insist that a team remain in Ottawa, which in the U.S. is regarded as the centre of hockey activities in the world."

The Senators would last another seven years in the NHL but their long slide into oblivion had begun. They would never again finish anywhere close to first in the NHL. They would never win another Stanley Cup. Like some of the other great professional hockey teams of the 1920s, the Cougars and the Metropolitans, the Eskimos and the Tigers, the Maroons and the Millionaires, the Senators were doomed to disappear. But they had made a lasting impact on the game. They had played a major role in establishing the NHL as the best of the competing professional leagues. They had put their names on the Stanley Cup. They had enjoyed a decade of glory.

5

AMERICA'S CUP

1928-41

As regulation time expired, and the final gong sounded to end the 1935 Stanley Cup final, three young men leapt from their seats in the rush end of the Montreal Forum. Each wore a Montreal Maroons sweater. Quick as a flash, they had scrambled over the boards and on to the ice. "For fully ten minutes, the rafters rang as the cheerleaders led the entire house in an ovation for the new Stanley Cup champions," wrote Marc MacNeil in the next day's Montreal *Gazette*. The dressing room of the victorious Maroons was quickly packed with players and well-wishers, reporters, and photographers. "Dress shirts and black ties confronted sweaty, discoloured underwear," MacNeil reported. "Overcoated, beaming faced admirers shook hands with naked, perspiring athletes." The mayor of Montreal, Camillien Houde, came by to congratulate the victors and, a few minutes later, Dick Irvin, King Clancy, and Charlie Conacher from the vanquished Toronto Maple Leafs arrived to offer their congratulations.

Outside the dressing room, a mob of fans occasionally surged and heaved against the door. Someone tossed out half-a-dozen sticks, which caused tug-of-wars with three or four men pulling on both ends of each stick. Gradually, the crowd settled down and, as MacNeil described it, "waited until the last player had emerged to run a gauntlet of deafening cheers and hammering hands that clapped their backs, heads, and arms."

For Montrealers, the triumphant conclusion of another hockey season meant that life was unfolding as it should, that the city had received its due. "The Stanley Cup came home last night," the *Gazette* told its readers, "home to the city that was the first to hold the famous old bowl that Lord Stanley of Preston offered for competition back in 1893." Yet the 1935 final between Montreal and Toronto was an oddity. It was the first time in almost a decade that two Canadian cities had met to do battle for the Stanley Cup, a trophy originally awarded to the hockey champion of the Dominion. It had last happened in 1926, when an earlier version of the Montreal Maroons beat the Victoria Cougars. And it would be twelve more years before there was another all-Canadian final.

American-based teams had begun pursuing the Stanley Cup in 1914 when Lester and Frank Patrick admitted the Portland Rosebuds to their Pacific Coast Hockey Association, followed by the Seattle Metropolitans, and the short-lived Spokane Canaries. By the late 1920s, American-based teams dominated the hunt. Canada still provided the athletic and managerial talent but most of the players were migrating south of the border to play before enthusiastic, if untutored, crowds in major U.S. cities. The combination of big arenas, big crowds, and big money in America had spelled the end of major league hockey in most parts of Canada, particularly the West, a fact sadly noted by the Edmonton *Journal* in March 1927. "New York pro hockey outdrew the combined attendance of any four cities of the Western Hockey League," the *Journal* lamented at a time when the WHL was on its last legs.

Professional hockey had operated on an transcontinental East-West axis between 1914 and 1927, but the NHL's expansion into the United States, starting in 1924, gradually turned the game into a North-South sport. This fundamental realignment is reflected in the list of Stanley Cup winners between 1928 and 1941. Clubs based in the United States won ten of fourteen Cups during those years. For the Canadian-based teams, this was a generally dismal era. The Ottawa Senators did not make the final between 1927, when they won their last Cup, and 1935, when the team finally folded. The Canadiens won back-to-back Cups in 1930 and 1931, then endured a thirteen-year drought. The Leafs won in 1932, their first season in the new Maple Leaf Gardens. They appeared in six more Cup finals during this era but lost every time. The Maroons won their second, and last, Cup in 1935, and folded three years later.

The transformation of Canada's winter sport into a continental spectacle, dominated by American money, was frequently lamented or scorned by Canadian writers of a nationalist bent. Writing in *Maclean's* in December 1927, Frederick B. Edwards noted: "There is no Pacific Coast league today. Instead, there exists a ten-club organization [NHL], with six of the clubs representing United States cities, which will play this season to something like two million people. Millionaires back the organizations. Fine ladies in evening gowns, with polite gloved palms, applaud the efforts of the skating roughnecks. Hockey has put on a high hat."

A decade later, again in *Maclean's*, Elmer Ferguson of the Montreal *Herald* would lament the fact that only two major league hockey teams had survived in Canada, the Leafs and the Canadiens, and the Canadiens were losing money. Added Ferguson: "Within the past twelve years, six Canadian cities that ranked as major professional hockey centres have vanished from the pro hockey picture, a withdrawal that involved seven teams fading off into mere memories of golden nights and glamorous figures. They have been replaced by the spectre of starkly empty rinks, their glories lost, their stars moved thence, leaving behind a trail of red where many a promoter's bank roll bled."

Some of the damage was caused by the NHL's expansion into the United States. Teams based in small Canadian cities simply could not generate the revenue required to keep the best players. But the Great Depression, which wreaked havoc on the entire Canadian economy for most of the 1930s, also contributed to the demise of some of the professional teams, particularly the Ottawa Senators and the Montreal Maroons.

Yet, for a few fortunate young Canadian men, professional hockey provided a fabulous alternative to the dreariness of life in the Depression. In 1934, when he was nineteen years old, Alex Shibicky was working in a Winnipeg factory that made wooden boxes used for packing fish. He was earning fifteen-and-a-half cents an hour, or $6.20 for a forty-hour week. That fall, Lester Patrick held a tryout camp in Winnipeg for graduating junior players. Shibicky was one of twenty-six players invited from across the country and one of the six whom Patrick took to New York. He recalls receiving a $1,000 signing bonus and a contract that would pay him $2,500 a season if he made the Rangers or $75 a week if he was sent to the minors. "I had to grab it," says Shibicky. "The NHL was like strawberries and whipped cream. There were no decent jobs around. Nothing. The wages were terrible."

Between the years 1928 and 1942, the NHL achieved a level of parity among its members that has rarely been reached since then. There were no dynasties, no perennial powerhouses like the Canadiens, or the Leafs, or the Islanders, or the Oilers who in succeeding decades would win the Cup and cling to it year after year. Back-to-back wins were the best the teams could do, and there were only two of them, the Canadiens and the Red Wings.

It was an era of colourful coaches, managers, and front office executives. There was Conn Smythe in Toronto, Jack Adams in Detroit, Lester Patrick in New York, and Tommy Gorman, who ran the Ottawa Senators, the New York Americans, the Chicago Black Hawks, the Montreal Maroons, and the Canadiens, and was a hit everywhere. All these men produced winning hockey teams, and all had a streak of showmanship in them. They spoke for their teams and were just as well known as their star players.

This era also produced some of the most memorable events in Cup history. There was a string of record-setting overtime marathons, starting with a 1930 semi-final game between the Canadiens and Rangers that lasted 128 minutes and 52 seconds. Two years later, the Leafs and Bruins played 164 minutes and 46 seconds of hockey before Toronto prevailed. In 1936, the Red Wings and Maroons played a game that lasted 176 minutes and 30 seconds, a record that was still intact fifty-five years later.

The first landmark event of these years occurred in the spring of 1928 when the New York Rangers and the Montreal Maroons met in the finals. The Rangers began the best-of-five series at a serious disadvantage: they were forced to play the entire final in the Montreal Forum, which by then had artificial ice, because Ringling Bros. Barnum & Bailey's Circus had temporarily taken over Madison Square Garden.

The Rangers lost the first game 2–0, and disaster befell them in the second. The game was a scoreless tie when their goaltender, Lorne Chabot, was seriously injured midway through the second period. "Chabot jumped into the air to stop a back-handed shot from the stick of Nels Stewart," the Montreal *Gazette* reported. "Chabot misjudged it and the puck caught him over the left eye. He fell in a heap to the ice, writhing in agony."

Chabot was finished, the Rangers had no substitute, and the Maroons refused to let them dress Ottawa Senator goalie Alex Connell, who happened to be in the stands. In an act of courage borne of utter desperation, New York's forty-four-year-old coach Lester Patrick, his playing days several years behind him, stepped into Chabot's blood-stained, sweat-soaked gear and played goal for the first time. Odie Cleghorn, coach of the NHL's Pittsburgh Pirates, filled in behind the Ranger bench, while a tense group of league executives, including Toronto's Conn Smythe, the Canadiens' Leo Dandurand, and Detroit's Jack Adams, offered advice from the first row of seats.

With each Maroon attack, Patrick darted from side to side in his crease shrieking wildly: "Make them shoot! Make them shoot!" At the same time, Cleghorn could be heard roaring: "Don't let them shoot! Don't let them shoot!" The Ranger players quickly realized that both Patrick and Cleghorn wanted them to force the Maroons to shoot from a distance or from bad angles. So the forwards lined up across their own blue line and the defencemen played right behind them. "Patrick handled a few tricky shots," the *Gazette*'s man observed, "by lunging on the puck and always looking behind him to see if it had trickled through."

Thirty seconds into the third period, New York's ace winger Bill Cook put the Rangers in front 1–0 by beating Montreal's Clint Benedict. The lead held until, with less than two minutes to play, the Maroons' big gun, Nels Stewart, rifled a rebound by a grounded and helpless Patrick. The teams played out the clock then battled through seven minutes of overtime before New York centre Frank Boucher scored the game winner. "The Rangers gave vent to their joy by pounding the ice with their sticks and smashing one another lustily on the back," the *Gazette* reported.

With the approval of the Maroons, the Rangers picked up minor league goaltender Joe Miller to replace Chabot for the rest of the series. The teams split games three and four to set up the decisive fifth game before eleven thousand rabid fans at the Montreal Forum. "From the first whistle, the Maroons lashed out a ferocious attack . . . and raked Joe Miller with shots," the *Gazette* reported. But it was New York's clever centreman Frank Boucher who opened the scoring with one of only three Ranger shots in the first period.

The Maroons put one by Miller early in the third but the referee disallowed it, prompting the crowd to unleash what a *New York Times* writer described as "a blizzard of torn paper and programs, not to mention several hats and a chair." Attendants spent ten minutes clearing the debris off the ice. When play resumed, the rejuvenated Rangers scored an insurance goal and went on to capture their first Stanley Cup.

A year later, in late March 1929, the Rangers and Bruins squared off in what was billed as "the first all-American playoff for hockey's most prized trophy." The league agreed to a best-of-three final, because both teams were about to be ousted from their rinks. A track meet had been scheduled for the Boston Garden while the circus was due to make its annual appearance in Madison Square Garden. The series opened in Boston before a highly partisan crowd of eighteen thousand. "Profound silence greeted the Rangers as they skated out on the ice," the *Times* reported. "A great roar welcomed the Bruins."

The teams played through a scoreless first period. But five minutes into the second Boston's star right winger Dit Clapper scored. A little more than five minutes later, Bruin sub Jim Gainor added another. "Their goals sent the rabid Boston fans, who packed the house, into frenzies of excitement," the *Times* noted. "The spectators came well supplied with torn pieces of paper and a veritable snowstorm descended from the galleries as the Bruins scored."

Immediately after the game, the teams boarded the midnight train for New York. Ranger president Colonel John Hammond had insisted on playing again the following night in order to get a match into Madison Square Garden ahead of the circus. With fourteen thousand New Yorkers on hand for game two, the teams again played a scoreless first period. Bruin centre Harry Oliver scored midway through the second, and Ranger sub Butch Keeling tied the game early in the third. "The crowd roared itself hoarse, and was looking forward to overtime when Boston's Bill Carson dashed their hopes with a flashy shot with less than two minutes to go," the *Times* said. "It was a shot that seemed to come from nowhere but it settled the Stanley Cup issue."

The defending champions, the Boston Bruins, were even

stronger in the 1929-30 season. They lost only five of forty-four games, and finished first overall with seventy-seven points, way ahead of the Maroons and Canadiens, who both earned fifty-one points. Boston's Cooney Weiland won the scoring championship with a record seventy-three points, Dit Clapper finished third, and netminder Tiny Thompson had the league's best goals-against average. Some members of the hockey establishment and the sporting press were describing the Bruins as "the greatest team of all hockey history," and they were heavy favourites going into the best-of-three final against the Canadiens on the night of April 1, 1930.

The Canadiens were playing their fifth game in ten nights. One of their playoff matches against Chicago had lasted 111 minutes and another against the Rangers had gone 128 minutes, both of which were new records for the N H L. Furthermore, Montreal had lost seven straight games to Boston. Despite all the odds against them, the Canadiens roared to a 3–0 win in game one. "Light and fast, the Montrealers swept around the champions like a Texas cyclone," the *Gazette* reported. "It was a stunned, silent crowd of seventeen thousand that sat in the Garden and watched the favoured Boston team rendered almost helpless against the amazing vitality of the Flying Frenchmen."

A noisy crowd of loyalists greeted the Canadiens at Montreal's Bonaventure Station the following day, and the excitement over game two grew from there. The Forum's rush seats were gone well before noon hour on game day, and by early evening the line-up for standing-room tickets circled the Forum twice. A record crowd, described in the *Gazette* as "row upon row of hockey-mad humanity," watched the Canadiens pile up a 3–0 lead by the ten-minute mark of the second.

However, a goal by Boston's fearsome defenceman Eddie Shore revived the Bruins, and they swarmed all over the Canadiens net throughout the third period. "The crowd was hysterical as the rubber was sent in on [Canadien goalie] George Hainsworth from all directions," the *Gazette* reported.

Seemingly beaten, the Bruins scored two more goals and pushed the Canadiens to the limit before surrendering 4–3. When the gong sounded to end the game, and the series, the crowd erupted. "Shattered nerves gave way to singing, shouting and noise of any kind," the next day's *Gazette* said. "Music played, different groups sang and danced, and the rafters fairly shook with the excitement."

Montreal and Boston were the two top teams the following season, but it was the Canadiens and the Black Hawks who met in the 1931 final, a best-of-five series. Based on regular season point totals, the series should have opened in Montreal. However, the Canadiens agreed to play the first two games in the Chicago Stadium because the arena's ice surface was about to be removed. Although the Black Hawks had a roaring crowd of 16,500 behind them, they could not hold off a vigorous Canadien attack, and lost 2–0.

In game two, Chicago's manpower advantage, coach Dick Irvin's quick line changes, and a tumultuous crowd carried the Hawks to victory. Chicago had dressed sixteen players, plus a goaltender, while Montreal only had a total of thirteen players in uniform. The teams battled to a 1–1 tie in regulation time, then played twenty-five minutes of overtime. Finally, Chicago forwards Johnny Gottselig, Rosario Couture, and Doc Romnes broke down the ice "to leave the leg-weary Canadien forwards behind in the Hawks territory." Gottselig rifled a shot that whizzed by Hainsworth into an unprotected corner and the game was over.

As the teams prepared for game three in Montreal, Hawk coach Dick Irvin told the press that his seventeen players were healthy and injury-free. The Canadiens, meanwhile, were troubled by a rash of injuries. League scoring champion Howie Morenz had a bad shoulder, Wildor Larochelle had wrenched his back, Gus Rivers had a charleyhorse, and Pit Lepine had a broken finger. Armand Mondou, who had suffered rib and shoulder injuries, and Albert LeDuc, who had suffered a concussion, had just been released from hospital. As well, Morenz hadn't scored in seven games, the longest drought of his career. "I feel I've got a good game coming to me," he told the press. "If I just smell that goal once, I think I can fling in a couple."

Despite the injuries, the depleted Canadiens almost ran off with the third game. They led 2–0 with four minutes to go when the Hawks rallied to tie the game. The teams then dragged themselves through fifty-three minutes of overtime. "When the third overtime started both teams were on their last legs," the *Gazette's* L. B. Shapiro reported. "Neither team seemed to have enough left in them to carry the puck effectively. Players were falling at the least pressure, and the crowd sank back in silence when Chicago's Cy Wentworth made the play that broke up the game."

Trailing 2–1 in the series and facing elimination, the Canadiens fell behind 2–0 in game four before they rallied. "While a capacity crowd looked on, at first hushed and later wild with enthusiasm, the Flying Frenchmen thrust aside physical injury, forgot their utter exhaustion, and skated in lightning fashion out of the shadow of defeat to gain a 4–2 victory," Shapiro wrote. "The final gong sent the crowd into a huge roar and the exhausted Frenchmen were half carried and half pushed to their dressing room by a group of jubilant supporters."

On the day of the fifth game, fans were lined up outside the Forum all day hoping to buy tickets for rush seats and standing room. The city's newspapers promised their readers special post-game editions. And Foster Hewitt, described as "one of the leading sports broadcasters of the continent," handled the play-by-play commentary, which was carried via railway transmission wires to all of English Canada. This was one of the first times Hewitt's voice was heard coast to coast. It was almost two years later, in January 1933, that he began his national Saturday night broadcasts from Maple Leaf Gardens.

With all Montreal on edge, and with fans across the country tuned in, the Canadiens were unbeatable. They shut down the Hawks 2–0 and drove the Forum crowd delirious. "The greater the odds, the greater the inspiration for the gallant Frenchmen," Shapiro concluded after the Canadiens had won their fourth Stanley Cup, and their last one for thirteen long years.

In fact, the Canadiens were about to begin the darkest decade in their long history. As the Depression worsened in the 1930's, the Canadiens began losing money, and there was talk in Montreal of selling the franchise.

A year later, the Rangers ousted the Canadiens to earn their third trip to the finals in five years, while the Leafs made their first appearance in a Stanley Cup series. The press and the public saw the 1932 series as a showdown between the NHL's top two lines: Toronto's Kid Line, comprised of Charlie Conacher, Joe Primeau, and Busher Jackson; and the polished New York veterans Bill Cook, brother Bun Cook, and Frank Boucher. Although the teams had finished with almost identical point totals in the regular season, the Rangers entered the series with enormous confidence.

Before the opening game at Madison Square Garden, the Rangers big, mean defenceman, Ching Johnson, stuck his head in the Leaf dressing room and said: "Listen bozos, listen to the Ranger theme song." From down the hall, the Toronto players could hear a chorus of voices singing a verse that ended with the line: "When the Leafs come tumbling down." The Rangers paid dearly for their arrogance, however, when the Leafs ran up a 5–1 lead on Busher Jackson's hattrick then held on to win 6–4. Afterward, veteran Frank Finnigan, who joined the Leafs at the start of that season, opened the Rangers' dressing-room door while his teammates bellowed: "Ain't that a shame, a measly shame."

The annual arrival of the circus forced the teams to move to Boston Garden for game two, and a crowd of twelve thousand watched the youth, speed, and persistence of the Leafs prevail over the age, savvy, and experience of the Rangers by a margin of 6–2. The series then shifted to Maple Leaf Gardens where 14,366 Toronto fans witnessed a brilliant game. "Both teams turned loose a bewildering display of beautifully timed combinations,"

The Montreal Amateur Athletic Association hockey team was awarded the Stanley Cup in 1893, and won again in 1894. (Hockey Hall of Fame)

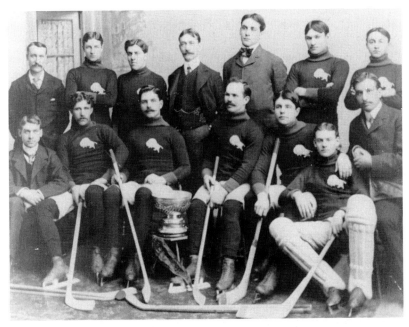

The Winnipeg Victorias, shown here after winning the cup in 1901, were one of the best teams in Canada during the first decade of Cup play. (Manitoba Hockey Hall of Fame)

The Ottawa Senators, now known as the Silver Seven, successfully defended the Cup nine times, and were renowned for their toughness. (Hockey Hall of Fame)

The Kenora Thistles, noted for their speed and slick passing, were the only small-town team ever to capture the cup. (Hockey Hall of Fame)

In 1917, the Seattle Metropolitans of the Pacific Coast Hockey Association became the first American-based Cup winner. (Hockey Hall of Fame)

Lester Patrick's Victoria Cougars changed hockey forever in 1925 by using regular line changes to defeat the Montreal Canadiens in the Cup final. (Hockey Hall of Fame)

The Ottawa Senators were the best team in hockey in the 1920s. They won four Stanley Cups and finished first in the NHL seven times. (Hockey Hall of Fame)

After winning the Cup in 1930 and 1931, the Montreal Canadiens went thirteen years without a championship. (National Archives of Canada/ C-38097)

NHL president Frank Calder presents the Cup to the Rangers' Bill Cook at Madison Square Garden in November 1933. (UPI/Bettman)

Coach Tommy Gorman, shown here with his 1934 Stanley Cup champion Black Hawks, was one of hockey's most colourful figures in the 1930s. (National Archives of Canada/C-38113)

Lester Patrick, wearing the famous bowl in this photo, celebrates the New York Rangers' last Stanley Cup triumph in 1940. (City of Toronto Archives/G&M 65350)

Clarence Campbell presents the Cup to Ted Kennedy after the 1949 final. The Leafs had just become the first NHL team to win three straight cups. (Hockey Hall of Fame)

Turk Broda, the Maple Leafs' goalie through most of the 1940s, sips champagne from the Cup during a victory party. (City of Toronto Archives/G&M 132810)

Conn Smythe and the wives of the Leafs' players after the 1951 Cup win. The Leafs and their fans did not celebrate another championship for eleven years. (Hockey Hall of Fame)

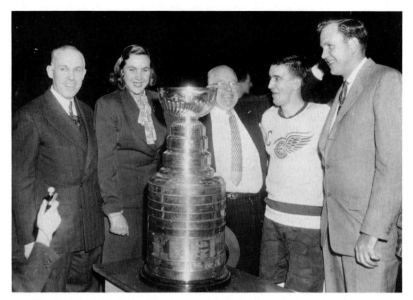

Marguerite Norris, the only woman to have her name engraved on the Cup, is seen here after the Red Wings' 1954 victory. Ms. Norris was president of the Red Wings that year. (UPI/Bettman)

The Red Wings of the early 1950s, seen celebrating a Cup victory, were one of the best teams ever assembled. (UPI/Bettman)

Star sports editor Lou Marsh wrote. "Every goal was scored by sheer wizardry of stick, blade and brain. Individual heroes were as scarce as anteaters in Alaska. Everybody was a star at times." But there was only one winner: the Leafs by a score of 6–4.

Afterwards, a microphone was placed on the ice near the penalty box. With the Leaf players surrounding them, coach Dick Irvin, team president Conn Smythe, and captain Hap Day addressed the crowd and Canadians listening at home on their radios. Mayor William J. Stewart was the last to speak, and he called for three cheers for the Leafs. "As the last faint echoes of the rousing cheers died away, then and only then did the fans begin to depart," the *Globe* reported.

A year later, after battling through a forty-eight-game regular schedule and the post-season preliminary rounds, the Leafs and the Rangers reached the finals again. The series opened April 4, 1933, in New York, but the Leafs were frazzled and in no shape to play when they got off the train at Grand Central Station a few hours before the opening face-off. The previous evening in Toronto, they had played a 164-minute marathon before beating the Bruins 1–0 in the fifth game of the semi-final. Almost sixty years later, at the age of eighty-two, former Leaf defenceman Red Horner recalled that long overtime game as the single most memorable event of his twelve-year NHL career.

"It was a thrilling evening," he says. "It looked as if it would go on all night. There was some question, around one o'clock in the morning, about whether we would toss a coin for it, and I remember one of our forwards, Harold Cotton, standing up in our dressing saying 'No we won't toss for it. We'll play it out.' Ken Doraty was one of our substitutes and hadn't played hardly at all during the regular game. So when they put Doraty on he was fresh, and he scored the winning goal about two o'clock in the morning. He went around Eddie Shore, who had played a brilliant game but was exhausted by this time.

"We went straight from the Gardens to Union Station, and the train left around three in the morning. Normally it would have taken off around eleven, but it was held for us. We didn't arrive in New York until four or five o'clock the next afternoon and then had to play at eight-thirty that night. Consequently we lost the game."

The arrival of the circus forced the teams to play the rest of the series in Toronto. But even with three days' rest and a friendly crowd behind them, the Leafs were no match for Lester Patrick's Rangers and fell by a score of 3–1 in game two. The rarely used Doraty, described by the *News's* Lou Marsh as "the pint-sized blond with the hippity-hop style of skating," scored Toronto's only goal. He also scored two goals in the third game, which the Leafs won 3–2. However, Toronto had only postponed the inevitable.

Two nights later, the teams battled to a scoreless draw in regulation time. Eight minutes into overtime, the game was decided. "Bill Cook, wily captain of the Rangers, drove home the goal that gave the visitors the triumph," Marsh reported, "beating Lorne Chabot, the tall net guardian for the Leafs, with a blistering side shot after taking a neat rink wide pass from Butch Keeling." The following day, most of the Rangers left from Toronto's Union Station for their homes in various parts of Canada, with another Stanley Cup to their credit, and $1,500 bonuses in their pockets.

The following year, 1934, the four Canadian clubs had already been eliminated by April, setting up an all-American final between Tommy Gorman's Chicago Black Hawks and Jack Adams' Detroit Red Wings. The Wings had been the superior team during the regular season and had a psychological edge on the Hawks because the first two games of the final were scheduled for the Detroit Olympia, where the Hawks had not won a game in over four years. However, Chicago surprised the Wings and their highly partisan fans by taking the first game 2–1 in overtime, and winning the second game by a comfortable margin of 4–1.

Detroit's forwards finally broke through Chicago's close-checking, defensive game to beat the Hawks 5–2 in game three.

The hero of the evening was undoubtedly Red Wing netminder Wilf Cude. Late in the second period he dropped to his knees to block a shot, when Hawk forward Rosario Couture accidentally clouted him across the nose and above the right eye with the blade of his stick. Cude was carried to the dressing room unconscious. Ten minutes later the Detroit goaltender returned with the right side of his face swollen, and his eye blackened and nearly closed. "He was in intense pain," the *Detroit News* reported, "but he kicked out twelve shots in the final period when Hawks rushed with four and five men seeking the tying goal."

In game four, both Cude and Chicago goalie Charley Gardiner were unbeatable through regulation time and thirty minutes of overtime. The break in the scoreless game occurred on a faceoff in the Detroit end with Red Wing Ebbie Goodfellow benched for tripping. Chicago centre Doc Romnes won the draw and pulled the puck back to linemate Mush March. The right winger eluded a check and drove a hard, low shot by Cude's outstretched foot and into the net. Having won their first Stanley Cup, the jubilant Hawks leapt on to the ice to celebrate.

"Players who had scarcely been able to skate danced the length of the ice," the *News* reported. "Louis Napoleon Trudel, the young Frenchman who plays left wing on the Hawks' third line, grabbed the Stanley Cup as soon as it was brought on the ice for the presentation and skated wildly around the rink. March tried to escape the celebration. He wanted to go to the dressing room. Thousands stood and shouted 'We want March' and the hero of the Hawks was forced to circle the rink arm-in-arm with Trudel as the fans gave him a thunderous ovation."

Strangely, winning the Cup was not enough to keep Hawk coach Gorman in Chicago. During the off-season, he joined the Montreal Maroons, taking with him defenceman Lionel Conacher. He lured Ottawa firefighter and former Senator goalie Alex Connell out of retirement and made a couple of other minor additions to a lineup comprised of solid veterans and promising young players. Gorman's Maroons were hardly worldbeaters, but they advanced to the best-of-five final against a much stronger Maple Leaf team. The Leafs had finished first in 1934-35, Charlie Conacher of the Kid Line had won the scoring championship, and goalie George Hainsworth had been in the Toronto nets for a league-leading thirty wins.

Nevertheless as he watched his team's workout on the day before the final began, Gorman leaned over the boards at the Forum and told an eager group of reporters: "That Toronto team can't hold this speed. Look at the balance we've got. Mind you, it's going to be a tough battle." When he saw those remarks in print, Conn Smythe had a blunt reply: "He had better do his talking now before the series starts because it will be too late after. Our boys were never in better shape."

Game one was played in Toronto before 14,500 fans, who witnessed a tense, tight battle that was tied 2–2 after sixty minutes of play. Five minutes into the overtime, Maroons' sophomore centre Russ Blinco picked up the puck at the Leaf blue line, stickhandled in, and drew the Toronto defence toward him before firing a pass to linemate Dave Trottier. "This time Hainsworth was beaten," the Montreal *Gazette*'s D. A. MacDonald wrote. "Trottier blew out the twine of the Toronto goal with a quick wristshot that caught the far corner."

Afterwards, the exuberant Gorman scampered around the dressing room in his shirt sleeves, slapping his players on the back, and chortling like a side-show barker: "We had it all over them tonight, all over them. What a team, what a team." The Leafs' room resembled a morgue, and the loss seemed to cast a pall over the entire city, according to MacDonald. "The so-called Queen City was as dismal today as Toronto on a rainy Sunday afternoon," he wrote the day after the game, "and Toronto on a Sunday afternoon is about as dull as any place can be."

From there, things only got worse for the Leafs. They outshot the Maroons 34–14 in the first two periods of game two, but Alex

Connell, the Ottawa fireman, held them off, and Montreal prevailed by a margin of 3–1. Nobody was more frustrated than Conn Smythe. At one point in the game, he leapt from his seat behind the Leaf bench, charged up the aisle, and attacked a fan who had been heckling his team all night. After a brief scuffle, Smythe returned to his seat, and the ushers ejected the noisy fan.

Having been pushed to the brink of elimination, Toronto mounted one last, frantic assault on the Maroons before capitulating. "The Leafs all but swept the Maroons out of the rink in the first half of the second period," MacDonald reported after game three. "They rattled shots off Connell's big black pads, they thumped drives off his chest, they drove sniping shots into his lean body as he sprawled across the goalmouth. But for 12 minutes and 59 seconds, seemingly at times by miracle, they could not beat the old fireman." Four minutes later, Baldy Northcott, a seven-year veteran who had never won the Cup, tipped in a rebound that decided the first all-Canadian final in ten years in favour of the Montreal Maroons.

In the spring of 1936, the Maroons advanced to the semi-final against the Detroit Red Wings, only to be swept 3–0 in a series that began with the longest game on record. The Maroons and Wings faced off at 8:30 on the evening of March 25 before a crowd of nine thousand at the Montreal Forum. They played until 2:25 the following morning: three periods of regulation time; almost six periods of overtime; a total of 176½ minutes. Montreal fired ninety shots at Detroit goalie Norm Smith. The Wings unloaded sixty-seven shots at Lorne Chabot before Modere Bruneteau finally broke the scoreless tie.

Fifty-five years later, at the age of eighty-two, former Red Wing Wally Kilrea still remembered Bruneteau's goal in photographic detail. "Montreal had dumped the puck into our end and my brother Hec picked it up," says Kilrea. "Hec outskated two Maroon forwards, Hooley Smith and Baldy Northcott. When he was coming out of our end, Jack Adams told Bruneteau to jump on, and he pulled off the right winger. Bruneteau was pretty fresh because he hadn't played much that night. When Hec carried the puck over the blue line, the two defencemen moved up a little. He whipped it over to Bruneteau, and it was on his stick and in the net so fast the goaltender didn't even make a move."

The Wings had won five in a row when they lined up against the Leafs in game one of the final April 5 at the Detroit Olympia. The Leaf players barely had time to get their bearings before the game was practically over. Detroit scored three goals, including a short-handed marker by defenceman Bucko McDonald, in the first seven minutes and twelve seconds of the game. Ten seconds later the Leafs scored their only goal of the night.

Afterwards, in the Wings' steamy and noisy dressing room, Jack Adams sat with his arm around McDonald, a former Leaf reject, posed for photographers, and bellowed at the Toronto reporters: "This is the guy you tossed away. This is the guy you Toronto guys didn't want." Over in the Leaf dressing room, the players dressed quickly and quietly while a pensive Conn Smythe told the press: "You know what beat us. We forgot how fast that Detroit bunch can break."

In game two, the fast-breaking Wings scored twice in the first five minutes and ran up a 4–1 lead after twenty minutes. By the end, they had thrashed the Leafs 9–4. "What's the matter with us?" an exasperated Buzz Boll shouted in the dressing room after the game, a question that neither his teammates nor the press could answer. Coach Dick Irvin had nothing to say after the game, but Smythe offered this assessment: "We simply ran into an express train that was driven by a cyclone."

Two nights later in Toronto, the Wings appeared to be unstoppable. "With seven minutes left to play in the third period the Wings were leading 3–0," Lloyd Northard of the *Detroit News* wrote. "Employees of Maple Leaf Gardens had placed the Stanley Cup on a table and were ready to carry it to centre ice where

Frank Calder, president of the National Hockey League, was to make the formal presentation to James Norris, Sr., owner of the Red Wings. Then there was a slip on the defense."

Leaf forward Bob Davidson made a blind pass from the corner. Joe Primeau, left unprotected in front the Detroit net, pounced on the puck and slipped it by a diving Norm Smith. Two minutes later, Frank Finnigan picked up a loose puck just inside his own blue line and fired a pass to teammate Pep Kelly, who streaked down right wing, cruised by McDonald and drove the puck past Smith. Then with the Wings a mere forty-two seconds away from the Cup, the puck bounced to Kelly in front of the Detroit net. He took a wild swing, and Smith made a desperate lunge. "There was an opening inches wide," Northard reported, "and into that opening Kelly rolled the puck and the score was tied."

Thirty-one seconds into overtime, Toronto's Buzz Boll got the puck during a scramble in front of the Detroit net, waited for Smith to make a move, and fired a perfect shot into an open corner. The Gardens crowd went wild, and an hour later fans were still hanging around outside the Leafs' dressing room. Inside the room, a jubilant Smythe kissed Boll on the cheek for a mob of photographers, and repeated the performance several times before Boll, a Saskatchewan farm boy, said, "That's enough," and walked away.

The Leafs had won a reprieve but it was a brief one. They took a 1–0 lead in the game four, but the poised and confident Wings came back to win 3–2 in what was described as the best-played game of the series. After ten NHL seasons, Detroit had won its first Cup, and both the coach and his players were jubilant. "Adams shouted in glee for a good five minutes after he and his Wings pounded into a dressing room filled with well-wishers," Canadian Press reporter A. E. Fulford wrote. "Deliriously happy and still somewhat dazed by it all, the Wings posed for pictures, singly, in groups, dressed and partly nude." Later that evening,

Frank Calder presented the Cup to the victors in his suite at the Royal York, and the following afternoon the Wings arrived at Michigan Central Station in Detroit to an enthusiastic welcome from two thousand noisy fans.

The Red Wings were the top team in the league again the following season. They lead their rivals in games won and points accumulated. Linemates Marty Barry and Larry Aurie finished third and fourth respectively in the scoring race, and goaltender Norm Smith had the best goals-against average and tied for the league lead in shutouts. And, again, Adams led his team to the final. This time they faced the New York Rangers, a team in transition. Lester Patrick's former stalwarts, Frank Boucher, the Cook brothers, Ching Johnson, and Murray Murdoch, had been eclipsed by some sparkling new recruits: Edmontonians Mac and Neil Colville, Manitobans Alex Shibicky and Babe Pratt, and Montrealer Phil Watson.

The series opened with a single game in Madison Square Garden, a move made to accommodate the Rangers, who were about to be displaced by the circus. As the players skated out for game one, equipment for the trapeze and other aerial acts hung from the Garden roof, while a menagerie including lions, tigers, elephants, seals, and camels was stored in the Garden basement. A crowd of more than seventeen thousand fans packed the stands, and before the game started, gamblers loitered in the lobby, offering six-to-five odds in favour of the Rangers.

New York skated to an easy 5–1 win, and Adams was forced to replace Norm Smith, who could barely move his left arm because of an injury, with minor league goaltender Earl Robertson. But the young and unproven goalie held the Rangers at bay in the second game, and the Wings won 4–2. When the players returned to the dressing room, a mob of photographers was standing on tables and benches with cameras ready. A moment later Adams was in front of the cameras and bellowing over the din around him: "We've cut them down to their level. They've been playing two thousand miles over their heads. We won the big game. We're back on stride."

Goaltending was the decisive factor in the next two games. The Rangers won the third game 1–0 on Mac Colville's second period tally, prompting Lester Patrick to strut around the dressing room afterward shouting: "The pressure is on them now. We're in the driver's seat." To emphasize his point, he waved his arm as though he were cracking a whip and yelled, "Gee haw." However, Patrick had underestimated the resolve of the Red Wings, who battled back to tie the series at two games apiece with a 1–0 win.

A few minutes before the fifth and deciding game, Adams delivered a daring and inspired pep talk. He brought the Stanley Cup into the dressing room and set it on a table in front of his players. "Every one of us, from the time we were kids shooting pucks on icy sidewalks, has wanted to get his name on that Cup," he said. "You can make history tonight by winning it two years in a row. Let's see what you've got. Let's bring this Cup back in here after the game."

With that, the fired-up Wings roared on to the ice and proved unbeatable. Marty Barry scored a power-play goal on a hard, low drive with less than a minute to go in the first period. The Wings added two more insurance goals and goalie Robertson shut out the Rangers. "He broke the hearts of the Ranger forwards with his cat-like ability," reporter John McManis wrote in the *Detroit News*. "Earl Robertson, the obscure rookie, the man not considered good enough for major league hockey, dominated the game."

The Wings' triumph was short-lived, however. The 1937-38 season proved to be a catastrophe for them. They plummeted from first place to last in the NHL's American division, finishing two points behind the Chicago Black Hawks, who snuck into the playoffs with a lamentable record of fourteen wins and thirty-seven points over a forty-eight-game schedule. By early April

1938, however, the press was describing the formerly feeble Black Hawks as the "miracle men" and the "wonder team." After upsetting two opponents, the Hawks had advanced to the Stanley Cup final against the Toronto Maple Leafs, a team twenty points better than them during the season. "If we win," Chicago forward Paul Thompson told a reporter before the series opened, "we'll all go nuts, just plain and fancy screwy."

The Hawks arrived in Toronto for game one with a major crisis on their hands. They didn't have a goalie. Their regular netminder, Mike Karakas, was out with a fractured toe. The only other goalie under contract to the Hawks, Paul Goodman, was with a minor-league team in Wichita, Kansas. Black Hawk vice-president Bill Tobin and rookie coach Bill Stewart, a former NHL referee and major-league umpire, asked the Leafs for permission to use New York Ranger Davey Kerr, one of the league's top netminders. The Leafs flatly refused. However, Leaf executive Frank Selke told Tobin and Stewart that minor-league goalie Alfie Moore was in Toronto and available. Selke then performed what he thought was a gentlemanly act. He phoned Moore and told him to show up at the Gardens with his equipment in case the Hawks decided to use him.

Forty-five minutes before game time, the goaltender issue remained unresolved. With the fans already arriving, Tobin and Stewart met Smythe and Selke near the Gardens' press box. Selke again suggested they use Moore, at which point Stewart blew up. He accused Selke of bringing in a half-sober goaltender, and lying to him earlier in the day. Then Smythe exploded. "Nobody calls Selke a liar in my presence," Smythe roared as he threw off his topcoat and lunged and swung at Stewart all in one motion.

"In a moment, they were struggling fiercely," reporter Andy Lytle told *Toronto Star* readers the next day. "Three or four men grabbed Smythe. Baldy Cotton, Joe Primeau and King Clancy grabbed Stewart and tried to haul him away. It was a difficult task. Stewart was fuming and struggling like a man gone mad." The executive-level fisticuffs seemed to set the tone for the entire series. Game one, Lytle said, was full of "thundering collisions, slashes and trips." Moore played goal that night, superbly as it turned out, even though he admitted to having had a couple of beers in the afternoon, and Chicago won 3–1.

The Hawks played minor-leaguer Goodman in goal in game two, under orders from league president Frank Calder, and lost 5–1. It was a game marked by "hard fierce battling and vicious high sticking," according to Lytle. Heading back to Chicago, the Hawks had a long casualty list: Louis Trudel had received a four-stitch gash in his head; Alex Levinsky had seven stitches in his lip; Doc Romnes had a broken nose; Art Weibe had suffered a severed artery above one eye; Johnny Gottselig had a severely bruised foot; and Cully Dahlstrom had injured his knee.

Game three was scheduled for Sunday, April 10, and the Chicago newspapers that day carried long, lurid accounts of "the slaughter in Toronto." Tobin had helped colour the coverage by pumping the local reporters with inflammatory statements about the savagery of the Leafs. The *Chicago News* ran a huge photo showing six Black Hawks in dressing gowns, resting side by side in hospital beds, but never mentioned that five of them would be in uniform that night.

The sensational coverage clearly enflamed the fans, who arrived at the Stadium bent on causing havoc and mayhem. Line-ups stretched for several blocks outside the building all afternoon. When the doors were opened, ushers confiscated beer cans, tomatoes, bags and bags of confetti and paper, as well as iron bolts, pieces of brick, and blocks of wood. But plenty of contraband was smuggled in despite the ushers' efforts. The crowd of 18,402, a new NHL record, unloaded a deluge of apples, popcorn, paper, and programs when the Leafs appeared. "The booing grew in volume until it seemed that we were caught in a horrible miasma of hate and fury," the *Star*'s Lytle wrote. "The Hawks came out and it was like an armada of roaring aeroplanes above the earth blotting out sky and earth and human reason."

In the first minute of play, Romnes clubbed Red Horner over

the head, knocked him unconscious, and the crowd screamed its approval. In the press box, there was a miniature uproar, Lytle later admitted to his readers. "We Torontonians screamed for Romnes' punishment," he wrote. "Romnes got a minor. We knew then it was a mad world and we were its victims." The Chicago writers viewed the incident somewhat differently. "Romnes waved his stick at Horner and the big Canadian fainted," one writer told his readers.

Although the game was frequently delayed by showers of debris from the stands, the teams managed to play tight, solid hockey. The score was knotted at one apiece late in the third period when Romnes scored his so-called phantom goal to win the game. He fired the puck along the ice and it appeared to whiz by Toronto goalie Turk Broda. But the goal judge hesitated for a second before flipping on his light. The puck was then spotted in the corner of the rink, and the Leafs argued furiously that it had never gone in. But the goal judge was not going to change his mind, not when he was surrounded by an angry, screaming mob.

A couple of nights later the Hawks put the Leafs away for good by a more convincing score of 4–1. "Wild scenes of jubilation marked the end of the game," the *Globe and Mail*'s Tommy Munns wrote. "Fans went wild. The Hawks threw their arms around one another. They kissed goaltending hero Mike Karakas, who played the final two games. They hoisted Bill Stewart high on their shoulders and behaved with all the elation of a school team winning its first title."

After the miracle of 1938, the Hawks slid to the bottom of the league standings and missed the 1939 playoffs altogether. The Leafs, still pursuing their second Stanley Cup, overcame a mediocre season and advanced to the final again. This time their opponent was the Boston Bruins, who had eliminated the Rangers in a dramatic seven-game semi-final. Four of those games went into overtime. Boston won three of them, and rookie winger Mel Hill scored all three winning goals, a feat that earned him lasting fame and the nickname Sudden Death Hill.

"I gave him the passes on all three of them and I remember the first of those goals as plain as if I'd played last night," says Hill's centreman Bill Cowley, now a retired hotelier living in his hometown of Ottawa. "I went into the corner during the second overtime period, and I rustled the puck from a Ranger defenceman, and I laid a perfect pass on his stick. He had an open net to shoot at, and he missed it. At two o'clock in the morning we came tumbling back into the dressing room. Our asses were dragging when we went back out. I rustled into the corner again and got a pass to Hill that was about eighteen inches off the ice. He picked it out of the air and knocked it in."

Hill's heroics made him an overnight celebrity in Boston, and the overtime wins aroused enormous interest in the best-of-seven final. Fans began lining up outside Boston Garden for rush seats eighteen hours before they went on sale, and by the time the ticket windows opened hundreds of fans were waiting. A capacity crowd of more than seventeen thousand packed the building for the opening game but the fans were surprisingly quiet. The *Star*'s Andy Lytle attributed the abnormal calm to the heat, noting that "the air was fetid with smoke and human fumes."

He also speculated that the ushers may have deflated the crowd by stripping its rowdier members of "their weapons of joy and tumult." In a hallway near the Leaf dressing room, the ushers had dumped several piles of confiscated debris, including fruit, vegetables, tin cans, and paper, all intended to be hurled to the ice. Harold Ballard, an ardent Leaf fan who had travelled to Boston for the game, found a brick among the debris, had an usher autograph it, and took it home.

The Bruins won the opener 2–1, but the Leafs bounced back for a 3–2 overtime win in game two. A *Toronto Star* headline nicely summarized the second match: "Conny Smythe talked turkey and Doc Romnes delivered the bird." Smythe summoned his troops to the dressing room an hour before game time, gave them a lecture, and the players responded by holding the Bruins in check until Romnes tipped in the winner. "Nobody knows what the dynamic Smythe said," Lytle wrote, "but it must have been enough. No fiercer fight by the Leafs has ever been witnessed by this reporter."

The sting of Smythe's pep talk quickly faded. The Leafs lost the next two games at home by scores of 3–1 and 2–0. For Boston rookie Roy Conacher, a Toronto native and the league's top goalscorer that season, it was a sweet homecoming. He scored both Bruin goals in game four while his parents, his five sisters, his twin brother, Bert, and his famous hockey brothers, Lionel and Charlie, watched from the stands.

Three nights later in Boston, the powerful Bruins finished off the Leafs to win their first Cup since 1929. Conacher scored the winner, with Cowley and Shore assisting. "I remember the Stanley cup winner," says Cowley. "I was in the corner and got the puck. Conacher broke from the blue line. I passed the puck back and laid it on his stick. He was coming at full speed and picked the top corner."

Throughout the final minutes of the game, the fans were on their feet, yelling, tossing firecrackers, blowing horns, ringing cowbells, and showering the ice with debris. Then the crowd began chanting for the man they called the Edmonton Express, thirty-eight-year-old Eddie Shore, who had played a magnificent series. When he skated on to the ice after the game, Shore received "one of the greatest ovations ever tendered an athlete," according to the New York *Herald Tribune*'s Kerr Petrie. Finally NHL president Frank Calder presented the Cup to Bruin captain Cooney Weiland at centre-ice. Calder tried to make a presentation speech, but the roar of the crowd drowned out his voice as it was carried over the public address system.

The Bruins finished first in the 1939-40 season for their third consecutive league title, but they were eliminated by the New York Rangers in a six-game semi-final. The Leafs, meanwhile, breezed through two preliminary rounds to earn their third straight trip to the final. A day before the series opened, a group of sportswriters surrounded Lester Patrick in the Ranger dressing room and asked him to predict the outcome. Patrick wrapped a towel around his head to mimic a fortune teller, gazed into a spherical inkwell, and said: "The Rangers will win in six games because they are the better hockey team."

Patrick's prediction proved to be dead on. The Rangers won the first two games at home then vacated Madison Square Garden for the circus. The homeless Rangers dropped the third and fourth games in Toronto. But they overcame injuries, adversity, and a highly partisan crowd to sweep the next two games. The most seriously wounded player was right winger Alex Shibicky, a smooth-skating Winnipegger, who broke his ankle in three places in the third game. "I missed the fourth game because my ankle was so swollen I couldn't get it into a skate," he recalls. "I couldn't put any weight on it, but the team kept it out of the papers.

"For the fifth game, we got the Toronto team doctor to freeze it with pain killer, and he gave me five shots, right up to the knee. Funny thing, the doctor never told the Leafs and they didn't know I was hurt. We won the game, but boy did I suffer afterward. I told Lester Patrick about it, and he brought in our own doctor from New York. He just gave me two shots for the sixth game. It picked up our players because they knew I was injured, and they just gave that much more."

The wandering Rangers left Toronto's Union Station the morning after the sixth game. They were the third Ranger club to win the Stanley Cup, but they arrived in New York almost unnoticed. "A handful of fans were there to greet us," recalls Mac Colville, another member of that team. "They didn't go out of their way to do anything for us after we won. We got good crowds for our games, but New York is a cold town." Most of the players packed up and left for their homes in Canada, but seven players required hospital treatment for an assortment of injuries and ailments.

With the passage of time, the Rangers 1940 Stanley Cup has become a source of both pride and embarrassment to the team. In 1990, the club issued Stanley Cup rings to the surviving players to commemorate their victory. "There were only eight of us left," Shibicky says. "I had a lot of phone calls from all the New York papers." For the players who have worn the Ranger colours over the ensuing decades, the 1940 Cup has served to remind them of their misfortune, bad luck, or ineptitude, for Shibicky and his mates were the last Rangers to win the Cup. At fifty-one years and counting, the New York franchise has endured hockey's longest losing streak.

The 1928 to 1941 era, a period when Stanley Cup competition was dominated by the U.S.-based teams, came to a fitting end with an all-American final between the Bruins and Red Wings. Boston entered the series as the clear favourite, having finished first overall for a fourth consecutive season, and having set a new record of twenty-three games without a loss. Bill Cowley, one of the league's smoothest playmaking centres, won the league scoring championship with sixty-two points, the second highest total recorded up to that time, and earned a record forty-five assists.

The Bruins swept the first two games at home and the goaltenders were the heroes of both games. After the first game, *Detroit News* reporter Mark Beltaire wrote that "Red Wing goalie Johnny Mowers was magnificent, with 39 saves as compared to 24 for Frank Brimsek. Mowers robbed the Bruins time after time." Following game two, Beltaire was equally complimentary toward the Bruin goalie: "It was one man alone, Frank Brimsek, who kept the Wings from scoring at least four goals in the first two periods. The Boston goaler was superb. Of his 35 saves, at least half were pure magic."

After winning the third game 4–2, the Bruins were in complete command and full of confidence. In the midst of Boston's noisy dressing room, defenceman Flash Hollett yelled: "Where'll we go tonight, fellows?" Hollett then snapped his fingers, as though suddenly remembering something, and said: "Oh, I forgot. We have another exhibition game here Saturday." One of his more prudent teammates, Woody Dumart, warned Hollett against becoming overconfident, and added: "Don't spend all your playoff money yet."

But the powerful Bruins defeated the Wings 3–1 in game four and became the first NHL team to sweep a best-of-seven final. The team arrived in Boston the following afternoon, and stepped off the train to an enthusiastic welcome from five hundred horn-tooting, bell-ringing fans. The players shook hands and signed dozens of autographs as they waded through the throng to automobiles outside the station. Over the next two days, the players attended a couple of quiet, private banquets. Then they scattered to their homes in various parts of Canada, having brought Boston its first professional sporting championship of any kind in more than a decade.

6

HAVES
AND HAVE NOTS
1942-55

The headline in bold, black type two inches high blazed across
the top of the *Toronto Star's* front page on December 1, 1949.
"BRODA GETS DOWN TO 189 POUNDS," the paper trumpeted
with a mixture of joy and bluntness. The Broda of the headline
was christened Walter Edward, but was known to millions of
hockey fans from coast to coast as Turk, a nickname he had
acquired as a youth in Brandon, Manitoba because his face was
freckled like a turkey egg. The stocky, five-foot, nine-inch Turk
had blossomed in his mid-thirties, an age when most players
have either quit or been canned, to become, in the words of
sportswriter Trent Frayne, the "oldest, fattest, baldest and best
goalkeeper in professional hockey."

The gregarious, down-to-earth Broda was the nearly impen-
etrable netminder who had backstopped the Toronto Maple
Leafs to Stanley Cup triumphs in 1947, 1948, and 1949. The Leafs
were the first team in forty years to retain the Cup for three consecutive years, the first since the Ottawa Silver Seven and the
Montreal Wanderers. But in December 1949, the defending
champions hardly looked like they were on their way to a fourth
straight Stanley Cup. They had a losing record in regular season

play, the press had taken to was calling them "the lamentable Leafs," and their pudgy puckstopper, who had always had more trouble with his weight than opposition snipers, had ballooned to 197 pounds.

In order to shake up his sagging troops, Leaf general manager Conn Smythe benched Broda. "We are not running a fat man's team," Smythe barked during an impromptu Monday morning press conference in late November, a good four months before the Stanley Cup playoffs. "Broda is away overweight at 197 pounds. He is off the team until he shows some common sense. He's been ordered to reduce to 190 pounds."

For three days, Broda's arduous trek to 190 was front-page news in Toronto and a major sports story across the country. He was photographed working out in a gym, and his weight was charted season by season from the time he joined the Leafs in 1936. (It showed a steady rise from 167 pounds.) Betty Broda, called "Mrs. B" by the press and described as "a compact five-foot, three-inch bundle who weighs 128 pounds," gave the papers calorie by calorie reports of every meal her husband ate.

On November 30, Broda weighed in at 189 and was back in the nets for two weekend games. On Saturday night, he blanked the Rangers at home. More importantly, he shut down Toronto's archrivals, the Red Wings, in Detroit on Sunday night. Smythe's ploy had worked. He had jolted his slumbering champions and reignited their drive for a fourth straight Cup. The Leafs were in fifth place at mid-season but finished the year in second place and met their old foes, the Red Wings, in the Stanley Cup semi-finals.

On paper, the Leafs were no match for the first-place Wings, a well-balanced team with exceptionally good goaltending in Harry Lumley, a mobile defence corps led by Red Kelly, and an offence powered by the NHL's three top scorers, Gordie Howe, Ted Lindsay and Sid Abel. But the Leafs had history on their side. They had won eleven straight playoff games against Detroit. They had eliminated the Wings in each of the previous three years, and they had beaten them in five of seven post-season series going back to 1942. In the Detroit camp, it was known as the Leaf jinx.

The semi-final became an emotional confrontation fuelled by Leaf pride, by Red Wing ambition, and by a past that made these two teams intense rivals. It began with a horrible injury to Gordie Howe, who suffered a broken nose, a fractured cheek-bone, and a severe concussion in game one. It was marred by donnybrooks and vicious stick-swinging in game two as the Wings sought vengeance for Howe's injury. It ended as a gallant last stand by the Leafs, who shut out their superior rival three times, pushed the series to a seventh game, and then lost 1–0 in overtime. And it brought jubilation to the victory-starved Red Wings and their fans. "Pandemonium was released the moment the red light flashed," a *Detroit Free Press* reporter wrote after game seven. "The 18 Detroit players, who regard victory over Toronto as one of the ultimate delights of existence, went hyster-ical. In the stands were 14,734 fans, many of whom had stood all night for tickets, laughing and shaking their fists."

While Detroit and Toronto were arguably the league's fiercest rivals through the forties, Detroit and Montreal shared the league's most intense rivalry in the early fifties. What created, sustained and drove these rivalries was success. From 1942 to 1955, the NHL was a two-tier organization, with three strong and three weak teams. The Stanley Cup rotated among the Leafs, Wings, and Canadiens. Not once during this era did the Bruins, Rangers, or Black Hawks put their hands or their names on hockey's premier prize. It was an era of haves and have nots.

The start of this era was heavily influenced by World War II. By the fall of 1942, about eighty NHL players had enlisted and, on September 28, 1942, league president Clarence Campbell issued a statement saying that the suspension of the season appeared inevitable because of the war. However, government authorities in both Canada and the United States encouraged the NHL to continue operating because all types of popular entertainment, including professional sport, were seen as good for public morale.

Every NHL team lost players to the war effort, but the Rangers and Bruins were the most adversely affected. At the end of the 1930s and start of the 1940s, they were the two most powerful teams in the league. The Rangers finished first in 1941-42, but lost five top players during the off-season and wound up last in 1942-43. The Bruins lost Frankie Brimsek, one of the league's best goalies, and the so-called Kraut line, comprised of Milt Schmidt, Woody Dumart, and Bobby Bauer, one of the NHL's best forward lines. By 1943-44, Boston had joined New York at the bottom of the league.

A number of top Maple Leaf players, including Turk Broda, Syl Apps, and Sweeny Schriner, also joined the armed forces. But, because the Leafs were deeper in talent than the Rangers or the Bruins, they continued to assemble competitive and even championship teams during the war years.

In this era of have and have not teams, the most unlikely of the haves was unquestionably the Leafs, the team that finished first only once between 1942 and 1955 but won six Cups. They did it with desire and dedication and hard work, because the Leaf rosters of those years were filled with good players rather than great ones, and stars rather than superstars. The outstanding Leafs of this era were Syl Apps and Ted Kennedy, Turk Broda, and Max Bentley. The superstars of the day were Rocket Richard and Gordie Howe, Toe Blake, and Terry Sawchuk.

The Wings of this era were one of the greatest teams in hockey history. They won four Cups in six years, they finished first seven years in a row, and they became the first team to earn 100 points or more in a season, a feat they accomplished twice. Then there were the Canadiens, who began this era by winning two Cups in three years and finishing first four consecutive seasons before faltering in 1947-48, when they missed the playoffs. By the early fifties, the rebuilt Canadiens were a dynasty in the making and the chief rival of the Red Wings.

This was also an era when triumphant players began hoisting the Stanley Cup aloft to trumpet their victories. Now an integral part of hockey's landscape, this annual ritual began quite inadvertently on the evening of April 23, 1950, after a horrendously hard-fought final between the Detroit Red Wings and New York Rangers. Pete Babando's overtime goal in the seventh game triggered an avalanche of applause and cheering in the jam-packed Detroit Olympia and a volcanic eruption of emotion from the Red Wing players.

Amid the uproar, league president Clarence Campbell presented the Stanley Cup to Red Wing captain Sid Abel. Then Terrible Ted Lindsay, scoring champion and renowned ruffian, grabbed the Cup top and bottom and heaved it toward the rafters. With that simple, spontaneous, and heartfelt gesture, Lindsay changed the imagery of hockey forever. He created a powerful new symbol of victory that would capture the imagination of the post-war, baby-boom generation.

When Lindsay spontaneously grabbed the Cup and held it aloft, there was a new kind of spectator in the crowd, thanks to a new medium, television, which brought hockey to the public. Then in its infancy, television was about to become both the eyes and the oracle of a new era, an era in which visual information would become more immediate and compelling than the written word. Here, courtesy of Ted Lindsay, was a concise and arresting image for the television age: a victorious athlete holding aloft a trophy, a victory march with jubilant teammates, and an arena full of delirious fans.

Budd Lynch, a broadcaster who called Red Wing games from 1949 to 1975, described the play-by-play of that seventh game for the *Detroit News*' Channel 4. Lynch said that Channel 4 had begun televising the last period and a half of Red Wing games during the 1949-50 season, a year before the CBC televised its first hockey game. Over forty years later he still remembers Lindsay lifting the Cup: "In the excitement he just picked up the Cup to get the crowd going. He moved right along the boards so the fans could see the Cup up close. I guess other people saw it because of television, and it caught on."

Television was the furthest thing from anybody's mind in the early 1940s when this era began. Hitler was still on the rampage in Europe. Radio was still the most advanced means of mass communication. And the Toronto Maple Leafs finally made it to the top by mounting the greatest comeback in Stanley Cup history to win their second Cup.

The favoured Leafs had finished second in 1941-42, fifteen points ahead of the Red Wings, whom they met in the final. But Wings coach Jack Adams had devised a simple and effective strategy for the series: dump the puck in, chase it hard, and forecheck with a vengeance. His players were also hungry. "We'd rather beat them than anyone else," Wings captain Syd Howe snarled before the series opened, "and we hate to lose to them more than anybody else because they gloat so much."

The fired-up Wings walked into Maple Leaf Gardens for the first two games, and skated off with two victories. According to one observer, the *Star*'s Andy Lytle, the Wings made it look easy. "A league underdog is now belting the magnificent Leaf machine around with the same ease and hilarity that kids employ in the blissful sport of kick the can," Lytle wrote. Playing before their own fans in the third game, the Wings thoroughly thrashed the Leafs to take a 3–0 lead.

Then the mind games began. Wally Stanowski, a defenceman on that Leaf team, half a century later remembered clearly how the Leaf comeback started: "We were down three nothing, and Colonel W. A. McBrien, one of the directors of Maple Leaf Gardens, made a speech in the dressing room after the game," Stanowski recalls. "He said they were going to announce to the press that it was impossible for us to win. No team had ever come back and won four straight. This was to play on the confidence of the Wings, and it worked."

In the next day's papers, one Detroit sportswriter declared that the Leafs were whipped. Another said they had conceded.

Then Jack Adams got into the act. Bob Davidson, a Leaf centre at the time, almost fifty years later still remembered Adams' remarks in a radio interview the night before the fourth game. "Five or six of us were in a room at the Leland Hotel playing cards," says Davidson. "It was a Friday night, and Wes McKnight used to come on at quarter to seven with his sportscast for Beehive Corn Syrup. He was interviewing Jack Adams, and according to Adams the series was in the bag. Well, that stirred us up."

On the day of the fourth game, Leaf coach Hap Day went to work on his players. Bob Goldham, later a commentator for "Hockey Night in Canada," was a rookie defenceman that year and remembered Day gently taunting the players. "What had a lot to do with getting us going was Hap Day saying 'They've got the champagne in the room and they're going to have a party tonight after they beat us four nothing,'" said Goldham in an interview before his death in 1991. Davidson recalled another move by the coach. "Hap Day got a letter from a young girl from Toronto who was eleven or twelve years old, and he read it to us. She said she was going to be ashamed to go to school the next day if we lost another game."

Meanwhile, Jack Adams turned to a ploy that had worked for him in the 1937 final. Fifteen minutes before the opening face-off he strode into the Wings' dressing room with the Stanley Cup in his arms and set it on a table in front of his awestruck players. "There it is," he said in a subdued voice. "On it are the names of all the fellows you've heard and read about all your life. That's what you've been working for since you learned to skate. Don't muff this chance."

Perhaps thanks to all the psychological wiles, the game itself was a playoff classic until the final minute or so. Detroit led 2–0 half way through the second period. Toronto tied it before the period was over. Detroit regained the lead early in the third. Two minutes later Toronto tied it again. With just over seven minutes to go, Nick Metz put Toronto ahead 4–3. But the game ended in an ugly display of violence.

With sixty-nine seconds left, referee Mel Harwood gave Detroit's Eddie Wares a misconduct and teammate Don Grosso a minor. The players protested, and a long argument occurred near the penalty box. Suddenly Adams exploded. He leapt from the players' bench, dashed across the ice, and attacked Harwood. The referee managed to free himself from Adams' grasp only to have his shirt nearly ripped from his back. Adams punched one of the linesmen in the face, while Grosso and Wares tore the other linesman's sweater to shreds. The fans erupted and showered the ice with debris, and a female fan reached out and slapped a linesman across the face. It took a police escort to get the three officials to their change room.

NHL president Frank Calder suspended Adams indefinitely but allowed Grosso and Wares to continue playing. By now, however, something was drastically wrong with the Detroit team. Two nights later, back in Toronto, the Leafs hammered the Wings 9–3. The Leafs then went back to Detroit and blanked the Wings 3–0 to tie the series 3–3. On the day of the seventh game, Maple Leaf Gardens was under siege all day from ticket-hungry fans. "I wasn't able to call my wife," said Frank Selke. "There were so many incoming calls I couldn't get a line out."

That night almost seventeen thousand fans packed the Gardens. Jack Adams was too nervous to watch the game. He paced back and forth in the Wings' dressing room listening to Foster Hewitt's broadcast. The teams played a scoreless first period before Syd Howe gave Detroit the lead less than two minutes into the second. The Wings then waged the battle of their lives to hold on to the lead. But a few minutes into the third, Sweeney Schriner tied it. Two minutes later, Toronto's Pete Langelle scored the winner. With less than four minutes to go, Schriner added an insurance goal.

"Shortly after 10:20 on Saturday night," Lytle wrote, "before the greatest throng that ever looked at a hockey game in the Dominion of Canada, Leaf coach Hap Day went flying over the ice. He caught Sweeney Schriner with one arm over his shoulder.

Hap brought his other fist affectionately to Sweeney's cheek and playfully punched it.

"'Hello champ,' he said to his left winger.

"'Champ yourself,' Schriner replied." Moments later the Leafs had the Stanley Cup in their hands, ending the greatest playoff comeback in the history of the game and erasing the grim memories of six straight Stanley Cup defeats.

After their humiliating collapse in 1942, the Wings extracted a modicum of revenge by ousting the Leafs in the semi-finals a year later. The NHL had become a six-team league in 1942-43 with the demise of the New York Americans, and the league adopted a playoff format that lasted until the expansion of 1967. The first-and second-place teams met the third- and fourth-place teams in the semi-final, and the winners advanced to the final. Detroit had lost fewer players to the war effort than any other NHL team and finished first that season, Boston came second, even though the Bruins had lost more players to the war than any of their rivals, and the two teams met in the final.

The Wings opened the series with an easy 6–2 win at the Olympia on the evening of Thursday, April 1. The Bruins put up a better fight in game two. They scored a couple of goals forty-eight seconds apart midway in the second and led 2–0. "The Bruins on the bench nearly batted down the boards with their sticks when the pair came," the Boston Globe's Tom Fitzgerald wrote. But the Wings, backed by a record crowd of 13,824, scored twice before the end of the period, and flattened the Bruins with two quick goals early in the third. The final score was a respectable 4–3, but amid the post-game gloom the Bruins' dejected coach Art Ross could only say: "We'll give them a run for their money in Boston."

It was an idle boast. Back home, the Bruins could do no better than chase the Wings. Detroit left winger Don Grosso led his team to a 4–0 victory in the third game by scoring three goals. After the game, Grosso told the press that his left wrist had been broken in two places and was encased in a cast during the semi-final against Toronto. He was slated for surgery in the off-season but the injury had been kept secret. Twenty-four hours later, Red Wing goalie Johnny Mowers blocked thirty Boston shots to lead Detroit to a 2–0 win. "One shot he stopped with his head in a tumultuous third period," writer John Walter noted in the *Detroit News.* "Blood poured from a gash under his eye. Mowers refused to delay the game to be sewed up. He tended goal the last five minutes with blood streaming down his face."

The victorious Red Wings skipped the traditional post-game presentation of the Cup. They were determined to catch the 11:00 p.m. train back to Detroit, and had only twenty minutes to make it. As the train pulled out of Boston's South Station, Jack Adams took a head count, then began opening a big box containing the Stanley Cup. "Here she comes, fellows," captain Sid Abel told his spellbound teammates.

The Cup was in two pieces, the bowl and the long, cylindrical base added in 1938. Adams lifted the bowl out first. He unwrapped it and held it up. "Here's the original bowl," he purred reverentially. For a moment his players were silent. Then they roared with delight. Someone poured a little water in the bowl, and the teetotalling Adams took a sip. After that, the Cup was filled with beer. Carl Liscombe, whose fourteen playoff points had equalled the record set by Bill Cowley in 1939, took the first drink, the first of many on that victorious overnight trip back to Detroit.

Adams tinkered with his line-up the following season, but the Wings were no match for the vastly improved Montreal Canadiens, who vaulted from mediocrity to excellence overnight. They accumulated a league record eighty-three points, twenty-five more than Detroit, and lost a mere five games. After thirteen seasons without a trip to the Stanley Cup finals, the Canadiens were back, and so were their fans.

Winnipeg native Glen Harmon was a defenceman on that Montreal team, and witnessed the remarkable rejuvenation of hockey's most hallowed franchise. "I joined the Canadiens in the latter part of 1942-43 after a couple of seasons with the Montreal Royals senior team," he said in 1991. "When I was playing senior at the Forum, we were getting bigger crowds than the Canadiens. The Canadiens were offering us tickets to go to their games on Saturday nights and we didn't have to pay for them. They just wanted to fill seats."

Montreal's turnaround coincided with the arrival of Maurice Richard, who was teamed up with Elmer Lach and Hector "Toe" Blake to form the famed Punch Line. Montreal *Gazette* sportswriter Dink Carroll observed that "Richard started the season slowly but by the time it was over he was the sensation of the hockey world." Blake paid Richard an even higher compliment: "I'm glad the Rocket is on a line with me. He'll make me good for another five years."

The other key addition to the team, according to Harmon, was the ambidextrous goaltender Bill Durnan, who joined the Canadiens from the senior Royals at the age of twenty-seven. "He wore two catching gloves," Harmon recalled. "He could catch the puck with either hand. If they were coming down the right side, he'd have the stick in his right hand and catch with the left. Then he'd switch hands." Durnan was also a defenceman's best friend. "We knew as long as we got back for the rebound, Bill would stop the first shot," said Harmon. "It was almost guaranteed."

The formidable new Canadiens met the Leafs in the 1944 semi-final and the Black Hawks in the final. Neither provided serious opposition. Toronto won the opening game of their series with Montreal. The Canadiens then reeled off eight straight victories, a playoff record, to claim their fifth Stanley Cup. The Punch Line racked up a record total of forty-eight points, Toe Blake earned an unprecedented eighteen points, and Rocket Richard scored twelve goals, another new record.

The Black Hawks tested the Canadiens only once, running up a three-goal lead in the fourth game. Montreal tied it in the third, and Blake scored in overtime to win it 5–4. "Blake's goal was the signal for the 12,880 spectators to let loose with a deafening roar that made the old building vibrate," Carroll wrote. But this would be a quiet celebration, compared with other Stanley Cup parties. With war raging in Europe, and food scarce at home, the Canadiens' management chose to lay on a low-key buffet luncheon, rather than a sit-down banquet.

A day after the luncheon, coach Dick Irvin boarded a train for Regina, where he spent the summer with his family. Most of the players had summer jobs with defence manufacturers. Elmer Lach and several teammates worked at an aircraft plant. Toe Blake worked in a shipyard. Rocket Richard and four others were employed in a munitions plant. For amusement, the Canadiens played softball together once a week, and contemplated their defence of the Cup.

At the end of the 1944-45 regular season, Montreal seemed destined to repeat their Stanley Cup victory. They had finished first with eighty points, Rocket Richard had scored fifty goals in fifty games, Elmer Lach had won the scoring championship, and Bill Durnan had the lowest goals-against average. But the third-place Maple Leafs knocked off the powerhouse Canadiens in the semi-final and went on to meet the Red Wings in one of the lowest scoring Stanley Cup finals on record.

The series went seven games, and each team scored a paltry nine goals. Toronto goaltender Frank McCool earned three shutouts, while Detroit's Harry Lumley blanked the Leafs twice. Both netminders were rookies. Lumley was a rosy cheeked eighteen-year-old kid from Owen Sound, Ontario, who had barely started shaving. McCool, nicknamed Ulcers, was a twenty-seven-year-old wartime replacement for Turk Broda, who was in the armed forces. Slender, high-strung, and a loner, McCool was racked by doubts all season about whether the fans regarded him as an adequate replacement for Broda.

Toronto won the first two games 1–0 and 2–0 in Detroit. Leaf coach Hap Day used a mere six forwards and two defencemen, and had them playing an extremely tight defensive game. Red

Wing coach Jack Adams was clearly disgusted with Toronto's cautious, stingy game. "Imagine me trying to explain to [team owner] Jim Norris how McCool shut us out twice," Adams said. "He's not that kind of goalie. The Leafs camped out in front of him all night while we beat our brains out trying to give the spectators a game for their money. The Leafs won't dare put on that kind of hockey in front of their own fans. They'd be hooted off the ice."

Adams was wrong on that count. Toronto played exactly the same game at home and won 1–0 on Gus Bodnar's third-period goal to take a 3–0 lead in the series. Then the Leafs briefly abandoned their defensive tactics, and the series almost slipped through their fingers. "Before the fourth game, Conn Smythe came into our dressing room with his son, Stafford, who had volunteered for the service and was going over to fight the Japanese," recalls Davidson. "He said 'I want you to put on a great show tonight.' Well, we put on a great show. We opened it up, but we lost the game."

The Leafs lost the fifth game 2–0 in Detroit, and lost the sixth game in overtime at Maple Leaf Gardens, despite Conn Smythe's attempts to rattle the youthful Lumley. "Smythe lurked behind Lumley's net in the late stages of the game and gave Harry the full benefit of his inimitable verbal blasts," *Globe* columnist Jim Coleman wrote. "Every time Lumley turned aside another Maple Leaf thrust he would turn and smile sweetly upon Smythe." The Leaf president's taunts proved harmless, and the Wings' Eddie Bruneteau snapped home a shot fourteen minutes into overtime to send the series back to Detroit for a seventh game.

A record crowd of 14,890 had barely taken their seats in the Olympia when Toronto's Mel Hill scored five minutes into the final game. The Leafs then withdrew into their defensive shell. They directed only one shot at Lumley in the second period, and held the Wings in check until the eight-minute mark of the third. When Detroit centre Murray Armstrong tied the score at one apiece, the Leafs were forced to open up. Four minutes later they got the deciding goal.

"Toronto's Babe Pratt launched a long pass from the Detroit blue line to Nick Metz at the left of the Detroit cage," Andy Lytle wrote. "As 18-year-old Lumley made a sprawling save on the corner, Pratt came racing in to jab the puck from under the Detroit goalie's pads and into the goal." Having played suffocating defence throughout the entire series, the Leafs had no problem closing the door on the Wings in the final eight minutes to win their third Stanley Cup.

The 1945 Leafs were more a playoff wunderkind than a genuine champion. The following season they missed the playoffs altogether. Montreal finished first for the third consecutive season while Boston wound up a close second largely thanks to the return of players from the armed services. The Bruins' best forward line from the 1941 Cup team, Milt Schmidt, Woody Dumart, and Bobby Bauer, was reunited for the 1945-46 season, and goaltender Frankie Brimsek was back in net. Boston demolished Detroit in the semi-final, and Montreal thrashed Chicago. So on March 30, 1946, the Canadiens and Bruins opened the final at the Forum.

The first two games were wide open, fast-skating, and low-scoring. Brimsek and Durnan each were brilliant in goal, and both games were decided in overtime. Montreal won the opener 4–3 after nine minutes of extra play. "Butch Bouchard fired a long shot from near the Boston blue line," Dink Carroll wrote in the *Gazette*, "and Maurice Richard, cruising near the goalmouth, snatched the rebound and jammed it under Brimsek. Delirious fans poured over the boards and hoisted him high in as spontaneous a victory salute as you'll ever see."

A couple of nights later, the teams battled to a 2–2 tie through regulation time. Montreal's rookie right winger Jimmy Peters finally scored after nearly seventeen minutes of overtime. "Kenny Mosdell carried the puck over the Bruins' blue line, was checked and the rubber rolled loose," Carroll wrote. "Peters scooped it up, spun around in a complete circle and fired a backhander that wound up behind Frankie Brimsek. For a moment, the big crowd was too stunned to realize what had happened. Then the Forum rocked with the triumphant roar of the Habitants' followers."

Hundreds of those same followers showed up in Boston hoping to see their team polish off the Bruins in four straight. "We've had a steady request for tickets, by phone, by wire, by letter, and by demands in person," Bruins manager Art Ross told the press. But most of the Montreal fans were unable to get into the sold-out third game to watch the Canadiens win again by a score of 4–2. Nor could they get tickets to see game four, another overtime thriller. This time the Bruins' Terry Reardon scored on a three-on-two rush to keep Boston's hopes alive.

The series resumed in Montreal, and there was a near riot before the fifth game. A crowd estimated at two thousand jammed the lobby of the Forum and refused to leave after tickets sales were cut off. Some people tore doors off their hinges, and others smashed windows in desperate attempts to get in. Those who had tickets came with bells, whistles, gongs, and in one case, an alarm clock. As the Canadiens left their dressing room that night, they walked by a chalkboard where someone had scrawled a blunt but forceful message: "This is it."

But the Bruins put up a gallant fight and went out with their dignity intact. "For 51 minutes and six seconds it was a terrific struggle," Carroll wrote. "Then Blake, hobbled by a spine injury and playing on nerve alone, pelted the puck past Brimsek to break a 3–3 deadlock." The Canadiens scored two more to win by a decisive margin of 6–3. As the final seconds ticked away, the huge Forum crowd stood and roared, and the thunderous ovation continued as league president Merv Dutton presented the Stanley Cup to Toe Blake.

Afterwards, dozens of well-wishers poured into the Canadiens' dressing room, and hundreds more fans attempted to push their way in. A French-language radio station set up a microphone, and the francophone players gave victory speeches that were carried live across the province of Quebec. A relieved Dick Irvin watched the celebration from the sidelines and quietly told Dink Carroll: "I lost eight pounds in the series." And someone had written a new message on the chalkboard. "This is it" had been rubbed out and replaced with "This was it."

The Canadiens skated to a fourth consecutive league title the following season, although they were chased hard by the Leafs, who finished six points back in second place. Both clubs advanced to the final in the spring of 1947, which was the first time the Canadiens and the Leafs had played off for the Stanley Cup. This was also the first all-Canadian final since the Leafs and Maroons had squared off twelve years earlier.

"We weren't supposed to win anything that year," recalled former Leaf Jim Thomson in an interview prior to his death in 1991. "There were seven rookies on the team. The defence pairings at the end of the year were Bill Barilko and Garth Boesch, Gus Mortson and myself. Four rookies. As a matter of fact, we got a sound whipping in each series that year. In the semi-finals, Detroit beat us in one game 9–1. In the first game of the final, Montreal beat us 6–0, and Bill Durnan was quoted in the papers afterward saying, 'How did these fellows ever get into the playoffs?'" With his flippant remark, Durnan inadvertently provided a spark that kept the Leafs fired up for the entire series.

Meanwhile, Montreal coach Dick Irvin tried to inspire his players with the battle cry "Let's win for Elmer." Irvin was referring to Elmer Lach, Montreal's star centre, who was home in Regina recovering from a fractured skull suffered in a late-season collision with the Leafs' Don Metz, whose brother Nick also played for Toronto. "Every player on the Canadiens would give every drop of blood in his body to win the Stanley Cup for Lach," Irvin told the press.

And Irvin's talk of shedding blood for a fallen comrade apparently put his players in a foul and vindictive mood. The Forum was hot and stuffy on the evening of game two, forcing the fans to remove their hats, shed their coats, and loosen their ties. Butch Bouchard, Montreal's big defenceman, took a penalty in the opening minute, and the Leafs popped two goals twenty-five seconds apart.

Just after six and a half minutes had elapsed in the second period, Toronto scored another power-play goal. Shortly after that, Dink Carroll wrote, "Rocket Richard blew his top." Richard clubbed Toronto's Vic Lynn, and the Leaf rookie "was carried from the ice unconscious with blood streaming from a cut over his left eye." With three minutes to play in the second period, Richard and Bill Ezinicki collided. The Rocket promptly walloped Ezinicki over the head and cut him for eight stitches. Richard was ejected from the game, which Montreal went on to lose 4–0.

League president Clarence Campbell fined Richard $250 and suspended him for the next game, which Montreal lost 4–2. Richard returned for the fourth game, but played poorly, and Montreal lost 2–1. Prior to game five, which was played at the Forum, the Canadiens honoured former greats Aurèl Joliat, Newsy Lalonde, and Jack Laviolette in a centre-ice ceremony. "The long history and great tradition of the club were dramatized for the present day colour bearers," Dink Carroll wrote. "In such circumstances, they had to win." A fired-up Richard scored at the start of the first period and added a second-period goal to lead Montreal to a 3–1 win. Afterward, the Rocket smiled for the photographers and held up a wad of bills that fans had collected to pay the fine he'd received along with his suspension.

The sixth game was played at Maple Leaf Gardens, and hundreds of fans waited in line overnight to buy tickets when the box office opened at 9:00 a.m. on the day of the game. That night, 14,546 fans watched a nerve-racking exhibition of hockey. Montreal opened the scoring twenty-five seconds into the game, but Toronto tied the score early in the second. Neither team could break the deadlock until, with less than six minutes to go in the game, Ted Kennedy, the Leafs' centre, fired a long shot that somehow eluded Durnan. That set up a tense and dramatic finale.

"Picture the last minute of play with every fan in the building standing and screaming for victory," Jim Vipond wrote in the *Globe and Mail.* "With forty seconds to go, Kenny Reardon breaks up a Toronto attack and rushes in on Broda only to be stopped at the last second as groans could be from fans expecting the red light to go on." The Habs pulled Durnan and threw a sixth attacker into the fray. They forced three face-offs in the Leaf end in the final thirty seconds but couldn't score. Finally, the siren sounded to end the game. "The noise was terrific," Vipond added, "as the players fell all over each other and the fans went wild."

But the Stanley Cup itself was nowhere near Maple Leaf Gardens. A superstitious Smythe had asked the league to leave it in Montreal rather than risk jinxing his club in game six. The Cup arrived the following day, and the players returned to the Gardens for photos and a quiet celebration. A rebuilt, rookie-laden team had beaten the mighty Canadiens. Jim Vipond called it "a modern hockey miracle," and his colleague Jim Coleman mused: "There's no telling how good this Maple Leaf team may prove to be."

The following winter, the youthful Leafs displayed both poise and prowess beyond their years. They finished first overall, five points ahead of the Red Wings. They were solid rather than flashy, reliable not erratic, and they were strong down the middle. Broda allowed fewer goals-against than any of his fellow goaltenders. The centremen, Syl Apps, Ted Kennedy, and Max Bentley, combined for seventy-four goals, giving the Leafs a more balanced attack than any opponent. Toronto was also a great checking team. "If we got a goal or two there was a chance we were going to win," says Gaye Stewart, who played in the 1947 Cup winner.

With their balance and composure, the Leafs completely overpowered the Red Wings in the 1948 final. They beat them 5–3 in the opening game and 4–2 in the second game. Detroit tried to intimidate Toronto in game two but failed utterly. "The Leafs met them half way and they smote each other with hips, fists, elbows, knees and high sticks," according to *Toronto Star* writer Red Burnett. There were also three fights, including a monumental mismatch between Howie Meeker and Gordie Howe. It was, according to Burnett, a mercifully brief scrap. "Howie swung once and buried his head in Howe's midriff," Burnett wrote. "Gord promptly hit him three on top of the noggin, raising a set of goose eggs."

Twenty-four hours later, the teams were on the ice at the Detroit Olympia. "It was a hard fought contest from start to finish," noted Jim Vipond, "with tempers simmering close to the boiling point for most of the 60 minutes." However, Turk Broda's superb goaltending made the difference, and Toronto won 2–0. Three nights later, the Leafs crushed the Wings 7–2 to sweep the series. While pandemonium prevailed in the Leafs' hot, stuffy, and crowded dressing room, a beaming Conn Smythe took off his coat and his hat, sat on a trunk, and addressed a horde of newsmen. "This is the greatest team I ever had," he said. "They never failed me and for the first time in my life I did not have to give a pep talk in the final series."

Smythe allowed his players to stay over in Detroit that night to celebrate their victory. But he had them on the train early the next morning. "The world champion Maple Leafs stepped off the Detroit train in mid-afternoon to be hailed by thousands of cheering citizens," the *Globe* reported. They rode up Bay Street in open cars, and a deluge of ticker-tape poured down on them from the office buildings along the way. A crowd estimated at ten thousand greeted the players at City Hall, and Mayor Hiram McCallum introduced them as "the Maple Leafs of Canada." With that, the first Stanley Cup parade in Toronto's history came to an end.

A year later, in 1949, the same two combatants squared off again in the Stanley Cup final. The Leafs staggered into the playoffs after finishing fourth, eighteen points behind the first-place Red Wings. But in the final, Toronto's balanced attack overpowered Detroit's one-dimensional offence. The Leafs had three strong centres in Ted Kennedy, Max Bentley, and Cal Gardner, and three good lines, whereas the Wings relied excessively their big line of Gordie Howe, Sid Abel, and Ted Lindsay.

The series opened in Detroit, and a large contingent of Leafs fans followed their team to the Olympia, including a Mr. and Mrs. Jack Watson, who had set out from their home in Stoney Creek, Ontario, by car. When it broke down near Brantford, they hired a taxi for twenty-five dollars to take them to an airport near London. The Watsons flew to Detroit and arrived on time to watch their Leafs score a 3–2 win on Joe Klukay's overtime goal. After the game, police and ushers formed a cordon outside the Leafs' dressing room. But one determined fan slipped through and strode around the room patting the players on the back and bellowing: "That's the big one, you champs. That's the big one."

Game two belonged to left winger Sid Smith, a "Toronto kid with a crew cut," as one writer described him. Smith scored three shorthanded goals in a 3–1 Toronto win, and the Leafs headed home with a 2–0 lead in the series. In the third game, thirty-four-year-old Turk Broda was the saviour. "For thirty minutes, the Leafs looked bad," Vipond wrote in the *Globe.* "The Wings were in command and peppering the rubber at Broda, who tossed it aside with amazing feats of goaltending legerdemain." The Leafs finally woke up and struck for three goals in five minutes and seventeen seconds to sink their adversaries.

By that point in the series, Detroit coach Tommy Ivan had pushed his big line of Howe, Abel, and Lindsay to the brink of exhaustion, and his other two lines weren't producing. Detroit's desperate braintrust borrowed an oxygen gas tank for the fourth game, and the team trainer gave the players bursts of pure oxygen throughout the match. "But even mechanical strength-reviving gadgets have their limits when the cause is hopeless," noted Vipond. The powerful Wings, who owned three of the game's greatest players, were undone that night by twenty-year-old Torontonian Ray Timgren, described as "the fair-haired kid from the east end of town." Timgren, a senior Marlboro for most of the winter, scored the Leafs' first goal and set up the third one in a 3–1 win.

At the end of the game, the military band that had played the anthems broke into an exuberant rendition of "Happy Days Are Here Again." The Leafs quickly retreated to their dressing room, where Conn Smythe could be heard above everyone. "You did it," he roared repeatedly. "You've done what no other NHL team has done. You've taken the Cup three years in a row!" According to Al Nichleson, a sports writer for the *Globe*: "There wasn't a happier fellow in the world than Smythe. His eyes were shining and his face was red as he pushed through the mob in the steamy, hot room to congratulate each of his boys."

The post-game uproar in the Leafs' dressing room continued for an hour. The team's accomplishments would stand for years. These Leafs were the first NHL team to win three straight Cups, the first to win six Cups, and the first to sweep seven-game finals in the minimum number of games two years in a row. "The Toronto Maple Leafs, the team the all-star selectors annually ignore, have ripped the NHL record book asunder," Vipond wrote in postscript to the season.

The Leafs were the NHL's first post-war powerhouse. The Red Wings were the second. After the Stanley Cup defeats of 1948 and 1949, the Wings broke Toronto's hold on the Cup in the seven-game semi-final of 1950. They went on to prove, in a seven-game final against the Rangers, that they were champions.

The Rangers came into the series as underdogs and orphans. They finished twenty-one points behind the Wings on the season. Come the playoffs, they were bounced from Madison Square Garden by the circus. The series opened in Detroit, but the second and third games were played in Toronto, which served as the Rangers' home ice. The Red Wings won two of the first three games and headed back to Detroit confident they could end the series in five. But the homeless Rangers proved surprisingly resilient. They won the next two games in overtime to take a 3–2 lead.

Faced with their third straight loss in a Stanley Cup final, the Wings finally asserted themselves. Lindsay and Abel came through with two goals each to lead Detroit to a 5–4 win in the sixth game. "By all standards, it was the fastest, most fiery and hardest played encounter of the final round," Paul Chandler wrote in the *Detroit News.* "It was witnessed by 12,045 fans who found it difficult to remain in their seats more than a minute at a time. To add to the general din, both clubs beat a tattoo on the boards with their sticks all night."

The finale was even more nerve-racking for both players and fans. The score was tied 3–3 through forty minutes of play, and remained knotted through the third period and the first period of overtime. The Olympia scoreboard showed that eight minutes and thirty seconds of the second overtime had been played when Detroit's George Gee and New York's Buddy O'Connor lined up for a face-off in the Ranger end. Gee asked his left winger, Pete Babando, to line up directly behind him, then drew the puck right to his teammate. Babando sprang forward instinctively and fired the winning goal before he had time to look at the Ranger net.

Just as quickly as Babando had unleashed his shot, the rest of the Wings vaulted over the boards to celebrate Detroit's first Stanley Cup in seven years. "In the view of 13,095 fans, weary, worn and aching Red Wings kissed and embraced, threw equipment to the ceiling and hoisted coach Tommy Ivan to their shoulders," Chandler wrote. Clarence Campbell presented the Cup to captain Sid Abel. The Wings' manager, Jack Adams, and its owner, Jim Norris, joined the centre-ice celebration, and the crowd began a thunderous chant of "We want Howe. We want Howe." Wearing a suit, a fedora, and a modest smile, Howe appeared on the ice for the first time since the opening game of the Toronto series. (In that game he had suffered a serious head injury, for which he had later undergone surgery.) Amid the post-game frenzy, while cameras were flashing and the fans were cheering, Ted Lindsay seized the Cup and heaved it above his head. He held it there and skated around the boards, followed all the way by a television camera. In so doing, he unknowingly created a potent and enduring image of victory.

The Wings set a new standard for regular season excellence in 1950-51 by earning 101 points over a seventy-game campaign. But in the opening round of the playoffs, they fell in six games to the Canadiens, who had finished the season in third place. Toronto coasted by Boston in the other semi-final to set up the NHL's second Stanley Cup showdown between the Leafs and Canadiens. It lasted a mere five games, but is remembered as one of the closest finals ever. Each game was decided in overtime.

The teams split the first two games in Toronto by identical scores of 3–2. Leaf centre Sid Smith led his club to victory in game one. "Smith, a Toronto-born player with a flair for the dramatic, opened the scoring after fifteen seconds of play and sent 13,939 perspiring fans heading for the exits 65 minutes and 13 seconds later," Jim Vipond wrote.

In game two Rocket Richard scored his third overtime goal of the 1951 playoffs. "It was a beautiful goal," wrote Dink Carroll of the *Gazette*. "Doug Harvey's long pass put the Rocket a half step ahead of Gus Mortson, the Leaf defenceman. He shifted into high gear, pulled away from Mortson, raced in on Turk Broda, faked him into a pretzel and flipped the puck into the empty net." After witnessing that goal, a dazzled Conn Smythe declared: "There's no comparison between the Rocket and Gordie Howe. Richard is the best in the game today."

Hundreds of Montreal fans lined up for almost twenty-four hours to purchase tickets for game three. When the "sold out" sign went up, a few desperate fans offered as much as seventy-five dollars for a pair of seats worth five dollars. Those who did get in witnessed another tight contest. Richard and Smith scored during regulation time, and Toronto captain Ted Kennedy netted the overtime goal that put the Leafs ahead in the series. Two nights later, the Leafs and Canadiens established a new NHL record by pushing a fourth straight game into overtime. Toronto's Harry Watson scored the winner early in the first extra period to send the Leafs home with a 3–1 series lead.

The Canadiens were far from finished, however. They led the fifth game 2–1 until the final minute of regulation time. But with a mere thirty-two seconds left, and Leaf goalie Al Rollins on the bench in favour of a sixth attacker, the Leafs' Tod Sloan tied the game. The capacity crowd at Maple Leaf Gardens showered the ice with debris, and the pandemonium continued right into the overtime period, which lasted two minutes and fifty-three seconds.

Defenceman Bill Barilko ended the game and the series with one of the most famous goals in Leaf history. Former Leaf centre Cal Gardner was on the ice and forty years later still clearly remembered the play. "I was only six or seven feet from the puck when it came out from behind the net, but I was watching Richard," he said. "Barilko came in from the blue line like an eagle. When he let it go he was practically in the air. He was right off his feet. He put the puck up in the air, and Montreal goalie Gerry McNeil went down. He didn't have a chance."

The hair-raising, heart-stopping finale dazzled everyone, including the sportswriters. "All the excitement, all the thrills, all the drama that can come out of hockey were crammed into the last three minutes and twenty-four seconds," wrote Dink Carroll. "During that stretch, there didn't seem to be a sane person among the 14,577 witnesses. A seasoned and cynical reporter, unable to make himself heard by his next door neighbour in the press box, scribbled on a piece of paper: 'If the man from Mars were to walk in here what would he think?'"

It would be eleven long years before the Maple Leafs or their fans would again experience such an evening of triumph and joy. But the culmination of that evening, the Barilko goal, has become one of the most memorable images in the history of

Stanley Cup play. The Leafs' photographer, Nate Turofsky, captured Barilko in full flight; froze an image of him on film as he flew headlong across the ice. Barilko left his feet just inside the blue line and landed on his hands and knees in the slot. It was the final, frantic lunge in a nerve-racking final, and Turofsky's photograph of it appeared in newspapers across the country the next day.

During the summer of 1951, Bill Barilko was in the news again. But this time it was a story of tragedy, not triumph. One day in August, he left Timmins for a fishing trip aboard a small private plane, which crashed in the northern Ontario bush. Barilko's disappearance triggered one of the largest air searches in Canadian history. Dozens of aerial surveys failed to turn up the downed aircraft. The remains were finally discovered, quite by accident, eleven years later in the summer of 1962, a few months after the Leafs won their first Stanley Cup since Bill Barilko fired his overtime winner.

The decline of the Leafs occurred just as the Detroit Red Wings, the third member of the triumvirate that ruled the NHL in those days, reached the peak of their power. In 1951-52, the Wings won their fourth consecutive league title and hit the 100-point plateau for the second straight year. Gordie Howe won the scoring championship and Terry Sawchuk posted the lowest goals-against average.

"We played fifteen or sixteen road games before we lost one that year," Bob Goldham, a Red Wing defenceman on that team, recalled shortly before his death. "That was the best team I ever played for. Boston was in Detroit one night and we beat them soundly. Afterward a newspaper reporter asked the Bruins' Johnny Crawford what kind of game Detroit had played, and he said: 'They played the same old game. They wouldn't give us the puck.' The Bruins wound up with eleven or twelve shots that night because we had the puck all the time."

The Wings dominated their opponents in the regular season, and smothered them in the post-season play. They swept the

Leafs and Canadiens in eight straight games to set an NHL record for playoff proficiency. In the mind of one loyal Detroit fan, Jerry Cusimano, a fish merchant, the Red Wings had strangled their foes like an octopus. To prove his point, he tossed one on to the ice at the Olympia during the final game of the 1951 playoffs. "It flew out of Section 10 about the middle of the game, a blue-gray hunk of a thing about 14 inches long," wrote *Detroit News* reporter Paul Chandler. "Over the years, galoshes, girdles, beef-steaks and buttons, and all brands of normal fish have appeared on the ice, but never an octopus."

The cornerstone of the Red Wing juggernaut that spring was Sawchuk, who earned four shutouts and was beaten just five times in eight games for an astonishing goals-against average of 0.62. Rocket Richard had several good scoring chances in the first game, chances that would almost certainly have resulted in goals against any other NHL netminder, according to Chandler. Afterward, all the twenty-two-year-old netminder could talk about was the Rocket. "I'll be dreaming about him tonight," Sawchuk said. "Every time I looked up, there he was blasting away." By the end of the third game, it was Richard who was talking about Sawchuk. "He is their club," a sullen Rocket told the press. "Another guy in the nets and we'd beat them. They're just lucky. It's been that way all year."

After losing the fourth game, most of the Canadiens lined up at centre-ice and congratulated the triumphant Wings. But Richard, Elmer Lach, and Dick Irvin headed straight for the Montreal dressing room. "Have your fun," Irvin snapped at a group of spectators who heckled him in the corridor. The Montreal coach also barred the Detroit press from the Canadiens' room. Over in the Red Wing room, Jack Adams stood bellowing before a crowd of sportswriters. "What do you think of this club?" he asked over and over again. "For balance, for depth, for anything you want to call it, this is the best Red Wing team I have ever had."

And yet with virtually the same lineup, the Red Wings failed to defend the Cup in the spring of 1953. They won their fifth consecutive league title, but lost in six games to the third-place Bruins. Meanwhile, Montreal advanced to the final by eliminating Chicago in seven games. Although the Canadiens were favoured over the Bruins in the final, their goaltending was a major question mark.

The Habs regular netminder, Gerry McNeil, had taken himself out of the Chicago series after five games because of what was described as "a nervous crack-up." In his place, Irvin had inserted Jacques Plante, an untested twenty-four-year-old rookie. Plante allowed just one goal in two games against Chicago. In the opener against Boston, he held the Bruins to a pair as Montreal won 4–2. After the game, a cocky Plante told the press: "They had twenty-seven breakaways on me in Buffalo this season before they scored on me. Gerry is a great goaltender but he's so small that he has to move twice as fast as me to cover the same area."

Two nights later the Bruins brought the puffed-up Plante back to earth. Boston winger Leo Labine scored early in the first period, and the Bruins cruised to an easy 4–1 win. Irvin decided to bring in Gerry McNeil for game three, and a relieved Plante said: "That playoff pressure, you can't imagine what it is until you've felt it." In the crucial third game, played in Boston, the previously jittery McNeil blanked the Bruins 3–0 to give Montreal the series lead. Even the taciturn and sometimes surly Irvin was swept away by McNeil's performance. "I was amazed when I found myself running out on the ice to grab Gerry when the game was over," he said later. "I haven't done that since 1931."

McNeil played the remainder of the series even though he had injured his right ankle stopping a Rocket Richard shot in practice. He had his ankle frozen before the fourth game, and needed another shot late in the third period when the pain became excruciating. In the fifth and final game, McNeil and Bruin goalie Jim Henry both played with injured ankles, yet they kept the game scoreless for sixty minutes. But one minute and twenty-two seconds into overtime, Richard fed a perfect centring pass to Elmer Lach, who fired the winning goal into the Bruins' net without even looking. "The 35-year-old centre raised his stick high in the air then did something between a cartwheel and a somersault to go rolling and sprawling along the ice," Carroll reported in the *Gazette*. "The organist burst into a triumphant paean and hundreds of uninhibited fans vaulted over the boards."

The era of the haves and the have-nots ended with the seven-game finals between Montreal and Detroit in 1954 and 1955. The Wings completed their string of seven consecutive first-place finishes in those two seasons and so had the home-ice advantage both years. In the 1954 final, Detroit ran up a lead of three games to one only to have the Canadiens come back to tie the series. About five hundred Montrealers travelled to Detroit for the deciding game, but once there, most were unable to buy tickets and instead watched it on television.

A crowd of 15,791, the Olympia's largest hockey audience up to that time, saw Floyd Curry give Montreal a 1–0 lead midway through the first. At the start of the second, Red Kelly tied the score and it was still tied when regulation time expired. The hero of the night was tiny Tony Leswick, the Wings' five-foot, six-inch forward. The goat was Doug Harvey, one of the best defencemen ever to play the game.

Leswick was just inside the Montreal blue line, about forty-five feet from the net, when teammate Glen Skov passed the puck out from the corner. Leswick took a wild whack at the puck and sent it fluttering toward the net. Harvey tried to knock the puck out of the air. Instead, it bounced off his hand, changed direction, and fooled Montreal goalie Gerry McNeil. "When the disc passed over the goalie's right shoulder and hit the netting high up, the crowd erupted into the noisiest moments in Olympia's hockey history," wrote Harry Staples in the *Detroit News*.

Hundreds of fans jumped on the ice and began hugging the Red Wing players. Clarence Campbell presented the Stanley Cup at centre-ice to Jack Adams, Tommy Ivan, Ted Lindsay, and Red Wing president Marguerite Norris, who had replaced her brother, Jim, and became the only woman ever to have her name engraved on the trophy. Campbell tried to make a presentation speech but was drowned out by the crowd. The players and team officials left the ice a few minutes later, but the more exuberant fans, and there were several thousand of them, refused to leave the building until ushers began turning off the lights.

Amid the mayhem in the dressing room, Tony Leswick picked up a telephone and called his parents in New Westminster, B.C. They had listened to the game on radio, along with over a dozen relatives and friends, as well as Leswick's children, eight-year-old Gary and six-year-old Barry. His younger son was first on the line, and as soon as he heard his father's voice, the boy shouted with glee: "Daddy, you got a goal!"

The Red Wings roared into the final a year later riding a thirteen-game winning streak, one short of the record set by the Bruins in 1929-30. They promptly set a new record for consecutive wins by defeating the Canadiens 4–2 and 7–1 in the first two games of the series at the Olympia.

Dick Irvin had dressed a bare-bones team of nine forwards and four defencemen, and a day before the series opened told the press: "We're the weakest team, certainly the weakest in manpower, that the Red Wings have ever faced." Several Montreal players were suffering from minor injuries. On top of that, the Canadiens had a huge hole in their line-up that spring. On the night the final opened, Rocket Richard was playing in an old-timers' game in Ottawa with former linemates Elmer Lach and Toe Blake. He had been suspended for the balance of the season after a stick attack on Bruin defenceman Hal Laycoe and a fist assault on linesman Cliff Thompson during a March 13 game in Boston.

The Red Wings and their supporters were confident they could whip the Canadiens four straight, but Montreal won the third game at the Forum, cheered on by Richard, who sat in the stands with his wife, Lucille. Shortly before the game ended, Richard left his seat and headed for the Montreal dressing room. He stood at the door in a grey topcoat and grey fedora and congratulated his teammates, in French and English, as they entered. The Canadiens tied the series with a 5–3 win at the Forum two nights later.

But this proved to be a homers' series. Detroit won the next game at the Olympia and Dick Irvin was more doleful than usual. "We've hit the bottom of the barrel," he told a Detroit sportswriter. "We're infirm. We've gone as far as we can go." But Irvin's supposedly depleted Canadiens won again at the Forum to send the series back to Detroit, where the Red Wings had not lost since the previous December.

Alex Delvecchio opened the scoring for Detroit at the beginning of the second period, and Gordie Howe scored the winner with eleven seconds left in the period. Defenceman Marcel Pronovost picked up the puck just inside the Montreal blue line and fired a pass across the ice to Howe, who burst in on the wing with checker Floyd Curry draped all over him. "I went for the puck with the blade of my stick," Howe said later. "The puck hit the handle eighteen inches in front of my hands and caromed into the net." Delvecchio scored again in the third and Detroit coasted to a 3–1 win.

The Red Wings stood at the pinnacle of the hockey world. They had captured their seventh Stanley Cup, which tied them with the Canadiens and Maple Leafs. They had also left personal stamps on the NHL record book. Howe scored an unprecedented twenty playoff points. Lindsay tied a playoff record with twelve assists. Howe, Lindsay and centreman Dutch Reibel combined for fifty-one points, a new record for a forward line.

The Red Wings, and several hundred jubilant supporters, celebrated their latest triumph with a champagne party at Detroit's Sheraton Cadillac Hotel. Team captain Lindsay stood on a chair and held the Cup for those who wanted to sip champagne from the famous bowl. Red Wing owners Bruce and Marguerite

Norris delivered brief speeches. But the final word went to Jack Adams, who had run the Detroit franchise without interruption since 1927. Adams spoke glowingly of the future and the young prospects he was grooming.

He had a defenceman named Larry Hillman, a left winger named Johnny Bucyk, and a centreman named Bronco Horvath, who were all ready to play in the NHL. He also had a centreman in Edmonton named Norm Ullman, who looked like the best of the bunch. "If all of them come through, we'll be all right for the next few years," Adams told his audience. "But you never know how kids are going to pan out in this game."

These were wise words indeed, for there was another group of young players who were just reaching their prime playing years. Their names were Béliveau and Geoffrion, Harvey and Moore, Olmstead and Plante. Their leader was Rocket Richard, the team veteran and one of the most inspiring performers who ever played the game. And for the next five seasons, come playoff time, they would prove to be unbeatable.

7

SELKE'S SOLUTIONS
1956-60

One chilly morning in mid-March, when hard, dirty snow caked the streets and sidewalks of Montreal, Maurice Richard sat at his kitchen table and discussed the days when he was the most exciting hockey player in the world, when he was known as hockey's greatest scoring machine, the game's greatest money player, and its greatest opportunist. It is something he has done countless times before, something that has consumed innumerable hours of his life in the thirty years since he retired from professional hockey.

Even at the age of seventy, five years a pensioner and eight times a grandfather, Richard is never far from the game he once played with unparalleled fire and ferocity. He referees as many as fifty-five games a year between NHL oldtimers and teams comprised of middle-aged men in communities across Canada. He occasionally attends a hockey banquet where he ranks as a head-table guest, and he makes the odd appearance at a sports card show. He is still in demand, still held in high regard by a generation of Canadians who never had the good fortune to see him perform in his prime.

On this March morning, Richard is just back from a road trip with the oldtimers. He wears a cardigan and slippers. He has traces of grey in his hair and an expansive waistline. His face has lost the hard, angular edge that made him look so menacing when he played. He could be just another senior citizen, and this could be just another suburban home, were it not for the mementos of the past.

A photograph of one of the great Canadiens teams of the 1950s hangs on the wall near the back door. The mantle above the fireplace is lined with trophies. The centrepiece is a twelve-inch-high metal replica of the Stanley Cup, a souvenir of the 1957-58 season, with the names of the players engraved on it. On the wall to the left of the fireplace is a portrait in oil of a proud young Richard in his Canadiens' sweater. To the right, is a full-length painting of the Rocket in his prime, skating at full speed.

Richard and his wife, Lucille, live in a grey stone home that they purchased in the mid-1950s, the same thirteen-room home in which they raised their seven children. It stands at the end of a street on the north shore of the island of Montreal, about ten miles from downtown and the Forum. Lucille Richard, who missed two home games during her husband's eighteen-year career with the Canadiens, both times because she was in the hospital giving birth, shuffles about their spacious kitchen preparing the noon meal. As the warmth of the stove and the aroma of tomato sauce fill the room, Richard sheds his initial chill and warms to his subject.

"Hockey today is faster than when I was playing because the players only take twenty to thirty-five second shifts," he says. "We used to take one-and-a-half- to two-minute shifts, and we only had seventeen players plus a goaltender. I played with bad injuries. I played with bad knees, bad hips, a bad back, all kinds of injuries. When there was no break, you played. I was never the best player in the league. Milt Schmidt, Béliveau, my brother Henri, they were all better skaters than me. But other players didn't have the desire I had every game. I didn't like to lose at anything. I worked hard all the time to produce."

Desire and hard work. Those are the words Richard has always used to explain the player he was. But they have an air of inadequacy about them. They have been overworked, used by too many ordinary players to explain what got them to the NHL and kept them there for a few years and for a bit of glory. Rocket Richard was no ordinary player. He was an explosive athlete, a tempest on ice, a man driven by some dark, demonic energy that his fans loved, his opponents feared, and neither understood. He was the molten core of the greatest team in NHL history, the Montreal Canadiens who won five straight Stanley Cups between 1956 and 1960, a feat never accomplished before that time and never duplicated since.

For those five seasons, the Canadiens were the unquestioned kings of hockey. It was an era framed by two emotional watersheds, the Richard riot and the Richard retirement. One night in March 1955, after being cut by a Boston Bruin defenceman's high stick, Richard attacked his opponent and a linesman with such ferocity that the league suspended him for the final three games of the season and the ensuing playoffs. His suspension triggered a riot in downtown Montreal. His absence deflated his teammates, and contributed to their defeat in the 1955 Stanley Cup final. And his retirement, in September 1960, at the age of thirty-eight, after eighteen seasons and 544 goals, stripped a powerful hockey team of the energy and intensity necessary to win.

The Canadiens launched their reign by crushing the opposition during the 1955-56 season. They compiled 100 points during the seventy-game regular schedule to finish twenty-four points ahead of the second-place Red Wings, and fifty ahead of the last-place Black Hawks. Goaltender Jacques Plante allowed an average of 1.86 goals per game through sixty-four games to win the Vezina Trophy. Doug Harvey won the James Norris Trophy as the league's best defencemen, and Jean Béliveau won the scoring championship.

Montreal's power-play, composed of Richard, Béliveau, Harvey, Bert Olmstead, and Bernie "Boom Boom" Geoffrion, so devastated and demoralized the opposition that the league was forced to change the rules pertaining to manpower advantages. At the time, a player who committed a foul served his entire penalty, regardless of whether the other team scored while holding a manpower advantage. But the Canadiens frequently scored two or three goals during a single power-play, and virtually won the game in two minutes. So the board of governors decided that if a team scored with the manpower advantage, the penalized player could return to the ice immediately.

"Rocket was the home-run hitter, whereas the others could fake and shoot," says Dickie Moore, a former Canadien right winger who twice won the scoring championship and occasionally took Olmstead's place on the power-play. "Doug always played to make a pass. Boom had the shot and could pass. The same with Béliveau. When everyone can shoot and pass, who does the other team check?"

Beside talent, the Canadiens of this era possessed a camaraderie that was rare at the time, and even rarer today. "There was no jealousy in the dressing room," Boom Boom Geoffrion says. "It was remarkable for me to see a team that was so close. It was like one big family. Even the wives stuck together. My wife used to hang around with Lucille Richard and Kenny Mosdell's wife, Butch Bouchard's wife, Dickie Moore's wife. When we travelled by train, we were together all day long. In our time, the captain would say let's go to this restaurant or that restaurant, and there were eighteen guys there. I never heard one word in the dressing room of the Montreal Canadiens from a guy who said, 'I don't feel good tonight. I don't feel like playing.' If the Canadiens had seen a guy like that, he wouldn't have stayed with the team. Star or no star, they would have replaced him."

In the 1956 playoffs, the Canadiens rolled over the Rangers and Red Wings by identical margins of four games to one. In succeeding seasons, they kept right on steamrolling the competition. During their five-year rule, these Canadiens ran up a postseason record of forty wins and nine losses. They never fell behind in a series, and they ended their streak in more convincing fashion than they started it. In the spring of 1960, they thrashed the Black Hawks and Leafs in eight games.

"They were an awesome group," said Bobby Hull, who broke in with the Hawks when the Canadiens were at their peak. "They just kept coming at you. Five after five right down to their so-called third and fourth lines. They'd come back in their own end and they wouldn't stop. They'd turn, and that Harvey would just thread that puck up to them. He was fantastic. Going into Montreal, if we could keep the score under double figures we considered ourselves lucky. We were chasing red shirts all night. They'd beat us soundly."

This was a team of remarkable depth, talent, and character, a team that was created, not by chance or circumstance, but by patience and careful design. If Rocket Richard was the heart and soul of that team, then Frank Selke was the brains and the builder. In his appearance, his mannerisms, and his personal habits, the late Frank Selke was the antithesis of the high-speed, freewheeling, overwhelming teams he created. Sportswriter Trent Frayne once described him as "a trim and gloomy man of perhaps five foot five, a funereal mien, a soft high voice, and a habit of rubbing his hands while he talked. Selke is the colourless architect of the flaming Habitants."

The incongruous Selke joined the Canadiens organization July 26, 1946, at the age of fifty-three after his stint as general manager of the Toronto Maple Leafs had come to a turbulent conclusion. Conn Smythe, the Leafs' principal shareholder, was just back from Europe and World War II, and the team Selke built was about to become the NHL's first post-war powerhouse by winning four Stanley Cups in five years. But with Smythe back, Selke was out.

The Canadiens that Selke inherited had just won a Stanley Cup, but the new general manager decided before his first training camp ended that the team needed an overhaul. "When the team hit the ice, I called for an executive meeting," Selke revealed years later. "I told [club president] Senator [Donat] Raymond that no other team could come up with six players as good as his top six – Bill Durnan, Ken Reardon, Butch Bouchard and the Punch Line of Elmer Lach, Toe Blake and Rocket Richard – but that there were no good reserves in sight."

Selke's solution was a farm system, similar to the one he'd built for the egotistical and ungrateful Conn Smythe, but far more extensive. He envisioned teams at every level of minor hockey, in every province, and he found a willing backer in Senator Raymond. "We owe the people of Montreal a good hockey team," the Senator told Selke that day in September 1946. "Go ahead and build an empire."

It was a *carte blanche*, a dream assignment for the short man with the wire-rimmed glasses and close-cropped hair. Although he was a certified electrician, and practised his trade for a time, Frank Selke had hockey in his blood, and some might say his genes. He developed a passion for organizing and managing as a youth in Berlin, Ontario, a town that was renamed Kitchener during World War I. His first team was the Berlin Union Jacks, a bunch of kids primarily of German and Polish descent. Selke's Union Jacks were Ontario champions in 1913-14, and from then on he just kept producing champions, for the University of Toronto, the junior and senior Toronto Marlboros, and the Toronto Maple Leafs.

Senator Raymond had handed Selke a mandate that was broad enough to satisfy his grand ambitions. The diminutive general manager eventually built a Montreal feeder system that embraced ten thousand players, from peewees to pros, competing for 750 teams across North America. He controlled more players and more talent than the five other NHL teams combined. Rival executives were astonished at what Selke had created. When he was told in 1956 that the cost of operating the Canadiens and their farm system exceeded $600,000 annually, Detroit Red Wing coach Jimmy Skinner admitted, "We just haven't got that kind of money."

So extensive was his empire that he eventually developed his own crass version of the Canadiens' famous motto, "To you with failing hands we pass the torch." To those who tried to find some weakness in the Canadiens of the 1956-60 era, Selke would respond: "They can say what they want. When our old men stop producing, we'll bring up young men who will start producing. Canadiens will be the team to beat for the next ten years."

But the best system in the world won't produce a Stanley Cup championship if a team allows its emotional harmony, or what the insiders call chemistry, to be disrupted. That became glaringly obvious to Selke and the other men who ran the Canadiens in the final days of the 1954-55 season. During a game in Boston on March 13, Richard twice attacked Bruin defenceman Hal Laycoe with his stick. He also struck linesman Cliff Thompson and blackened one of his eyes.

After a hearing in his Montreal office, league president Clarence Campbell suspended Richard for the remainder of the season and the playoffs. "No sports decision ever hit the Montreal public with such impact," Sidney Katz later wrote in *Maclean's*. "It seemed to strike at the very heart and soul of the city. It touched off the most destructive and frenzied riot in the history of Canadian sport."

Campbell suspended Richard on March 16, the day before the Canadiens were scheduled to play a crucial game against the Red Wings. The two old rivals were tied for first place with only a couple of games to go in the season. In the hours between the suspension and the big game, the signs of trouble grew ever more ominous and menacing. The sports departments of both English- and French-language newspapers were besieged with calls and letters from furious fans. A French-language radio station, CKAC, asked listeners for their opinions, but the switchboards became jammed so quickly that the station had to plead with the public to stop calling.

On the afternoon of the game, Campbell's secretary, Phyllis King, took dozens of phone calls from angry Montrealers. Some issued death threats and others growled ugly epithets. Groups of young men loitered outside the Forum, some carrying signs, others merely shouting anti-Campbell slogans. By 4:00 p.m., radio station CKVL had set up a mobile sound unit in a Shell service station across the road from the Forum. "We were almost certain that there was going to be trouble," said Marcel Beauregard, the station's feature editor at the time. "It was in the air."

The problems began midway through the first period when a police officer escorted Campbell, his secretary, her sister, and another young woman to their seats in the Forum. Detroit was leading 2–1 at the time. But the crowd immediately forgot about the game, and the Montreal players could barely concentrate on their jobs. The building soon reverberated with a deafening roar as the fans shouted over and over: "Shoo Campbell. Shoo Campbell."

Spectators in the seats above and behind Campbell unleashed a deluge of vegetables, eggs, tomatoes, and even bottles. Many of the projectiles hit fans sitting around the NHL president. Campbell's grey suit and dark green fedora were soon splattered with tomatoes, eggs, and oranges. One young man dashed down from an upper row and threw several punches at Campbell. While all this was happening, Rocket Richard was seated in another section, unnoticed by the crowd. "This is a disgrace," he muttered in disbelief to team physiotherapist Bill Head, who sat beside him.

By the end of the period, Detroit was leading 4–1. Campbell remained in his seat for the intermission. As debris continued to rain down, another young man charged up to Campbell and crushed two large tomatoes against his chest. Then there was an explosion twenty-five feet from Campbell. Putrid smoke filled the air. The crowd bolted for the exits *en masse,* and the vilified league president was temporarily forgotten. Someone had hurled a tear-gas bomb. "At the height of the exodus," Katz wrote, "with tears streaming from everybody's eyes, the organist high in the loft began playing My Heart Cries for You."

The frenzied crowd pouring from the Forum exits collided with a mob of six hundred surly young demonstrators who had been hanging around outside the building all evening. The collision of those two crowds was the spark that ignited the worst sports riot in Canadian history, an eruption of destructive fury that lasted six hours and caused $30,000 in damage. A dozen police officers and two dozen civilians were injured. "At one time, there were as many as ten thousand people – patrons, demonstrators and onlookers – packed outside the Forum," Katz wrote. "Many of them rushed around in bands shrieking like crazed animals. Groups of rioters were savagely chanting in unison: 'Kill Campbell! Kill Campbell!'

"The windows of passing streetcars were smashed. For no apparent reason, cab drivers were hauled from their vehicles and pummeled. The mob smashed hundreds of windows in the Forum by throwing bricks, chunks of ice and bottles full of beer. They pulled down signs and tore doors off their hinges. They toppled corner newsstands and telephone booths, doused them in oil and left them ablaze. Across the street, CKVL broadcasters were busy giving the Montreal public a blow by blow description of the riot.

"When the mob grew weary of the Forum, they moved eastward down Ste. Catherine Street, Montreal's main shopping district. For fifteen blocks, they left in their path a swath of destruction. It looked like the aftermath of a wartime blitz in London. Hardly a store in those fifteen blocks was spared. Display windows were smashed and looters carried away practically everything portable – jewellry, clothes, radios and cameras. By 3:00 a.m. the last rock had been hurled, the last window had been smashed and the last blood curdling shriek of 'Kill Campbell' had been uttered. The fury of the mob had spent itself."

The riot made headlines around the world. It left many Montrealers stunned and embarrassed. It also forced Selke to make a major personnel change at the end of the season. He concluded that his old friend Dick Irvin, who had coached the Canadiens for fifteen years, was contributing to Richard's eruptions of temper and outbursts of violence. He believed that Irvin kept the Rocket wound up too tight and occasionally channelled his ferocious energy in the wrong direction. Selke persuaded Irvin to pursue a coaching opportunity in Chicago, and replaced him with Hector Blake, known to the public as Toe and to his peers as the Old Lamplighter for his ability to score goals and light up the goal judge's lamp. While Blake was a stern man and staunch disciplinarian, he also had the respect of his players.

"Toe Blake understood the players better than Dick Irvin," says Maurice Richard. "If you had a bad game, Dick Irvin would criticize you in front of the other players. Nobody liked it. Toe Blake was different. He never said anything critical of you in front of the other players. We played much better under Toe Blake. Dick Irvin was too strict, too severe." Jean Béliveau, who succeeded Richard as captain, adds: "We all admired Toe. We found that even if he was very strict he was very honest, and he would stand behind us if somebody attacked one of the players. I was captain for ten years so I was very close to Toe. I saw him cry after winning and I saw him cry after losing."

The Canadiens of 1955-56 were essentially the same team that had finished second to Detroit the previous two seasons and lost to the Wings in a seven-game final each year. However, there were four rookies on the team that year, defencemen Bob Turner and Jean-Guy Talbot, and forwards Claude Provost and Henri Richard. Of the newcomers, nineteen-year-old Richard, nicknamed the Pocket Rocket after his famous brother, Maurice, was unquestionably the best. One day during the 1956 final, former Canadien Ray Getliffe tried to convince a group of sceptical sportswriters that the younger Richard deserved to win the rookie-of-the-year award. After a lengthy discourse about the youngster's virtues, Getliffe concluded by saying: "It's hard to believe the Pocket can be as good as this at nineteen."

Besides a few new players and a new coach, the Canadiens

approached the 1956 final with a completely new outlook. A year earlier, Dick Irvin had been gloomy and had publicly expressed his doubts about the team. In 1956, the Canadiens' long-time captain Butch Bouchard told the press: "I don't think I have ever seen a Montreal team go into the final in such good condition." And while the Canadiens were awaiting the outcome of the Detroit-Toronto semi-final, a sportswriter asked Blake which opponent he would rather face. "When this team is going right," he replied, "we are ready for anybody."

However, the Canadiens didn't appear to be prepared for the Red Wings in the first two periods of the opening game at the Forum. "The Wings started as though they meant to chase Montreal out of the rink," the *Gazette*'s Dink Carroll wrote. Detroit held a 4–2 lead after forty minutes, but the Canadiens unleashed a four-goal fusillade within five-and-a-half minutes in the third to take the lead, and each goal was followed by an avalanche of debris from the fans. "Overshoes, peanuts, coins and programs were showered down on the ice and the crowd's roar assaulted the ears," wrote Carroll. "One female fan threw her Easter bonnet, though her escort managed to recover it."

The CBC then caused a much larger uproar by announcing that it would only be televising games played on Saturday night, or games in which the Cup could be won. Angry hockey fans promptly lit up the switchboards at the headquarters of CBC television in Toronto. The network received over one thousand telephone calls in a single evening and quickly reversed its decision. Every game would be televised, the chastened corporation hastened to announce.

Unfortunately, the second game was hardly a spectacle to hold the attention of a national television audience. Montreal thrashed Detroit 5–1, and the Wings could barely get the puck out of their own end in the second period. "The Canadiens skated them into the ice for most of the 60 minutes," the *Gazette* told its readers. The Wings' lamentable performance brought a blast from the still volatile Jack Adams, who told the press:

"Some of our guys have lost their desire. I wonder if they have any pride left. They weren't tired. They just quit."

As unflattering as it may have been, Adams' diatribe lit a fire under his players. In game three at the Olympia, Red Kelly opened the scoring for Detroit late in the first and Béliveau tied it before the period was over. Howe and Lindsay then added third-period goals to give the Wings a 3–1 win. "That's the big one," Lindsay boasted after the game. "It will make those guys think a little." The Detroit victory proved to be a mere distraction for Montreal rather than a turning point in the series. Three nights later, the Canadiens blanked the Wings 3–0 and returned home a single win away from the Stanley Cup.

For the first thirty-five minutes of the fifth game, the teams played scoreless hockey. "Then the lightning of Montreal's famed powerplay struck with devastating effectiveness twice within 52 seconds and the Red Wings were dead," Carroll wrote. Jean Béliveau and Rocket Richard scored the goals. Boom Boom Geoffrion added another at the thirteen-second mark of the third period, and Alex Delvecchio scored Detroit's only goal twenty-two seconds later. The Canadiens then protected their lead and ran out the clock.

The moment the siren sounded to end the game, the crowd of 14,157 stood and roared with delight while the Canadiens swarmed goalie Jacques Plante. Plante and Geoffrion then hoisted Toe Blake to their shoulders and carried the rookie coach to centre-ice as the crowd sang "For He's a Jolly Good Fellow." Stanley Cup trustee Cooper Smeaton presented the venerable old mug to the Canadiens' long-time captain Butch Bouchard, who "made a tour of the rink with it so the happy spectators could get a good look at it."

The hockey season officially came to an end in Montreal four days later, a Saturday, with a gargantuan Stanley Cup parade organized by Mayor Jean Drapeau. This was the fourth parade in the history of the Cup, the first having occurred in Montreal in 1907, the second in Ottawa in 1923, and the third in Toronto in

1947. It was unquestionably the largest and the longest. The parade was composed of four bands, six floats, and thirty-five convertibles, each carrying a player or a team official. Cars with a player aboard sported a placard bearing his name and sweater number.

The entourage started moving at 9:00 a.m. and was supposed to cover the thirty-mile route in four hours. But the crowds were so huge that it took six-and-a-half hours to complete. An estimated 250,000 people, one-quarter of the city's population, lined the route. "The parade was stalled time and time again when thousands swarmed into the streets and choked them from curb to curb," the *Gazette* reported. Crazed fans ripped the buttons off Rocket Richard's jacket, someone stole defenceman Tom Johnson's topcoat, and the cars were stripped of their placards. The day, and the season, ended on a more peaceful note as the players, their wives, and 250 guests enjoyed a civic dinner that evening.

The Canadiens added only one new player, left winger Andre Pronovost, to their roster for the 1956-57 season. But the defending champions slipped to second place in the standings, behind Detroit, and their point production fell to 82 from 100 the previous year. The playoffs brought the Canadiens back to life, however, and they knocked the Rangers out of the semi-final in five games. Rocket Richard scored the overtime goal that finished off New York, and he beat Boston almost singlehandedly in the opening game of the final. "The famed Rocket, at 35 the oldest player in the NHL, kicked gaping holes in such hockey shibboleths as 'It's a young man's game,' " Dink Carroll wrote in the *Gazette*.

Boston's Fleming Mackell opened the scoring seven-and-a-half minutes into the second, but Richard tied it three minutes later when he whipped a sizzling backhander past the Bruins' rookie goaltender Don Simmons. Another three minutes elapsed before the Rocket took a pass from Doug Harvey in the Boston end, eluded Mackell, and snapped his second shot by

Simmons. Boom Boom Geoffrion interrupted Richard's rampage by scoring fifteen-and-a-half minutes into the second, but the Rocket added his third goal before the period was over. He was heard from once more that night. "The Rocket's fourth and final goal came at 18:17 of the third period when he took a rink wide pass from the Pocket Rocket and fired a twenty-footer that went in between Simmons' pads and the goal post," the *Gazette* told its readers.

Badly rattled by the barrage he had just faced, the twenty-five-year-old Simmons told the press after the game, "It's a strange sensation to see Richard coming in on you with his eyes popping like headlights." An hour after the game, Richard's performance was still the main topic of conversation in the Canadiens' dressing room and the Forum directors' lounge. Asked for his assessment, Frank Selke told a group of sportswriters: "You just can't compare him to ordinary mortals."

The next two games belonged to Jacques Plante. His sensational goaltending compensated for Montreal's lack of offence in the second match, and the Canadiens prevailed by a margin of 1–0. When the offence recovered in the third game, Plante again handcuffed the Bruins, and Montreal won 4–2. The *Boston Globe's* Harold Kaese was so impressed that he devoted his entire column the following day to the wonders of Plante.

"He is the world's greatest advertisement for wandering goaltenders," Kaese wrote. "He plays in front of the net, beside it, behind it. Some night he'll probably be found on top of it. He retrieves loose pucks in the corners. He has been bodychecked near the blue line. He has yet to face off, score a goal or go up ice to help keep the puck in the Boston zone. But he has won the Vezina Trophy two years in succession and the average goals he has allowed in 238 games, including 41 playoff games, is 1.95 per game. The Bruins will have to solve Plante and his meanderings if they are to win the Stanley Cup."

The fourth game was slated for a Sunday night at Boston Garden, and the Canadiens were full of confidence. Toe Blake, speaking with a cigar hanging out the side of his mouth, told a group of sportswriters: "The boys are playing their best hockey of the season. They're going to try to finish this thing off in a hurry. If, and it's still a big if, we win Sunday it's too bad the Montreal fans won't see the big finish."

Hoping to witness the kill, several hundred Montrealers, including Mayor Jean Drapeau, drove to Boston for the Sunday game. Most of them took rooms at the Manger Hotel, where the Canadiens were staying, and cars with Quebec plates were visible on the surrounding streets all weekend. The Montreal fans made plenty of noise at the game but went home empty handed. Mackell jammed his own rebound by Plante early in the first, and Simmons made that slender lead hold up for the rest of the night. Mackell added an insurance goal when the Canadiens pulled Plante in the final minute.

The series then reverted to Montreal, which created a stampede for tickets. Public relations director Camil DesRoches complained that someone phoned him at three in the morning pleading for tickets, and box office salesman Don Smith said: "My phone didn't stop ringing from ten o'clock in the morning." With their fans in a mood for victory, the Canadiens did not disappoint. Moore and Geoffrion, two of the team's offensive stars, scored that night. But the Montreal checkers and grinders, Andre Pronovost, Donnie Marshall, and Floyd "the Honest Blocker" Curry, each scored in a 5–1 rout.

The Canadiens had won their second straight Cup. Afterward, their dressing room was said to resemble Times Square on New Years Eve. It was jammed from wall to wall with sportswriters, photographers, and well-wishers. Coaches of the farm teams joined in the jubilation. Clarence Campbell and Jean Drapeau made the rounds congratulating the players. The smell of sweat and champagne filled the air. And before the players had undressed, a special edition of the Montreal *Gazette* arrived with a front-page story trumpeting the Canadiens' latest triumph.

The first-place Canadiens and the fourth-place Bruins met

again in the 1958 final, and there was no doubt who was favoured to win. "We've got a good club and we're ready," Boston coach Milt Schmidt said the day before the final opened, "although man for man I must admit the Canadiens have a stronger team." The Bruins were overly reliant on their one big line, Fleming Mackell, Jerry Toppazzinni, and Don McKenny, who performed on the power-play, killed penalties, and accounted for seventeen of Boston's twenty-eight goals in the semi-final against New York.

Despite an injury-filled season, the Canadiens dashed into the final with their usual balance, depth, and spirit. During a high-speed workout before game one, a Montreal forward fired a sizzling shot that hit goalie Jacques Plante square on the forehead. Plante escaped injury but the shot split his face mask in two. The team doctor pronounced Dickie Moore, that season's scoring champion, fit to continue even though he had a fractured left wrist and was wearing a cast. More importantly, Rocket Richard had recovered from a deep cut to his Achilles tendon that put him out from November 13 to February 20. Although his injured foot was still tender, Richard scored seven goals during a four-game semi-final against Detroit. "I never saw anybody so goal hungry," Montreal coach Toe Blake said after the series. "You'd think he was still going for the first goal of his career."

Montreal won the opener on goals by Geoffrion and Moore, but the best player on the ice was Doug Harvey. "He checked and blocked and threw himself in front of Boston shots and he did it without the benefit of more than token rest in each period," wrote Red Fisher of the Montreal *Star*. "He was clocked for 15 minutes and 34 seconds of action in the first period, 15 minutes and 44 seconds in the second, and altogether was on the ice for more than 44 minutes. It was a glorious hour for Harvey. But he's had them before."

Boston tied the series with a 5–2 win on the strength of a great individual performance by goaltender Don Simmons. "That was the best job of goaling I've ever seen," said the Bruins backup net-minder Harry Lumley, a thirteen-year veteran. "Simmons won it for us," added Schmidt. But Toe Blake was more inclined to believe that his players had given the game away. On the train to Boston for game three he was still fuming over the loss and told the Montreal sportswriters: "When a team scores on you in the first twenty seconds of a playoff game you know you're not on your toes." He was particularly incensed at defenceman Jean-Guy Talbot. Rather than preparing for the game, Talbot had been scurrying around until six o'clock trying to scrounge tickets for friends.

The Richard brothers put the Canadiens back in front in the series by handling all the Montreal scoring in the third game. Maurice scored first, Henri got the winner early in the third, and Maurice scored again at fifteen minutes into the third. "Dickie Moore started the play by feeding the puck to the Pocket Rocket, who made a drop pass to the Rocket and his low sizzler hit the post and caromed in," Dink Carroll wrote of the Rocket's second goal. But Boston bounced back to tie the series at two games apiece and Simmons played another outstanding game. After-ward a jubilant Milt Schmidt said: "These guys don't know the meaning of the word quit. I guess the Canadiens know they have to do more than just put on their uniforms."

The crucial fifth game, played before 14,415 shrieking fans at the Forum, was described by one Montreal writer as "a bitterly fought, high-speed, hard-shooting battle." Another called it "Stanley Cup hockey at its fiercest." The score was tied 2–2 at the end of regulation time. It had been an evening of sparkling per-formances. But Montreal's old warrior, Rocket Richard, had been out of step with the swirl around him.

"He had been a weary, exhausted figure most of the night," Red Fisher wrote. "Passes had eluded him and he missed others. But seventeen times in other years, he had scored overtime goals in Stanley Cup playoffs and now the clock had passed the five minute mark of the overtime period and his line was tumbling over the boards. Richard moved along the left wing, strange territory for him, and suddenly the puck was at his feet. He cut sharply, fired, and the puck was a blur over the leg of goalie Simmons. It was Richard's 80th playoff goal."

Three nights later at the Boston Garden, the Canadiens finished the job of winning their third consecutive Stanley Cup. They ran up a 4–1 lead through two periods. Boston scored a couple of goals to make it close. But Doug Harvey's empty-net goal with a minute left put the game beyond reach for Boston. The Canadiens had become the second NHL team, and the fourth team ever, to win three straight Cups. Clarence Campbell hoped to make an orderly presentation of the Cup at centre-ice, but that proved impossible. "The players leaped over the boards, hugging and backslapping and pounding each other," Fisher reported. "Coach Toe Blake was mobbed and jostled and pushed by the players and nearly 100 giddy, hysterical Montrealers who swept onto the Boston ice in a mass display of devotion."

The Canadiens took an overnight train back to Montreal and arrived at 10:30 the following morning. A crowd of two thousand waited outside Windsor Station and greeted the players with thunderous applause as they appeared. The fans saved their loudest and longest ovation for Rocket Richard, who had scored eleven goals and led all playoff scorers despite his age and the serious injury he had suffered the previous winter. And that same morning, in the pages of the *Boston Globe*, columnist Jerry Nason paid tribute to Richard by comparing him to the great money players in other sports.

"The greatest of these is Richard, possibly an athlete whose production of clutch epics has never known an equal in any sport. Babe Ruth had a built-in production plant in the clutch, 32 runs batted in in 41 World Series games, but you doubt that Ruth, or anybody, rivals M'Sieur Richard at this sort of thing. At the age of 36, and out 42 games this season with a nearly severed Achilles tendon, he beat the Bruins with a sudden-death goal in the key fifth game. There may have been equal competitors along the way, Marciano possibly, but I suspect they threw away the pattern after they cut out the suit for Maurice Richard."

The 1958 final turned out to be Rocket Richard's last great playoff performance. On January 18, 1959, Richard fractured his left ankle in a game at Chicago Stadium and sat out the rest of the season, as well as the semi-final against the Black Hawks. He returned for the final against the Maple Leafs but barely resembled the Rocket of old. Richard took no more than a couple of shifts per game, and watched the last installment of the final from the bench. The Canadiens also had to play the 1959 final without Jean Béliveau, who had led the league with forty-five goals during the regular season. He had suffered two cracked vertebrae in the Chicago series.

Montreal eliminated the Black Hawks in a tough six-game semi-final that nearly ended in a riot at Chicago Stadium. The final game was tied 4–4 when Canadiens forward Claude Provost scored near the end of the third period. The crowd of 18,521, the largest to witness an NHL game since February 1947, had become increasingly noisy and hostile throughout the game over what was perceived as unfair officiating. Provost's goal seemed to unleash the crowd's anger. Two fans jumped on the ice and tried to attack referee Red Storey. They were quickly hauled away by the linesmen. A couple more came over the boards, but Montreal's Doug Harvey intervened. "That did it," Red Fisher wrote. "Debris of all shapes and sizes was hurled to the ice, and for nearly twenty minutes, the players were compelled to stand around perspiring while caretakers attempted to clear the rubbish."

The teams managed to play the final minute and twenty-eight seconds, and the Canadiens took the train home to await the winner of the other semi-final. Three nights later in Boston, the Leafs beat the Bruins in the seventh game, and immediately boarded a chartered aircraft for Montreal. It was Toronto's first trip to the Stanley Cup final since 1951. Although the Leafs had been awful most of the winter, and had earned a playoff spot only on the final day of the season, coach Punch Imlach was full of confidence. "I couldn't care less if Richard's back," he said after the Boston game. "I hope they have Béliveau back, too. I hope they have all their big guns. But it won't be enough. We're going to beat them in six games."

The Canadiens ignored Imlach's boast and casually dismantled the Leafs in the opening game. "The Leafs had occasional spurts of frenzied energy," Rex MacLeod wrote in the *Globe and Mail*, "but throughout it all the Canadiens conducted themselves with a poised nonchalance that suggested they would not be party to any more Leaf miracles." With superstars Richard and Béliveau unable to contribute, Montreal's second-string players took over. Left-winger Marcel Bonin, who was wearing Rocket Richard's gloves that spring and was "impersonating a superstar," according to one writer, scored his eighth goal in seven playoff games, including the winner.

Montreal overpowered the Leafs 3–1 in game two and would likely have won by a heftier margin were it not for Toronto's thirty-four-year-old goaltender Johnny Bower, who had just completed his second NHL season. "Bower was a magnificent figure for the Leafs all night," said Fisher. "He cut down the Habs grimly and beautifully starting in the first period. He beat Bernie Geoffrion time and again. In the third period when Geoffrion raced in alone, he gave him an open corner to shoot at then took it away with an electrifying stop."

Toronto scratched out an overtime win in the third game and battled gamely in the fourth. The Leafs were leading 1–0 early in the third period when they ran out of miracles. Boom Boom Geoffrion set up a pair of Montreal goals. Then he scored what proved to be the winner. "With the Canadiens in the process of changing lines, Carl Brewer of the Leafs was caught up ice," Fisher reported. "Henri Richard raced goalward with the puck and gave it to Geoffrion, who rocketed the puck at Bower. The goalie stood transfixed as the puck flashed by him on the left side."

Geoffrion was the offensive star of the fifth game as well, scoring twice and assisting on another. The Canadiens led 5–1 after two periods and were coasting toward an easy win. But the Leafs came back to life after scoring a couple of third-period goals. Imlach pulled Bower with just over two minutes remaining, and the Leafs kept the Canadiens captive in their own end but couldn't score.

When the final buzzer sounded, the Canadiens had won their fourth straight Stanley Cup. They had secured for themselves a special place in the history of the game, and the mayhem in the dressing room reflected the magnitude of their accomplishment. "It was one of the wildest dressing room scenes in Canadiens' history," Fisher wrote. "Hordes of newsmen and photographers and newsreel men clamoured for photos. A television camera was moved into the room to record the festivities. Champagne appeared as if by magic and was poured liberally into the Stanley Cup. Everybody satisfied their thirst."

For most of the Canadiens, this was becoming a routine end to the season. But at least one player, centre Ralph Backstrom, was experiencing it for the first time. "I'm thrilled to be on a Stanley Cup team," he told a pack of newsmen. "For a guy like me, only twenty-one, to be on a winner like this, well it's something I'll never forget."

The seemingly unstoppable Canadiens cruised to another league title in 1959–60, finishing thirteen points ahead of the second-place Leafs and twenty-three ahead of the third-place Black Hawks, whom they eliminated in a four-game semi-final. Having advanced to the Stanley Cup final for the tenth straight season, the Canadiens had only overconfidence and complacency to fear. On the day of the opening game, Toe Blake summoned his players for a verbal bracing. Their objective, he told them, was simple: a fifth straight Cup and the bonus money that went with it.

The Leafs had ousted Detroit in six games to earn their second straight berth in the final and Punch Imlach arrived at the

Forum on game day with four-leaf clovers pinned to his suit, his shirt, and his new fedora. The good-luck charms may have put smiles on a few faces but they did little else. Montreal bolted to a 3–0 lead before the game was twelve minutes old, and according to Red Fisher, "appeared intent on running the Leafs out of the rink." From that point on, the Canadiens coasted to a 4–1 win in a game that became so dull the Forum fans grew restless and discontented.

From the fans' perspective, game two was just as lacklustre. All the scoring took place in the opening twenty minutes. Dickie Moore and Jean Béliveau had scored before the game was six minutes old, and the Canadiens allowed the Leafs a goal in the final minute of the first period. "For the rest of the night, both teams were involved in a series of bad passing plays and erratic shooting," Red Fisher observed.

The Canadiens played with more vigour and precision in the third game, and thrashed the Leafs by a score of 5–2 before a Gardens crowd of 13,307. The only noteworthy incident in the game occurred at just after the eleventh minute of the third period, when Rocket Richard scored Montreal's fifth goal of the night and his first of the 1960 playoffs. "The goal capped a brilliant evening of work by the peer of National Hockey League scorers," wrote Red Fisher. "Five times earlier in the evening, twice in the third period within seconds of each other, the Rocket had been foiled by Bower. But finally, he finished a play he had started at the Toronto blue line and which had degenerated into a scramble around the goal, by grabbing a loose puck and firing it into the upper left hand corner of the net. Then, as a burst of wild applause by the Toronto fans was settling down, the Rocket picked up the puck and returned it to his bench for safekeeping."

Silent and inconspicuous through seven playoff games, the Rocket was now suddenly the centre of attention. The next day's papers were full of speculation about his future. Why had he retrieved the puck? Was this the end of the line for the game's greatest scoring machine? Richard remained evasive. "I don't know why I picked it up," he said. "I haven't got the puck that was used when I scored my first playoff goal but I'd like to have the one that was used when I scored my last one. But this doesn't mean I'm going to retire because I don't know what I want to do. I've felt awful for the last three years. It's not that I'm sick but I've been hurt so often. I just can't keep up the pace anymore. Some of the younger fellows can skate all night. I can't."

The questions about the Rocket's future were quickly set aside. Another day brought another game, and another victory for the Canadiens. Jean Béliveau scored for Montreal shortly after the eight-minute mark of the first period and Doug Harvey scored eighteen seconds later. Montreal scored twice more that night, but the rest of the game was a mere formality. The Canadiens had won their fifth straight Cup, and they had done it by eliminating two opponents in the minimum eight straight games, equalling the proficiency record set by the 1951 Red Wings. Victory had come so quickly and so easily that most the Canadiens hardly felt like celebrating. "When you win 4–0, in four games and after four previous Cup titles, you don't get too excited," explained Doug Harvey.

At the height of their success, the Canadiens were simply too powerful for their opponents. Before the series had even ended, the colourless little man who had built the powerhouse Canadiens put the issue in perspective for a group of sportswriters. "The Leafs are better than they were last year but they are playing the greatest team in all the history of hockey," Frank Selke declared. "It's the greatest team because it has more great players than any one team ever possessed. Some players that we use only occasionally would be stars with other clubs in this league.

"Then there's team spirit, and there's the strength that comes from two or more racial units on the club, each with a different approach mentally, to the play. The player of English or German or Polish or some other descent has the inborn urge to drive right in, to smash his way along. But on the other hand, there's the Gallic spirit of our French Canadian players. They like to set up plays in almost dramatic fashion by passing the puck. They're the artists of the game."

The Canadiens' campaign for a sixth straight Stanley Cup began September 12, 1960, when training camp opened at the Montreal Forum. The team's owners, managers, and legions of faithful followers had every reason to be optimistic about the coming season. The core players, Béliveau, Harvey, Geoffrion, and Plante, were all back. The top-notch secondary players, Henri Richard, Claude Provost, Donnie Marshall, and Tom Johnson, were all ready, willing, and able. And having subdued the doubts of the previous spring, Rocket Richard was back in camp. He was thirty-eight and injury prone but still possessed a work ethic. "He was coming to practice like he was twenty-five years old," Geoffrion says. "He was there first. He was first to get on the ice and last to get off. Rocket was always Rocket, even at the end of his career when he was going to retire."

The end came five days after training camp opened, and those who were there still remember Rocket Richard's final performance. "The morning that he retired in fall of 1960, boy what a practice he had," says Béliveau. "Toe thought that practices should be like a game, so we had a lot of scrimmages. That morning, Rocket scored four or five goals." Added Moore: "We all asked him why he was retiring. Who was he kidding?" But in his mind and his heart, Richard knew that time had caught up to him. "I was fifteen or twenty pounds overweight," he now says. "My reflexes were too slow, and I was afraid of getting hit. So I decided to quit."

Richard announced his retirement at a press conference at the Queen Elizabeth Hotel. He sat at a table with Blake, Selke, club president Hartland de M. Molson, who had purchased the team in 1957, and director David Molson. He spoke, simply and eloquently, for a total of four minutes, first in French, then in English. There were about fifty newspaper, radio, and television

reporters present. When he was finished, they gave him a standing ovation.

The Rocket's absence had scarcely any impact on the Canadiens during the seventy-game regular season. Montreal finished first with ninety-two points, exactly as it had done the year
before. Montreal was again the NHL's top offensive team. Geoffrion became the second fifty-goal scorer in NHL history and
won the scoring championship. Moore and Béliveau were third
and fourth respectively in goals scored. But once the playoffs
began it was apparent that these were not the Canadiens of old.

Montreal met the third-place Black Hawks who had finished
seventeen points behind them. The teams split the first two
games, and then played fifty-two minutes of overtime before
resolving game three. According to former Hawk Bobby Hull,
the third game was the turning point in the series. "We were leading them 1–0 going into the last thirty seconds of the game," Hull
recalled in 1991, "and lost a face-off in our own end. Our centreman, who would never do it again, got excited and rushed to the
point, out to Harvey, instead of staying with Henri Richard. The
right winger went out with him and that left Henri Richard
loose. He just looped around our defence. Harvey shot the puck
and Glenn Hall made the save. The puck lay there and the Pocket
knocked it in. Our line, Murray Balfour, Billy Hay, and myself,
we got the goal earlier to make it 1–0. Then in the third overtime,
at one something in the morning, Murray scored again to beat
them. That was the game that won the whole deal for us, beating
the Canadiens in that long overtime."

Montreal managed to bounce back in the fourth game,
outshooting the Hawks sixty to twenty-one and outscoring
them 5–2 at the Chicago Stadium. In the fifth game back at the
Forum, the Canadiens were flat and lifeless in a 3–0 loss. "I have
no excuses and no alibis," Toe Blake told the press. "They
outskated and outchecked us. We just died out there." Frank
Selke thought he had the found the problem and the solution.
"You can't score goals with the puck on your sticks," he told the

players. "You have to shoot. If you won't do it for me now, you can expect trouble when it comes to signing contracts next season."

But Selke's solutions had no effect on the troops. The momentum had clearly swung to the Hawks. Several hundred fans showed up at the Chicago airport at three o'clock in the morning on Easter Sunday to greet the Hawks when they returned from game five. Three nights later, fans four deep circled the stadium hoping to get standing-room tickets for the sixth game. The crowd began littering the ice with paper airplanes half an hour before the game began and started cheering wildly from the moment Glenn Hall was introduced as "Mr. Goalie." "The jammed-packed Stadium of some twenty thousand fans roared themselves hoarse when the Hawks took the lead and gave them a standing ovation through the last minute of play," wrote Pat Curran of the Montreal *Gazette.*

The Hawks won 3–0, and shut out the league's top offensive team for the second straight game. They had eliminated Montreal four games to two, and ended their string of Stanley cup wins at five. The Hawks had advanced to the final for the first time in seventeen years, and the Habs had missed the final for the first time in eleven seasons.

Neither Toe Blake, nor his players, had much to say when it was all over. But the little man who had built hockey's greatest powerhouse had an idea of what had gone wrong. "In other years," said Frank Selke, "injuries and bad breaks were overcome by sheer determination on the part of the players and the spirit instilled in them by Maurice Richard. This season our boys just didn't have that kind of drive."

The Black Hawks, led by Bobby Hull, Stan Mikita, and Kenny Wharram on offence, Pierre Pilote, and Elmer Vasko on defence, and Glenn Hall in goal, met the Red Wings in the final that year. Chicago prevailed in six games to capture its first Stanley Cup since 1938. "We competely dominated Detroit," said Hull. "We beat them in Detroit. We were supposed to go home right after the game but there was a lousy snowstorm that plugged us in. We couldn't get out of Detroit till the next day. They had a really big deal for us at the Bismark, the Wirtz family's hotel in Chicago, when we got back. It was a big do. They pulled out all the stops. I was very young, twenty-two years old, and didn't really appreciate what we'd done. I thought that was just going to be one of many Stanley Cups we were going to win."

The 1961 Black Hawks were a talented and youthful group of players who improved as the decade went on. But they never did make it back to the summit. "The reason we didn't win it is we'd have a breakdown for just one game or maybe one period where we didn't do things right," recalled Hull. "Either one guy or two guys would break down. Or the wrong guys would get out on the ice at the wrong time. That's all it took to lose it in those years."

8

THE
LEAFS' LAST WALTZ
1961-70

In the unforgettable spring of 1967, Canada celebrated its
hundredth birthday and the Toronto Maple Leafs hoisted
their last Stanley Cup. Canadians were happy; the Leafs were
ecstatic. They'd beaten the slick and speedy Canadiens, the
defending champions, a team with talents as diverse as the graceful Jean Béliveau, the blazing Yvan Cournoyer, and the bruising
John Ferguson. In a sport where thirty is old, they had done it
with a stable full of old workhorses.

Johnny Bower was still stopping pucks at forty-two. Allan
Stanley was a rock solid defenceman at forty-one. Red Kelly
could be a spellbinding centreman at forty. They were the oldest
of a bunch of aging wonders. Four other players, including captain George Armstrong, were thirty-seven. The Leafs had a
couple of token youngsters in their lineup, rookies Brian
Conacher, twenty-five, and Mike Walton, twenty-one. In that
unforgettable spring, the Leafs were living for the present, while
the country was embracing the future. The Leafs looked old, the
country felt young.

If this were theatre, the play would have been called *In Praise
of Older Men* and the playwright would have been Punch Imlach.

But this was sport. This was Punch Imlach's last miracle, and his timing couldn't have been better. Punch's Leafs met Toe Blake's Habs in the last act of the old six-team National Hockey League. The Leafs were beating the Canadiens in Toronto on the very weekend that Montreal was welcoming the world to Expo 67. In the first three days after the gates opened, a million and a half people visited the fair, including Haile Selassie, emperor of the impoverished and underdeveloped African nation of Ethiopia.

Time magazine sent a writer and a photographer, and devoted sixteen pages of its May 5 issue to Canada and Expo 67. Canada had finally acquired a modicum of self-assurance, an unnamed essayist wrote in the magazine. It had also staged "the greatest international exposition ever, the most spacious (six thousand acres), the costliest ($1 billion), the most imaginative and likely the most visited (some ten million people are expected). Its very existence is a symbol of the vigor and enthusiasm of the Canadians who conceived an impossible dream and made it come true."

Montreal had a party that wowed the world. Toronto settled for a Stanley Cup parade. At four o'clock in the afternoon on May 5, a squadron of Toronto's white-helmeted, mounted police set out from Maple Leaf Gardens, followed by a military brass band and twenty white convertibles. George Armstrong and his father, Fred, rode in the lead car, along with the Leafs' president, Stafford Smythe, and executive vice-president, Harold Ballard. Imlach and his trusted assistant, King Clancy, rode in the second car. The players, each one with a blue and a white carnation pinned to the lapel of his suit, occupied the rest of the cars.

Thirty thousand people lined the parade route, down Church Street to Wellington Street, west to Bay Street and north to City Hall. The awaiting crowd was so large that 250 police officers had to clear a path to the podium in Nathan Phillips Square. Mayor William Dennison, and several other civic dignitaries, greeted the players as they arrived. Then the mayor addressed the crowd. "It was a great win for the Leafs," he said. "Never before have they deserved such a reception as they do today, in this, Canada's centennial year."

Armstrong stepped up to the microphone next, and declared: "All the experts said we could not win. They said Chicago had too much scoring and Montreal had too much skating. But they forgot the most important ability of all, the ability to work and dig in when it counted." Stafford Smythe spoke last. He announced that every Gardens employee would get an extra week of paid vacation as a victory gift. Then a blue and white Maple Leafs flag was raised over the square as fireworks exploded overhead.

As the crowd dispersed on that warm, sunny day in early May 1967, Punch Imlach's last miracle with the Toronto Maple Leafs had come to an end. Neither the elated players, nor their adoring fans could envision the years of misery and mediocrity that lay ahead. But the following season, the defending Stanley Cup champions missed the playoffs altogether. In 1968-69, they were eliminated in the first round, and Punch Imlach was fired.

Imlach's reign over the Maple Leafs was the most dramatic and, in the end, disheartening hockey saga of the 1960s. The Boston Bruins and New York Rangers, the poor cousins of the league for most of the decade, rarely even made the playoffs. The Chicago Black Hawks and Detroit Red Wings endured their share of grief. Both put together strong teams but could never do more than mount serious challenges for the Cup. The Canadiens, managed by the brilliant Sam Pollock and still reaping the benefits of Frank Selke's organizational genius, remained a consistent powerhouse that captured four Cups during the 1960s.

The Leafs, on the other hand, were undone at the height of their success in the mid-sixties by the twin demons of dissension and discontent between the players and the coach. They rode a rollercoaster from the bottom of the league to the top and back to the bottom again, all within ten years, all under one man's guidance, all with the same core group of players.

Hired as Leaf coach and general manager a third of the way into the 1958-59 season, George "Punch" Imlach was an unlikely saviour of a venerable franchise. At the age of forty, he was a novice in the NHL, a man with no major league experience either on the ice or behind the bench. However, he had been a successful coach in the Quebec Senior Hockey League and the American Hockey League. Imlach inherited a team that had finished third, fourth, fifth, and sixth, in that order, over the previous four seasons. Nevertheless, in each of his first two seasons he took the Leafs to the Stanley Cup finals, only to be shredded by the Canadiens' juggernaut. In his third season he guided the team to a second-place finish, and in his fourth the Leafs were champions.

Imlach resurrected the team by blending youth with age, by turning talented young players into bona fide big-leaguers, and by resuscitating veteran players who had flopped or worn out their welcome with other teams. He inherited a group of young players that included Frank Mahovlich, Tim Horton, Bob Baun, and Carl Brewer. Later the farm system produced Dave Keon, Bob Pulford, and Eddie Shack. And he turned discards like Johnny Bower, Allan Stanley, and Red Kelly into Hall of Famers.

Bower turned pro with the Cleveland Barons of the American Hockey League in 1945 and played all but one of the next thirteen seasons in the minors before joining the Leafs midway through the 1958-59 season. Kelly was one of Detroit's top defencemen for twelve seasons before Jack Adams traded him to Toronto in February 1960 following a contract dispute. Stanley was booed out of New York, dispatched to Chicago, sold to Boston, and finally traded to Toronto in October 1958.

Imlach motivated his players by needling them. He kept them fit by working them hard in practice. He kept them in line with stern discipline. His ways worked wonders on losers but caused discontent when applied incessantly to winners. "He wasn't there to win friends," says former Leaf winger Ron Ellis. "He was there to be successful and to win a Stanley Cup. Punch had a gift for being able to assess talent. He frequently saw something in players that other people didn't see. And he was a great bench coach. He very seldom got outcoached behind the bench. But I don't think Punch was a great practice coach. He'd skate us hard. We were well conditioned. We were a very basic, basic team. Nothing fancy. We didn't work on the power play. He would just send a line out. It's your turn, away you go. His basic rule was take care of your own end and the rest of the game will take care of itself."

The Imlach years were tumultuous, but many Canadian hockey fans remember them as the most illustrious in the Leafs' history. It was an era in which the Leafs won three Stanley Cups in a row, and four in six years, and in which their popularity soared to new heights from coast to coast thanks to the advent of televised hockey. One avid Leaf fan from that era, CBC radio host Peter Gzowski, declared in *Maclean's* in March 1964, "The Leafs are a national institution. They are co-stars of the most popular television program any Canadian has yet thought up, Hockey Night in Canada, on which they alternate with the Montreal Canadiens." The country's second-favourite show, Gzowski noted, was Bonanza.

The Leafs were popular luncheon-club speakers, and were sought after by corporate sponsors. "Sixteen Leafs, for instance, recently lined up for a certain razor blade ad," Gzowski added in the same issue of *Maclean's*, "and they got their $50 each without even having to shave with one blade." Punch Imlach had a weekly television show in Toronto, and even the trainer appeared in car ads for a local dealership. Torontonians who couldn't get enough of the Leafs through CBC's Wednesday and Saturday night tele- casts could buy a seat at one of six Famous Players movie theatres in the city that regularly carried the games on giant television screens. One member of the team, Red Kelly, even got elected to Parliament as a Liberal in 1963.

They were English Canada's team just as the Canadiens were the pride of French Canada. And in many ways, the Leafs reflected the very spirit of English Canada. They were earnest, industrious, and successful. They hit their opponents hard, they forechecked tenaciously, and they made the best of their scoring opportunities. But they had no explosive players like the Black Hawks' Hull, no natural leaders like the Canadiens' Béliveau. "We didn't have any superstars," says Allan Stanley. "Clancy used to keep track of the hits. We found that if we lost a game we usually had no more than twelve to seventeen hits, which wasn't even one per player. When we won, we always had forty or fifty hits." Or, as Gzowski observed, the Leafs of the 1960s were "more mechanics than artists."

Punch Imlach's Leafs conquered all comers for the first time in the spring of 1962. They advanced to the final for the third time in four years, and squared off against the defending champion Black Hawks. They won the opening game 4–1 largely thanks to their relentless and intensive forechecking. As Chicago captain Pierre Pilote said later: "The Leafs kept charging us in our own end, applying pressure and we were forced into making mistakes. The answer is to stampede them in their own zone. We were doing that in the first fifteen minutes and we were in control of the game. I remember saying to myself, 'What the hell. This is going to be easy.' Then we ran out of gas." The Hawks played a more spirited game two nights later but still lost 3–2.

The series then shifted to Chicago, and Bobby Hull, who that season became just the third player in league history to score fifty goals in a single campaign, boldly predicted that the Hawks would tie the final at home. "Normally, I try to ignore crowd reaction but in Chicago it's impossible," he told the press. "You can't help but get a lift from it."

Chicago Stadium was hot, smoky, and humid for game three. The crowd was announced at 16,666, the maximum permitted under the city's fire regulations, but the sportswriters guessed that there were closer to twenty thousand in attendance. "Greeted by a standing ovation from hockey's largest, noisiest and most rabid audience, the Hawks sailed into the Leafs from the opening face off," the *Star*'s Red Burnett wrote. "Bobby Hull set the style by smashing into the Leafs' Bobby Baun three times. They crashed with the impact of railway engines and both fell on the first two meetings. Hull spun Baun into the dasher the third time and the Hawks never looked back." Stan Mikita scored early in the second, and nine hats landed on the ice. Ab McDonald gave the Hawks a 2–0 lead four minutes later, and a couple of more hats sailed out of the stands. Fans threw dozens of rolls of toilet paper after both goals. In the final minute of play, Chicago scored an empty netter to make it 3–0.

The Hawks fulfilled Hull's prediction by winning the fourth game 4–1 to tie the series. But it was far from a pretty spectacle. Leaf goalie Johnny Bower pulled a muscle in his left thigh and was replaced by Don Simmons. Referee Frank Udvari issued seventeen minors and two ten-minute misconducts, as well as five-minute slashing majors and games misconducts to Frank Mahovlich and Stan Mikita. Red Burnett said it was the nastiest playoff game he had witnessed in over ten years. The fans responded to all four Chicago goals by littering the ice with debris and hurling smoke bombs. Afterward, a dejected Imlach declared: "It's tough to play against the Hawks, three officials, and twenty thousand fans."

The management of Maple Leaf Gardens decided it wanted no part of the mayhem in Chicago and issued an unequivocal warning to Toronto fans. "We welcome all the vocal support our fans can give," Harold Ballard said prior to game five. "But any-body caught throwing things on the ice will be asked to leave." Leaf fans ignored Ballard's warning and tried to outdo their Chicago counterparts. The Leafs scored eight goals that night, compared to the Hawks' four, and the crowd showered the ice with peanuts, paper, firecrackers, shoes, and fruit after every goal. *Star* columnist Milt Dunnell bemoaned the fact that Toronto rowdies had trashed the "brightest, cleanest and most orderly sports arena in the world," while his colleague Burnett added: "It was one of the noisiest and most unruly crowds to occupy the Gardens since it opened in 1931."

The sixth game proved to be a tight-checking, scoreless duel through the first forty-nine minutes of play. Then Bobby Hull, hockey's most fearsome sniper at the time, unloaded a shot that caromed off the left leg of Leaf goalie Don Simmons and into the net. Hull's goal, scored from twenty feet out, gave the Hawks a 1–0 lead. The Chicago crowd, described by one Toronto sports-writer as "a hostile mob" of twenty thousand, responded to Hull's howitzer by littering the ice with empty beer cans, eggs, bottles of ink, a waterbomb, and twenty-six hats.

The outburst delayed the game and allowed a rattled group of Maple Leafs to regroup. Less than two minutes after play resu-med, Toronto forward Bob Nevin tied the score, and less than five minutes after that Dick Duff took a pass from defenceman Tim Horton and rifled a shot past Hawk goalie Glenn Hall. Duff's goal silenced the rabid Chicago crowd, and his team-mates' checking smothered the Black Hawks' awesome offence until time expired and the stadium's famous airhorn signalled the end of the game, and the series.

Three decades later, Allan Stanley still remembers the initial ecstatic minutes after the Leafs' 1962 Cup victory. "My dad was the first guy on the ice," says Stanley. "He was down from Tim-mins for the playoffs. He talked his way past a couple of guards, and when we won he went flying across the ice. He ran right into me and almost knocked me down. You'd think he'd won the Stanley Cup. People thought it was Conn Smythe throwing his arms around me."

In the Leafs' dressing room afterward, team captain George Armstrong had his first drink in five years, champagne from the Stanley Cup, and jubilantly declared: "I've worked all my life to be one of the top pros in this game and that's what I am tonight." Centres Billy Harris and Bob Pulford took pictures of their team-mates drinking from the Cup, while fourteen-year veteran Bert Olmstead sat smoking a cigarette and talked of retirement.

Coach and general manager Punch Imlach, who was drained and exhausted after the long season, took a moment to explain to a pack of reporters why he had restricted their access to the Leafs' dressing room during the final series. Pulford, he revealed, had played the last five games of the final with one shoulder frozen to ease the pain of an injury, and right-winger Ron Stewart had played that evening with a set of badly battered ribs. Imlach told the scribes that he felt it necessary to conceal Pulford's injury from them, lest they tip off the Black Hawks.

The Leafs caught a charter flight back to Toronto after the game. They arrived at the city's international airport at 3:30 a.m. and received an uproarious reception from two thousand boisterous fans who packed the terminal. Some of the players spent an hour trying to get through the crowd, and some were carried to their cars by enthusiastic Leaf loyalists.

Two days later, under sunny skies, a crowd estimated at a hundred thousand chanted "Go Leafs go!" and showered their heroes with streamers, ticker-tape, and confetti as they rode in a motorcade down Bay Street to City Hall. The next day's *Toronto Star* called it "the greatest reception in Stanley Cup history," and Metro chairman William Allen declared: "Even the Queen never had a crowd like this." For Toronto's victory-starved hockey fans, it was a day of triumph and jubilation after eleven years of dashed hopes and bitter disappointments. The Leafs had not won the Stanley Cup since April 21, 1951, when Bill Barilko scored his famous overtime goal against the Canadiens.

The Leafs finished first in 1962-63 and they were completely in command when the playoffs rolled around. They held the Canadiens, the league's highest scoring team, to six goals in a five-game semi-final series. And Imlach could not see his team having any problem playing against the Red Wings in the final. "I don't think Detroit has three centres to match Keon, Kelly, and Pulford," he said the day before game one. "And show me where they have five defenceman as good as the five I can put out on the ice. If you want to go all the way back to the net, our guys Bower and Simmons won't suffer by any comparison with Sawchuk." The oddsmakers were also impressed with the Leafs. They made them 13–5 favourites.

The Leafs almost put the opening game out of reach early as

left-winger Dick Duff scored two goals in the first sixty-eight seconds. "Those goals came off perfect shots," Sawchuk explained later. "On the first one, he had me on the move because I had to worry about Armstrong cutting in from the right side and he put the puck between me and the post. The second was another wristshot, this one to the far corner. He had to thread the needle, and did, to find the hole just inside the post." Toronto prevailed by a margin of 4–2, but the game was much closer than it should have been because of the Leafs' second-period lapse.

Imlach ordered everyone to attend an eleven o'clock practice the following morning to atone for their shaky second period. Having performed their penance, the Leafs then played with grim efficiency in the second game and dispatched the Wings by the same 4–2 margin. Imlach again rewarded his troops with a vigorous workout, while Red Wing coach Sid Abel sequestered his players in a Toledo hotel to rest before the third game at the Detroit Olympia.

The Wings knew there was no future for a team that falls behind 3–0 in a Stanley Cup final and played accordingly in the third game. The improbable hero for the desperate Detroiters was rookie centre Alex Faulkner, a 165-pound native of Bishop's Falls, Newfoundland. The crew-cut blond scored two goals, including the winner in a 3–2 Detroit victory. It was his third winner of the playoffs and each one was scored in a Sunday night game. "I just hope we're back here next Sunday for the sixth game so I can try to make it four Sunday winners in a row," the reserved rookie said to the mob of newspaper, radio, and television reporters that surrounded him after the game. Fellow Newfoundlander and former Leaf Howie Meeker, who attended the game, was considerably more exuberant. "They'll be dancing in the streets tonight," Meeker said. "Alex is to Newfoundland hockey fans what Babe Ruth was to baseball fans."

The Leafs felt they had let the third game slip away through overconfidence and had no intention of prolonging the series. The fourth game was a tight contest until the final ten minutes when Dave Keon broke a 2–2 tie. Kelly added another late in the game to give Toronto a 4–2 win. On the way back to their dressing room, the Leafs had to cross the lobby of the Olympia. A group of hostile Detroit fans showered the players with paper cups, programs, and food containers. One fan struck defenceman Carl Brewer in the face, and others shouted obscenities at Imlach. "Go on home," the Leaf coach yelled back. "You've just watched your last hockey game of the season."

The Wings, who were forced to rely excessively on their big guns, Gordie Howe, Alex Delvecchio, and Norm Ullman, could do no better than keep the fifth game close. Keon scored a shorthanded goal late in the first period and Detroit's Marcel Pronovost tied the game early in the second. With less than seven minutes left in the game, Eddie Shack inadvertently scored the winner. "I was cruising near the net," he explained afterwards, "and the puck hit my stick on the handle and went in. I never even saw it. All I wanted to do was get out of the way of Kent Douglas's shot." Keon scored another shorthanded goal, which was all the insurance the Leafs needed to capture their second consecutive Cup, and their first on home ice since 1951.

Clarence Campbell presented the Cup to George Armstrong, but Eddie Shack carried it off the ice and into the dressing room. A few players stayed on the ice for post-game television interviews that were carried over the Gardens' public address system. Johnny Bower made a brief speech. Gordie Howe was warmly applauded when he said: "For a team that wasn't even supposed to be in the playoffs we showed up rather well." Allan Stanley's remarks were drowned out by thundering chants of "We want Keon." The crowd got Keon, and drowned out his words too.

As the last players left the ice, and silence settled over the building, there was pandemonium in the Leafs' dressing room. "Everyone from the mayor to Maple Leaf Gardens sweepers sipped champagne from the Stanley Cup," Jim Proudfoot wrote in the next day's *Toronto Star*. "Millionaires, clerks, entertainers, fathers, brothers, sons, politicians, hangers on and scores of newspaper reporters surged through wild shouting and glaring flashbulbs." The players carried Imlach, Ballard, and Smythe into showers fully clothed. But one unfortunate Leaf missed the party. Carl Brewer, who had taken ten stitches in his mouth early in the game, broke his left arm with five minutes remaining and spent the night in hospital.

The players had one more appearance to make before scattering for the summer. The city had planned a parade up Bay Street and a reception at City Hall the next day. School kids, who were out for Easter break, began lining the route at 9:00 a.m. and by noon forty thousand people stood eight deep in the heart of the normally staid financial district. Police chief James Mackey had 600 of his 2,200 officers out to control the crowds. "Bay Street exploded in ticker tape and roars of hero worship for the Stanley Cup champs," the *Star* reported. After a brief ceremony on the steps of City Hall, the season was officially over.

Having won two consecutive Cups, the Leafs now stood shoulder to shoulder with the Ottawa Senators of the 1920s, the Montreal Canadiens and Detroit Red Wings of the 1930s, and the Wings of the mid-1950s. But winning that third Cup proved an arduous effort. The troubles in the 1963-64 season began in training camp when defenceman Carl Brewer held out for more money and even enrolled at the University of Toronto before rejoining the team. Frank Mahovlich suffered through several slumps and failed to measure up to Imlach's expectations. Toronto fans booed the Leafs during a loss to the Canadiens in late November and again in late January in another loss to the Canadiens.

The team's problems were exemplified by a mid-season 11–0 pasting at the hands of the then lowly Boston Bruins. That night the Leafs had a junior player from the Toronto Marlboros in their lineup. In the dressing room afterwards, Imlach told the youngster that he wouldn't be making the trip to Chicago for a game against the Black Hawks the following evening. On the overnight train trip to the Windy City, Imlach revealed to a reporter how he had conveyed the news: "I told him I didn't want to humiliate him by making him play with a team like this."

Despite a difficult regular season, the Leafs finished third and advanced to the final against the Wings. Both semi-final series went the full seven games. As a result, the two finalists were emotionally flat when the series opened on April 11, 1964, at Maple Leaf Gardens. The Leafs won 4–3 on Bob Pulford's breakaway goal with twelve seconds left in the third period. Despite the close score, it was a dull game that left the fans shuffling in their seats.

The next morning, Sid Abel and his players boarded a bus and went sightseeing in the Niagara Peninsula. Abel loved horse-racing, so the excursion included a stop at the track in Fort Erie. Meanwhile, Imlach had his troops on the Gardens ice by 11:00 a.m. for a stiff workout. When he was asked about the wisdom of practising hard near the end of a long season, Imlach snapped: "Hockey is my business, our business. That's why we work at it every day."

However, Abel's relaxed approach paid dividends in game two. The Wings completely dominated the Leafs for the first forty-five minutes, and had a one-goal lead with forty-three seconds to go. But Jerry Ehman scored for Toronto to send the game into overtime. The Detroit players regained their composure during the break, and eight minutes into the extra session Norm Ullman snared a loose puck at his blue line. He raced down the right side and fed a pass to Gordie Howe deep in the Toronto end. Howe pitched the puck across the goalmouth where an unguarded Larry Jeffrey tapped it in.

Afterwards, a disgruntled Imlach told the media mob that his forwards had stood around most of the night. The following morning, he put his players through a hard practice then held a team lunch. In the afternoon, he brought the players back to study the films of the second game. Meanwhile, Abel and the Wings took the train to Toledo, Ohio, sixty-five miles from

Detroit, and checked into the Secor Hotel, which had been the team's playoff retreat for fourteen years.

Some of the players went to the race track. Others wondered aloud at the folly of Imlach. "Those old guys like Stanley, Kelly and Armstrong can't take it," said defenceman Bill Gadsby, who was thirty-seven himself and a seventeen-year veteran. "When we came out for overtime we had plenty left. Even I wasn't tired. But I looked at some of them and they were bushed. Imlach must be nuts."

The rested and relaxed Wings threatened to run the Leafs right out of the Olympia in the third game. They ran up a 3–0 first-period lead, but the Leafs battled back to tie the game with four minutes remaining. That set the stage for another dazzling finish, the third in three games. Gordie Howe, called "The Great One" by newspaper reporters, stole the puck from Frank Mahovlich in the Leaf end and fed Alex Delvecchio for the winner with seventeen seconds to go. "His pass came right along the line of the goal crease," said Delvecchio. "All I had to do was touch it and it was in."

The Leafs tied the series with a 4–2 win in the fourth game and headed for home immediately afterwards. When their overnight train arrived at Union Station, the Leafs' car was shunted to a siding and the players slept for another hour or so. Then they got up and boarded a bus for Maple Leaf Gardens and a 9:30 a.m. practice.

The players responded to Imlach's work-'em-hard approach by completely outplaying Detroit the following evening. Keon and Mahovlich both had breakaways in the first five minutes, and Bob Pulford had a couple of clear runs at Sawchuk. But the Detroit netminder stoned the Leafs, Gordie Howe ran his point-scoring streak to eleven games and the Wings won 2–1. Abel hugged team owner Bruce Norris on the way to the dressing room afterward and said: "For the first time in the series I really feel we can beat them."

The Wings were one win away from their first Stanley Cup victory in nine years. A crowd of 15,222, the largest of the season, jammed the Olympia for game six. The score was tied 3–3 with less than seven minutes to go in the third when the game took a wildly improbable turn. Alex Delvecchio ripped a hard, low shot that cracked Bob Baun on his right ankle. The Toronto defenceman fell to the ice and was removed on a stretcher. Four minutes later, just as the sportswriters received a press release saying that the Leaf player had fractured his ankle, Baun returned to the ice. The game went into overtime, and Baun fired an early shot from the point that bounced once, hit the shaft of Gadsby's stick, took a crazy hop, and wound up in the net behind Sawchuk.

In the dressing room afterwards, Baun was mobbed by incredulous sportswriters. "There was a face-off in our end and I took it with Howe," he explained. "I wheeled around and my leg just turned to cream cheese. I collapsed and the next thing I knew they were carting me off on a stretcher." As two doctors were delicately examining the injured ankle, Baun curtly demanded an injection of pain killer. He returned to the bench and jumped on the ice without even waiting for instructions from Imlach. "Nothing could have held Baun back," the coach said. "He had a charge in him that would have blown up the rink."

Prior to the seventh game at Maple Leaf Gardens, Baun received several injections of novocaine to freeze his leg right to the hip. Red Kelly, who couldn't sleep the previous night because of the pain from twisted ligaments in his left knee, required a shot, too. Carl Brewer, who had damaged ribs, and George Armstrong, who had a shoulder injury, also received injections. Still, the wounded Leafs and their healthy teammates thoroughly thrashed the Wings that night by a score of 4–0. For the third year in a row, the Leafs had carted off hockey's most valuable piece of silverware, which put them in the same select company as the 1947-48-49 Leafs.

Defenceman Allan Stanley carried the Cup to the dressing

room, and a riotous celebration erupted. Brewer sprayed his teammates with champagne. Leaf co-owners Stafford Smythe, John Bassett, and Harold Ballard were carted off to the showers. Friends, family, and hangers-on packed the room. Mayor Philip Givens came by to congratulate the players. So did Liberal Prime Minister Lester B. Pearson. As the prime minister made his way through the crowd shaking hands, the Liberal MP Red Kelly, who represented York West, barely acknowledged his leader. He was in too much pain. Ninety minutes after the game ended, an ambulance arrived. Kelly was wheeled out on a stretcher and spent the night in hospital.

Two days after the team's triumph, the city held its third consecutive parade and civic reception for the Leafs. The club itself had a rather odd policy when it came to rewarding the players. In 1962, each player had received a Stanley Cup ring made of a gold band with a white gold, raised maple leaf as the centrepiece. The following year, the returning players handed in their rings and management had diamonds installed in the centre of the maple leaf. In 1964, the players turned in their rings again and management had larger diamonds inserted. New rings were presented only to players who had joined the team in 1963 or 1964. Conn Smythe had done the same thing when the Leafs won three straight Cups starting in 1947. Each player got one ring. Each time he played on another Cup winner, a bigger diamond was installed.

As they pursued their fourth straight Stanley Cup during the 1964-65 season, the defending champions were dogged by turmoil and discord. The team's biggest offensive star, Frank Mahovlich, missed ten games because he was in hospital from mid-November until early December recovering from stress, depression, and exhaustion. The Leafs staggered to the mid-season mark having won only four of their past fifteen games. Imlach threatened a major shakeup, through trades or demotions to the minors, unless the players improved. The Leafs broke out of their skid, played better for a while in the new year, but still finished fourth. A rookie, Ron Ellis, tied Mahovlich for the team lead in goals. Both had twenty-three.

By the spring of 1965, as they faced the Canadiens in the Stanley Cup semi-final, the age of the Leaf players was becoming an issue. Pat Curran noted in the Montreal *Gazette* that the Toronto lineup included ten players over the age of thirty, six over the age of thirty-five, and one, Johnny Bower, who had celebrated his fortieth birthday. Imlach had a curt response to anyone who questioned the wisdom of sticking with aging athletes. "I don't care how old a player is," he barked. "I'm only interested in results and so far I've been getting them. I'm paid to win now, not in the future."

But that spring, Imlach's veterans were no match for Toe Blake's freewheeling Canadiens. The Montrealers dethroned the defending champions at Maple Leaf Gardens on the evening of April 13, 1965. After sixteen minutes of overtime play, defenceman Jean-Claude (J. C.) Tremblay dumped the puck into the Leaf end. Henri Richard won a battle in the corner and threw the puck to Red Berenson in front of the net. Berenson tipped it over to Claude Provost, who rifled it by Johnny Bower from twenty feet out. "Hail to the winners," Imlach snarled sarcastically afterwards, "and to hell with the losers."

While the Leafs licked their wounds, the Canadiens prepared to meet the Black Hawks. Their principal concern was Bobby Hull, who had scored eight goals in a seven-game semi-final against Detroit. Toe Blake gave Claude Provost the job of silencing the Golden Jet, as Hull was dubbed, and the dogged rightwinger held Hull to one shot on goal in the first game and four in the second. None of those shots eluded Montreal netminder Gump Worsley, a twelve-year veteran who was appearing in his first final. The Canadiens won both games, and then boarded a train for the nineteen-hour trip to Chicago. The Hawks caught a charter flight after the second game and arrived home by 1:30 a.m. Although his big gun had been shut down, Chicago coach

Billy Reay was confident that Hull would shake his shadow and score a few. "I don't believe there's a player in the league who can stay with Hull game after game after game," Reay said.

Provost covered Hull in game three and again the shadow prevailed over the sniper. Hull was held scoreless but his teammates were inspired by a roaring crowd of eighteen thousand and beat the Canadiens 3–1. Prior to the game, NHL public relations officer Ron Andrews was besieged by calls from Montreal, mainly from bookies, after a rumour circulated that Béliveau had broken his leg. The story was untrue but the bookies were unable to set the odds for the game until they had checked it out.

A couple of Chicago players did suffer painful injuries that threatened to keep them out of action, possibly for the series. Ken Wharram, right-winger on the Hawks' top line, twisted his left knee and captain Pierre Pilote suffered a badly bruised left shoulder. Team doctor Myron Tremaine came to the rescue with a newly developed drug called dimethyl sulphoxide, a red liquid applied externally to the injured part of the body. "It's pretty strange stuff," Pilote told a sportswriter. "For about twenty minutes after you put the stuff on, your skin burns. Then in a couple of hours it must get all through your system because you can taste it and your breath smells of it."

Strange it may have been, but the doctor's medicine worked, and both players were in the lineup for game four. The score was tied 1–1 after forty minutes of play when Chicago erupted for four goals in the third period. Bobby Hull provided the spark by scoring on a seventy-foot slapshot twenty-six seconds into the period. He added another later in the period as the Hawks skated to a 5–1 win.

The series then shifted to the Forum and the Canadiens waltzed to a 6–0 victory. The turning point, according to some observers, occurred early in the first period when Montreal's John Ferguson hammered Eric Nesterenko to the ice with a furious flurry of punches. Nesterenko, who stood six foot two and weighed almost two hundred pounds, was cut under the right eye for six stitches and virtually disappeared for the rest of the evening. As the Canadiens stormed into their dressing room after the game, a jubilant Ferguson bellowed: "Just one to go. Just one to go." And amid the post-game clamour, the Canadiens welcomed a distinguished visitor. Prime Minister Lester Pearson made the rounds and shook hands with all the players.

The Hawks battled back on home ice to tie the series and force a seventh game on May 1, 1965, which was the first time that the Stanley Cup playoffs had lasted beyond April. For both the players and the fans, it proved to be a memorable evening. "I wasn't supposed to play that final game," Gump Worsley recalls. "I was sitting in a coffee shop at the Forum a couple of hours before game time with my wife and Toe Blake's wife. Larry Aubut, who was our trainer at the time, comes into the restaurant and says, 'Hey Gumper, you better get in there. You're playing tonight.'"

Another key figure in that series, Bobby Hull, also remembers the prelude and the start of that game. "Chico Maki and Phil Esposito and I drove up to the Forum in a cab and we could taste the champagne," Hull remembers. "We said all Billy Reay has to do is start our line. They put their checking line out against us. We get through that first shift without getting scored on, and everybody gets through that first shift, then we're okay. Because we just had the momentum going. Well, Billy started another line and they got scored on. Fourteen seconds and it was in our net. They got three more and the period ended 4–0. That's the way the game ended."

For Hull and his teammates, it was a grim end to another season. "The Canadiens almost seemed compelled to win," he says. "A lot of it had to do with the pressure the fans and media put on them, the nostalgia that has been built up. There was a tradition that every Canadiens team had to live up to. Plus the fact they weren't paid as well as some of the other teams. For them to make as much money as the other guys in the league they had to win the Stanley Cup and get those extra bonuses. French Canadian kids would go in and say, 'I want so much money.' Management would say, 'You take this, or that's it.' They'd say, 'That's it,' and they'd go home and say, 'They're going to trade us.' Well the wives would say, 'No, no they can't trade us. We can't go anywhere else because we can't speak English.'"

For Worsley and the thirteen other members of that Canadiens team who had never been on a Cup winner, it was dream come true time. "I'll tell you one thing," Worsley says, "the last five minutes of that hockey game were the longest five minutes of my life. I'd been around for twelve years and was wondering if I was ever going to win." As the siren sounded to end the game, Worsley and defenceman J.C. Tremblay met in a flying, mid-air embrace at the blue line. Forum organist Leo Duplessis played "Auld Lang Syne" as the players shook hands. He played "*Prendre Un P'tit Coup*" when the Canadiens hoisted Toe Blake to their shoulders. When Jean Béliveau held the Cup aloft and skated around the rink, Duplessis played "Happy Days Are Here Again."

Two days later, the city held its first Stanley Cup parade since the thirty-mile, six-and-a-half-hour epic of 1956. This time, the route was only seven miles long and took only a couple of hours to complete. Fans standing three to ten deep lined the streets. Office workers in the St. James Street financial district showered the cars with confetti, ticker-tape, and paper. And Mayor Jean Drapeau summed up the city's expectations: "Not only do we want you to win next year, but in 1967 as well. When you win your third Cup in a row, we can give you an absolutely tremendous reception at the world's fair."

The Canadiens finished first in the 1965-66 regular season and then eliminated the Leafs four straight in the semi-final. But their momentum evaporated during a ten-day layoff, and they lost the opening game of the final at home against Detroit. They were rusty and no match for the brilliant goaltending of the Red Wings' Roger Crozier. But the Montreal players also claimed they were distracted by changes in the Forum lighting. NBC broadcast the game live, in colour, across the United States, and had installed lights that were four times as bright as those required for black and white telecasts. The Canadiens complained that the intense illumination caused glare in some parts of the rink, and shadows in others. They also maintained that the ice, which had been tinted blue to accommodate NBC, was soft, sticky, and slow.

The Red Wings stunned the Canadiens and their fans by winning the second game 5–2, and jumping into a commanding 2–0 lead in the series. Afterward, the ecstatic Wings celebrated in their dressing room as though they'd won the Cup. "It was sheer bedlam for better than ten minutes inside while newsmen and photographers cooled their heels outside," the Montreal *Star*'s Charlie Halpin wrote. When the doors finally opened, the Wings were still backslapping and embracing, and a few, like Bill Gadsby and Alex Delvecchio, puffed on victory cigars.

Over in the morgue-like Montreal dressing room, the Canadiens were still shaking their heads over the marvellous performance of Crozier, the five foot eight, 160-pound Red Wing netminder. With the score tied 1–1 in the opening minute of the third period, he had robbed both Gilles Tremblay and Jean Béliveau of what looked like sure goals. "I still do not believe it," Béliveau muttered. "I don't think I ever shot a puck harder. I put everything into it. It was streaking for the upper right-hand corner, but Crozier threw out his hand, made a perfect catch and tossed the puck away. How did he stop it?"

The Canadiens were desperate for a victory when they skated on to the ice at the Detroit Olympia two nights later. Another defeat would have put them too far behind to have any realistic hope of coming back. The Canadiens won the third game 4–2, and then tied the series with a 2–1 win in game four. After that game, Toe Blake explained the Canadiens' recovery to Elmer Ferguson, the Montreal sportswriter who had been covering professional hockey since 1917 when the NHL was formed. "It was Canadien pride, nothing else, that stirred the team to find itself and go headlong, top speed, to break Detroit," Blake said. "The

Rocket Richard pours champagne after one of Montreal's five straight Stanley Cup victories in the late 1950s. (*Montreal Gazette*/National Archives of Canada/PA-175907)

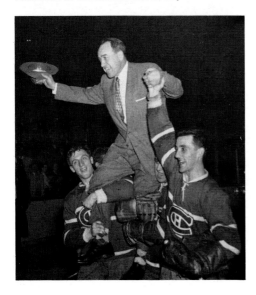

Dickie Moore (left) and goalie Jacques Plante (right) hoist coach Toe Blake after winning the 1956 Stanley Cup (*Montreal Gazette*/National Archives of Canada/PA-175909)

Forum fans surround Marcel Bonin (left) and Bernie Geoffrion (right) after another Canadiens' Cup victory in 1959. (*Montreal Gazette*/National Archives of Canada/PA-175908)

Marcel Bonin embraces the Cup and Toe Blake holds up four fingers after the Canadiens had made it four victories in a row in 1959. (*Montreal Gazette*/National Archives of Canada/PA-175910)

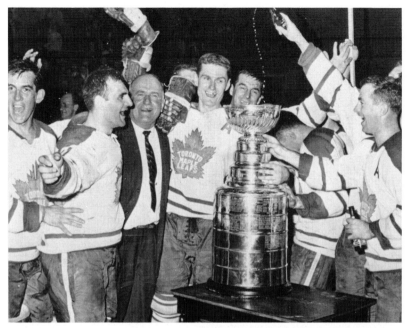

William Stanley, wearing the suit, hugs Bobby Baun (left) and his son Allan (right) on the ice at Chicago Stadium after the Leafs' 1962 Cup victory. (*Montreal Gazette*/National Archives of Canada/PA-175901)

Leaf captain George Armstrong, who is carrying the Cup here, tries to reach the stage at Toronto City Hall during a civic reception for the victorious Leafs in the 1960s. (*Montreal Gazette*/National Archives of Canada/PA-175902)

Montrealers celebrate one of the Canadiens' four Stanley Cup wins during the 1960s. The city's longest victory parade covered thirty miles and lasted six hours. (*Montreal Gazette*/National Archives of Canada/PA-175906)

A familiar sight for Montreal fans: Jean Béliveau hoisting the Stanley Cup. The Canadiens won five Cups while Béliveau was captain. (*Montreal Gazette*/National Archives of Canada/PA-175900)

The jubilant Bruins mob Bobby Orr after the defenceman scored a brilliant overtime goal to win the Cup in 1970. (UPI/Bettman)

Phil Esposito kisses the Cup as teammate Ken Hodge looks on after the 1972 final. (UPI/Bettman)

(Top Left)
Goalie Bernie Parent and team captain Bobby Clarke lead the Flyers' victory skate following the 1975 final. (UPI/Bettman)

(Top Right)
Philadelphia fans take over the Spectrum ice surface after the Flyers win the 1974 Cup. (UPI/Bettman)

The Canadiens and thousands of their fans celebrate one of Montreal's four consecutive Cup victories during the 1970s. (*Montreal Gazette/* National Archives of Canada/PA-175899)

An ecstatic Bob Nystrom leaps with joy after scoring the Cup winning goal in 1980. (Bruce Bennett Studios)

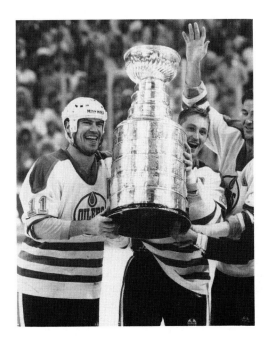

Mark Messier and Wayne Gretsky raise the Cup after the Oilers' 1988 win, their fourth in five years. (Bruce Bennett Studios)

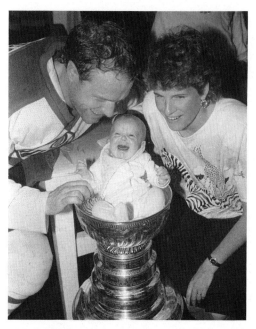

Oiler defenceman Randy Gregg and a new addition to his family try out the Cup for size in 1988. (Bruce Bennett Studios)

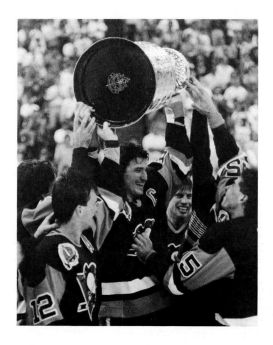

Mario Lemieux and his triumphant Penguin team-mates skate a victory lap following the 1991 final. (Brian Miller/Bruce Bennett Studios)

Canadiens are a great hockey team. They are a proud hockey team. Defeat does not rest lightly on Canadien shoulders. You could feel it as we journeyed to Detroit. There was no joking, no laughing on the trip, none in the motel where we're staying. This was a grim, even bitter team that felt it had been pushed around by an inferior team, and determined it wouldn't happen again. Our meeting before the third game was the shortest we've had this season. All I told them was, 'Boys, remember, you're the greatest team in hockey. You've proved it. Don't get pushed around.'"

The Canadiens demolished the Wings 5–1 in the fifth game at the Forum with an awesome display of speed and skating. "No question about it," said team president David Molson, "they were remarkable. Their skating was a beautiful thing." As for dejected Sid Abel, he had this to say: "We were humiliated. We couldn't have beaten a girls' team." Although the momentum in the series had clearly shifted, the Red Wings came back with a gallant effort in the sixth game at the Olympia.

The Wings fell behind 2–0 by the midway mark in that game but rallied to tie the score with just under ten minutes to go. Regulation time expired with the teams deadlocked. After two and a half minutes of overtime, Henri Richard scored one of the strangest winning goals in Stanley Cup history. "It was a fluke," the Montreal centre admitted after the game. "Dave Balon let go this shot from the left boards and I tried to deflect it. That's when I was tripped. The puck hit my leg and the next thing I knew I was in the net and so was the puck." While the Canadiens savoured another triumph, Detroit's Bill Gadsby announced that he had played his last game after twenty seasons in the NHL. His only regret: he never won a Stanley Cup.

The city of Montreal celebrated the Canadiens' latest Stanley Cup with another mammoth parade, this one eleven miles and three and a half hours long. It was held on a Sunday afternoon, and police estimated that half a million people attended. At a civic reception for the team and 300 invited guests that same evening, Mayor Jean Drapeau gave each player a passport to Expo 67, and made them promise they would win the Cup again the following season. Béliveau handled the mayor like a diplomat. "I do not want to put my foot in anything at this time," he said, "but next year, I think we can do it."

The Canadiens were shaky and inconsistent for most of the 1966-67 season. Still, they finished with a flourish, an eleven-game unbeaten streak that assured them of second place. But their chances of repeating as Stanley Cup champions appeared to be slim. The powerful Chicago Black Hawks, who had finished seventeen points ahead of the Canadiens, were heavily favoured. The Hawks had scored a league record 264 goals. Bobby Hull had surpassed the fifty-goal plateau for the second straight season, and Stan Mikita had romped to the scoring championship.

However, the Hawks' hopes were dashed in the semi-final by the longshot Leafs, who were coming off another turbulent season. "Punch really wore the players down," says Allan Stanley, one of the veterans on that team. "Of course, he was fighting some losing battles at the time. He was fighting the attempts to bring in a players' association. He was fighting long hair, beards, and moustaches. I think the whole league, the owners, the lawyers, everybody was resigned to these things, except Punch. He was the last guy to fight right to the last ditch. He got a lot of unnecessary flak because of it. He was the boss. Everybody knew that. But you don't have to prove every day that you're the boss."

The turmoil in the team affected the players' performance in the regular season, and finally Imlach's health. The Leafs lost ten straight games between mid-January and early February 1967. A week later, Imlach checked into a Toronto hospital suffering from stress and exhaustion, and stayed until March 18. While he was out of commission, the Leafs went ten games without a loss. In the final two weeks of the season, however, they reverted to their inconsistent ways, and most observers predicted that Chicago would eliminate them quickly.

The teams split the first two games at the Chicago Stadium,

then moved to Maple Leaf Gardens and won a game apiece there. The crucial fifth game was played on a Saturday afternoon in Chicago before nineteen thousand fans. CBS televised the game to a national audience in the United States, and Terry Sawchuk staged one of the greatest performances of his long career in goal. He replaced Bower at the start of the second period and stopped forty-nine shots in forty minutes. Nobody was more frustrated or flabbergasted afterward than Bobby Hull.

"I'd never had any trouble scoring against Sawchuk, ever, when he was with Detroit," Hull says. "We started the period on a power play and I drilled a shot that hit him in the shoulder, and he lay on the ice for about fifteen minutes. He got up and he was as loose as a goose. I had eleven shots on him and couldn't put a pea past him. I broke the handle of his stick twice. He was laying prone on the ice, and I fired one upstairs. He threw his leg up, and I stuck the puck right on the end of his skate. He just played fantastic. They beat us 4–2."

Sawchuk's performance that spring left a lasting impression on other players as well. "He was probably one of the worst practice goalies you ever saw in your life," says Ron Ellis. "He didn't like getting hit by the puck in practice. What made this stand out in my mind was the way he came out and challenged Hull time after time in that Chicago series. He knew he was going to get hit. When everything was on the line, he sacrificed his body. He was black and blue all over. I'll never forget it."

With the Black Hawks out of the way, the Leafs set their sights on the Canadiens and goaltending quickly became an issue. The day before the final opened, Imlach was sitting in the corner reds at Maple Leaf Gardens watching his players work out. He was surrounded by sportswriters who were trying to prod him into saying something controversial about Toe Blake. Instead, Imlach took aim at Montreal netminder Rogatien Vachon, a twenty-one-year-old rookie who had been playing junior B in Thetford Mines the previous spring. "You can tell that junior B goaltender he won't be playing against a bunch of peashooters when he plays against the Leafs," Imlach bellowed. "We'll take his head off with our first shot."

The Canadiens had eliminated Detroit four straight in the spring of 1967, Canada's centennial year, to set up an all-Canadian final. They promptly hammered the Leafs 6–3 in the opening match of the final. Sawchuk complained of fatigue and took himself out of the game midway through the third. And Blake had the satisfaction of sniping back at Imlach. "Vachon's got to be the only junior B goalie in history who has come up and won five straight games in the Stanley Cup playoffs," Blake told reporters.

The Leafs tied the series at one game apiece two nights later, and goaltending was again the decisive factor. Imlach started the forty-two-year-old Bower, who turned aside thirty-one Montreal shots in a 3–0 win. Despite his age, Bower was playing without a mask, and three times that night John Ferguson accidentally rapped him above the shoulders with his stick. The third one opened a bloody gash on Bower's nose. Leaf trainer Ron Haggart vaulted over the boards and scurried across the ice with a towel. Haggart asked Bower if he needed a few minutes on the bench to recuperate. "I'm hot," the ancient wonder hissed. "Hot. Leave me alone. Don't bother me."

Toronto took a 2–1 lead in the series with an overtime win at Maple Leaf Gardens, and Imlach was suddenly bursting at the seams with confidence. The next morning, he and Clancy were sitting in the coffee shop at the Gardens when Imlach spotted a Montreal sportswriter.

"How's your team?" the Leaf coach blurted out. "Ask them if they want to be humiliated any more."

"For crying out loud," Clancy gasped, "will you cut that out."

"There's no way we can lose to them," Imlach boasted before taking another shot at Vachon. "He's up to junior A now. He's graduated from junior B to junior A."

During the warm up for the fourth game, the red hot Bower pulled a muscle in his left thigh and had to turn over the starting assignment to Sawchuk. But after his brilliant performances in the semi-final, Sawchuk was suddenly ordinary. The Canadiens pumped six goals by him, including a couple of soft ones, and the teams were back on even terms.

The Montreal players were elated to learn that Sawchuk was starting game five at the Forum because they considered him a much softer target than Bower. "They thought a whirlwind start would unnerve him," Rex MacLeod commented in the *Globe and Mail.* "It distracted some of the Leafs and stupefied others but it made no impression on Sawchuk." The Leafs eventually took control of the game with oppressive checking that completely nullified Montreal's speed and slick passing. According to MacLeod, Marcel Pronovost's short-handed goal midway through the second "destroyed the Canadiens' last shred of resistance." The Leafs prevailed by a margin of 4–1, and went home perched on the brink of their first Stanley Cup since 1964.

After two periods of play in the sixth game, Ron Ellis and Jim Pappin had given Toronto a 2–0 lead. Montreal's Dick Duff cut the lead to 2–1 early in the third, and the Canadiens battled furiously for the equalizer right down to the final minute. Their last chance came when they forced a face-off in the Leaf end with fifty seconds left. Toe Blake pulled his goalie for an extra attacker and Punch Imlach decided to make a statement to the media who had criticized him, to the fans who had doubted him, and to the owners questioned him.

As Allan Stanley tells the story, Imlach walked the length of the bench and carefully selected the players he wanted on the ice. "He puts out Pulford, Armstrong, Kelly, and Horton," the former defenceman says. "Then he looks down and he says, 'Stanley. You take the face-off.' I look at him and he says, 'Yeah, yeah. You take the face-off.' So I give him another look because I haven't taken a face-off in four years. Defencemen always used to take the face-offs because the centremen were usually a little smaller. The ref would drop the puck, and you'd run the centreman right out of there. That was before they brought in the face-off interference rule.

"So I'm going out there, skating very slowly, saying, 'Jesus Christ what am I going to do here?' because I haven't taken a face off in four years and there's big Béliveau standing out there. By the time I got to the face-off circle, I figured I should put on a little show. Kelly was standing even with me, so I asked him to line up a little behind me and I said that's where I'm going to put the puck. Then I said to myself there's only one way I can do it and that's the way I always did it.

"I'm watching the referee and when he drops the puck I played Béliveau so he couldn't get his stick on it, and I ran the son of a bitch right out of there with my stick between his legs. The puck came back right to Kelly, just like I said it would. Kelly threw it up to Pulford, who threw it to Armstrong. Armstrong put the puck in the net, and Béliveau was chasing the referee around hollering, 'Face-off interference! Face-off interference!' I could hear him hollering all over the ice.

"That was the last game of the season and it showed what kind of a guy Punch Imlach was because he had been under a lot of pressure for years to get rid of his old guard. The press was after him. The owners were after him. But Punch comes out to the press and says, 'I don't care how old a guy is. If he produces, he plays for me.' To prove this, he sent out his old guard to take the last, most important face-off of the whole goddamned season. The one with the Stanley Cup riding on it."

Clarence Campbell presented the Cup at centre-ice to Leaf captain George Armstrong, who was accompanied by his twelve-year-old son, Brian. A few minutes later, the players, the press, a few politicians, and family and friends jammed the dressing room. Imlach and Stafford Smythe posed with champagne glasses, toasting Toronto's eleventh Stanley Cup. "The old-fellows athletic club played pretty well," Imlach hollered. "They're the best bunch of players I've ever had." Terry Sawchuk sat quietly, puffed on a cigarette, sipped on a Coke, and told a reporter he didn't care whether he ever played another game.

The Leafs' victory party began that night at the Gardens' Hot Stove Lounge and continued until five o'clock the next morning at Imlach's Scarborough home. Several hours later, the players were back at Maple Leaf Gardens for a team photo. Afterward, Imlach asked the photographer to take a shot of him surrounded by his veterans, Bower, Stanley, Pronovost, Armstrong, and Horton.

For both the old and the young members of that Leaf team, the 1967 Stanley Cup win was immensely gratifying. "There's nothing more exciting than your first Stanley Cup," says Allan Stanley. "But the most satisfying one for me was the last one because we were the underdogs. After every game we won the media said, well, the Leafs won another one, but they might as well have said it was all over. It was most satisfying, too, because it was the last year of the six-team league." Ron Ellis, who had just completed his third season with the team, adds: "It was the year of Expo in Montreal and they wanted the Stanley Cup bad. We had a lot of veterans who were going to retire in the next year or so. We weren't supposed to win. When you put all those ingredients together, it was a very nice win."

For the Canadiens, it was a depressing defeat, a loss that still lingers in memories of some of the players. "Of all the years that I lost, 1967 is the one that hurt the most," Jean Béliveau says a quarter of a century later. "We had just as good a team as the Leafs. But they had Terry Sawchuk, and I remember a save he made on me in the first period of a game in Toronto. I still try to figure out how he could have stopped that puck. I walked in on him and he made a hand save. I don't know where that hand came from. Nineteen sixty-seven hurt me, and I know it hurt my teammates, because we had a good team and we had no reason to lose."

But the Canadiens bounced back from their centennial-year loss to finish first overall in the new twelve-team NHL of 1967-68. They then breezed by the Boston Bruins, and Chicago Black Hawks before crushing the new St. Louis Blues in the final. The following season, Montreal finished first again and eliminated the Rangers, Bruins, and Blues with the same ruthless efficiency. The Canadiens completed the 1960s with four Cups in five years. Had it not been for the Leafs of 1967, they may well have won five in a row.

As for the Leafs, their long and ignominious descent into mediocrity had begun. Punch and his old fellows were mere spectators for the 1968 playoffs. They made the playoffs in 1969 but were cut to shreds by a dynamic young Bruin team that included the likes of Bobby Orr, Derek Sanderson, and Phil Esposito. The Bruins beat the Leafs twice in Boston, outscoring them 17–0, then beat them twice more in Toronto.

The final game was played on Easter Sunday. When it ended, Imlach kicked a coffee cup that lay on the floor behind the Leaf bench then went and stood in the hallway between the two dressing rooms. "Hell of a series," he told Sanderson as the Bruin player walked by. "Keep going," he told Esposito. Then a grim-looking Stafford Smythe appeared and summoned Imlach into his office. A *Globe and Mail* reporter followed the Leaf coach but was immediately asked to leave.

The meeting between the two men lasted five minutes. Smythe emerged to tell the press that Imlach had been fired. The new general manager was thirty-four-year-old Jim Gregory, and the new coach forty-year-old was John McLellan. "We need young men to do the job," Smythe said. "They've got to know where the young players are. We lost 4–0 to a bunch of young kids."

Punch Imlach walked around the Leaf dressing room and shook hands with his players, without revealing that he had been fired. He then went back to his office to collect his briefcase and overcoat. He and King Clancy left the Gardens with Imlach's wife, Dodo, and his daughter, Marlene. As the foursome approached the Imlach family car, a couple of police constables on foot patrol recognized the former Leaf coach and stopped.

"I sure hope they don't blame you for this," one officer said, who was already aware of the outcome of the series but unaware that Imlach had just been fired. "It's not your fault."

"Thanks a lot," the Leafs ex-coach said as he slid into his car. With that, the Imlach era was over, and the Leafs would win no more.

9

SKILL VERSUS SKULDUGGERY
1971-79

Forty minutes into the Montreal Canadiens' biggest game of the decade, the nominally objective observers in the Forum press box were reeling with anger and disbelief at the spectacle unfolding on the ice seventy-five feet below them. In this, the seventh and deciding game of the Stanley Cup semi-finals on May 10, 1979, the visiting Boston Bruins were on the brink of administering a final, fatal blow to a Montreal dynasty. The Bruins, a team considered inferior to the mighty Montrealers in every category save one, desire, were leading 3–1 with twenty minutes to play. "The Canadiens had been written off," Montreal *Gazette* columnist Tim Burke recalled later. "They were scorned in a seething press lounge." And he probably spoke for the entire crowd of over sixteen thousand when he added: "There wasn't a commentator in the lot who gave them a hope of ever coming back."

Before that game was over, however, the Montreal Canadiens had proved that miracles are possible in the world of sport, and that the spirit of past triumphs and the memory of former superstars can lift a nearly defeated, thoroughly flustered group of professional athletes to inconceivable heights. They had proved that there was substance to the mystique surrounding hockey's most hallowed franchise. After being checked mercilessly for two periods, after being roughed up, outmuscled, and outscored by one of the most tenacious opponents they had ever faced, the Canadiens roared back to tie the score in the third.

Boston took the lead again with four minutes remaining in regulation time. But the Canadiens got a reprieve. The Bruins were penalized for having too many men on the ice, a foolish mistake that has come to be regarded as one of the game's all-time great blunders. Guy Lafleur tied the score 4–4 on a power play with seventy-four seconds left. Finally, less than ten minutes into the first overtime period, a Montreal buzzsaw named Mario Tremblay fired a pass across the front of the Boston goal to a grinder named Yvon Lambert, and the big left-winger deflected the puck past the outstretched Gilles Gilbert in the Boston net.

"Everyone rushed onto the ice," recalls former Canadiens left-winger Bob Gainey. "We were all behind the net to the side and we were all laughing. That was all we could do. We looked at each other and we laughed and laughed. I don't know whether we were happy because we'd won or happy because we hadn't lost. I don't know. It was ecstasy, really."

The Canadiens had won more than just another game and another series. They had kept their Stanley Cup victory streak alive. This team had won three straight Cups, and eleven days later, after a rather routine five-game final against the New York Rangers, they made it four in a row. For a victory march, they hoisted the unexpected hero of that series, Bob Gainey, the defensive specialist, to their shoulders and carried him around the Forum ice.

By winning a fourth consecutive Cup, this particular collection of Canadiens, which included such superstars as Ken Dryden, Larry Robinson, and Serge Savard, Guy Lafleur, Steve Shutt, and Bob Gainey, had earned lasting glory. They could rest assured that they would always be remembered, that they would be regarded as one of the greatest hockey teams ever assembled.

In winning those four Cups, the Habs compiled a record of forty-eight wins and ten losses. In an era of ambitious and occasionally foolhardy expansion, they met and defeated the Blacks Hawks and the Flyers, the Islanders and the Rangers, the Blues and the Wings, the Leafs and the Bruins.

However, no opponent gave the Canadiens as much trouble as the Bruins, whom they met in the 1977 and 1978 finals and again in the exhilarating 1979 semi-final. The feverish finish to the seventh game of that series left the players, the fans, and even the press-box observers momentarily delirious. In a column written immediately after the game, the *Gazette*'s Tim Burke triumphantly declared: "The Canadiens dug deep from somewhere not apparent to the naked eye, from a reservoir that can only belong to a dynasty that stretches back so far. They came from behind three times against one of the noblest of opponents, and in the process restored to the game of hockey the greatness that has been so badly undermined in recent years. It was one of hockey's finest hours."

As the 1970s ended, so they had begun, with a monumental and unforgettable showdown between the Canadiens and the Bruins. In the spring of 1971, however, it was the Bruins who were the powerhouse, who owned hockey's biggest stars, the incomparable Bobby Orr, the unstoppable Phil Esposito, the irreverent Derek Sanderson. The Bruins were the defending Stanley Cup champions, a team that seemed destined to become a dynasty, to achieve greatness.

They had won the Stanley Cup in 1970, the first Bruin team to do so in twenty-nine years, and they had done it in convincing fashion. These Bruins had beaten New York in six games, Chicago in four, and St. Louis in four. In the 1970-71 season, they finished first overall in the fourteen-team NHL with 121 points, well ahead of their nearest rivals, the New York Rangers, who earned 109 points, and they scored 399 goals, 108 more than the Canadiens, who finished with the second highest total. This was a team that had scored more goals in a single season than any other team in NHL history, that had the highest scoring line in league history, that won more games and earned more points than any previous NHL team, and set more league records in one season, thirty-seven in all, than any team before them.

The Bruins won five of six regular season games against the Canadiens, and thrashed the Montrealers 7–2 on the final weekend of the season. Esposito scored a hattrick in that game, his seventh of the season, to finish with an incredible seventy-six goals and seventy-six assists in seventy-eight games played. Rick Smith, a 200-pound Boston defenceman, had almost run Bobby Sheehan, a 155-pound Montreal centre, through the end boards, while Bobby Orr administered a vicious slash to the Canadiens' J. C. Tremblay and laughed about it. According to one Montreal sportswriter: "The Canadiens were humiliated physically and mentally by the brilliant Bruins."

Four nights later, the Bruins and the Canadiens faced off again in the opening round of the Stanley Cup playoffs. Small wonder, then, that the oddsmakers declared the Bruins 4–1 favourites and Montreal *Gazette* hockey writer Pat Curran predicted that Boston would eliminate the Canadiens in five games, or less. For the first five periods of the series, events unfolded as almost everyone had assumed they would. The Bruins won the first game 3–1, and before game two was half over they had cruised to a seemingly insurmountable 5–1 lead, thanks to the playmaking wizardry of the twenty-three-year-old Orr. Nor did anything seem amiss when Montreal's crafty veteran Henri Richard stole the puck from Orr at the Boston blue line late in the second period, waltzed in, and deposited it behind Bruin goalie Eddie Johnston.

But in the final twenty minutes of that game, in the hot, steamy confines of the Boston Garden, before a rabidly partisan Bruin crowd, the Canadiens mounted one of the most astonishing comebacks in hockey history. The thirty-nine-year-old Jean

Béliveau, who told coach Al MacNeil before the game that he was tired and run down, launched Montreal's rally by scoring two goals early in the third to make the score 5–4. Centre Jacques Lemaire added another to tie the game. Then Béliveau won a skirmish against defencemen Dallas Smith behind the Bruin net. Even though he was pinned to the boards by Smith, Béliveau flipped a pass with one hand to linemate John Ferguson, who batted the puck past Johnston from his position at the corner of the Boston crease. And with time running out, Frank Mahovlich scored again to make it 7–5.

Afterwards, in the Canadiens' dressing room, a jubilant Béliveau described the winner: "I just saw a red sweater out of the corner of my eye and gave the puck to him. It could have been Yvan [Cournoyer] or Fergy." Amid the merriment, general manager Sam Pollock, his voice hoarse from cheering, repeated again and again as if in disbelief: "Class, class, class." As for the Bruins and their fans, Boston sportswriter Tom Fitzgerald probably summed up better than anyone the impact of that dreadful defeat. When he arrived at Dorval Airport in Montreal prior to games three and four, Fitzgerald had to clear customs. "Have you anything to declare," asked a customs officer, to which Fitzgerald replied: "Only my humility."

With their air of invincibility shattered, the Bruins never fully recovered the confidence and momentum they had had coming into the series. The teams split the next four games, setting up a seventh and deciding game on Sunday afternoon, April 18. The Bruins opened the scoring seven minutes into the game, giving themselves and their fans a huge but shortlived lift. They were quickly overpowered by the fired-up Canadiens. Jacques Lemaire, who played the best road game of his career up to that point, set up three goals, including one by a hungry rookie named Réjean Houle, to lead the Canadiens to a 4–2 victory and a series win.

When it was over, Lemaire sat in full uniform in the crowded Canadiens' dressing, amazed at what had happened. "It's like a dream," he said. "I can hardly believe we beat this team." For thirty-three-year-old Frank Mahovlich, whom the Canadiens acquired from the Red Wings in a mid-season trade, victory was an elixir. "I feel eighteen," Mahovlich said as he puffed on a cigar. "If we'd lost, I'd feel dead."

Besides being an upset of historic proportions, this was a series that was distinguished by brilliant individual performances. There was Bobby Orr's three-goal outburst in game four, a first for a defenceman in Stanley Cup play, which prompted Henri Richard to describe Orr as "the best all-round player I've ever seen." There was Béliveau's Trojan performance in the third period of game two, and Henri Richard's dogged and effective checking of Esposito throughout the series. There was Mahovlich's penalty killing against "hockey's most terrifying power play," as one sportswriter put it, and his goal-a-game contribution on offence.

But the most memorable performer of all was a tall, lanky, studious-looking goaltender named Ken Dryden, who began the series as a virtually unknown player with unusual credentials. The six-foot, four-inch Dryden was a graduate of Cornell University who was attending law school at McGill University in Montreal. On weekends that winter, he had played goal for the Canadiens' minor-league affiliate, the Voyageurs. And during the previous summer, he and his wife, Linda, then a teacher at Montreal's Holy Family School, had travelled from Luxembourg to Istanbul in a Volkswagen van. They had slept in a tent, cooked their own food, and spent an average of $10.17 a day.

With only six late-season NHL starts to his credit, the twenty-four-year-old law student was given the job of stopping the most prolific scoring machine the hockey world had ever seen, an awesome offensive team that had more twenty-goal scorers, more thirty-goal scorers, more forty-goal scorers and more fifty-goal scorers than any team in history. Yet Dryden allowed only twenty-six goals and stopped 260 shots. He was as unflappable as he was unbeatable. Asked if he had been able to relax the night before the critical third game, Dryden told a reporter: "I was reading a book on trusts and I fell asleep. There's nothing like trusts to put you to sleep."

As the series progressed, the once omnipotent Bruins became as vulnerable and bewildered as Samson without his locks. Right-winger John McKenzie, sporting two black eyes and a seven-stitch gash across his nose, said: "Four games with the best scoring chances in my life and I've got one lousy goal. Twice I had my hands in the air. Each time, I had lifted the puck to the most empty part of the net. Each time, this guy is there." Johnny Bucyk, another big gun for the Bruins, added: "For a big man, he's got incredible reflexes. Trying to jam one in is like trying to walk between two streetcars. Incredible, eh?" And after the fourth game, Esposito described how he felt being robbed of a sure goal: "That was the greatest save that's ever been made off me in my life. My God, he's got arms like a giraffe."

Montreal hockey fans also recognized that they had seen something special. When the Canadiens arrived at Dorval shortly after 7:00 p.m. on the evening of April 18, several hours after eliminating the Bruins, a crowd of ten thousand showed up to welcome them. They cheered and applauded as the players entered the terminal, and eventually they began to chant: "*On veut Dryden. On veut Dryden.*"

The Canadiens went on to defeat the Minnesota North Stars in a six-game semi-final, then went seven games against the determined Chicago Black Hawks before carting off their seventeenth Cup. Dryden continued his excellent play, although some of the novelty had worn off. During the final, Henri Richard became the centre of attention when he was benched for a game and responded by lashing out at Al MacNeil's coaching methods. Richard redeemed himself by scoring the tying and winning goals in the seventh game, but he and MacNeil never worked together again because the rookie coach was fired at the end of the season.

Montreal and Boston owned the Cup in the early 1970s, but both teams proved incapable of a successful defence. In 1971-72, the Canadiens fell to the New York Rangers in the opening round of the playoffs and the Bruins had changed their ways after the debacle the year before. "We were pretty hungry after being beat out in the first round," Orr says. "It was a good lesson for us. Going into the next season and the playoffs, there wasn't going to be any chance of a letup. We knew we had to keep our intensity up and stick to our game plan. If we get knocked down, get back up and stick your nose in. And we did that. We were really grinding."

In the spring of 1972, the Bruins beat the Leafs in five games, the Blues in four, and the Rangers in six to win their second Cup in three years. The following season, the Bruins remained a powerful team even though they had been stung by defections to the upstart World Hockey Association. But they faltered badly in the playoffs, losing to the Rangers in five games in the opening round. The Canadiens dominated both the regular season and the post-season in 1972-73. They finished first overall then beat the Buffalo Sabres, Philadelphia Flyers, and Chicago Black Hawks to capture the Cup again.

The Bruins and the Canadiens of the early 1970s were both powerful teams with some great individual performers. But neither left a lasting imprint on the game. Neither had the impact of the Philadelphia Flyers, the next truly dominant team. The Flyers were one of the most despised, one of the most maligned, and one of the most colourful teams ever. What they lacked in speed and skill, they made up for with aggressiveness and sometimes outright brutality.

In 1973-74, they were one of the most heavily penalized teams in the history of the game, largely because of the antics of enforcers like Dave "the Hammer" Schultz, who grew up in a Saskatchewan Mennonite community and attended Bible camp in the summers, and Bob "the Hound" Kelly, who was described by a teammate as "the most dangerous eleven-goal scorer in hockey." Schultz set an NHL record in 1973-74 by earning 348 penalty minutes, then surpassed himself the following season by getting 472 minutes. Kelly, who usually dropped his gloves in a season more often than he put the puck in the net, was 14–1 in the fight department in 1973-74.

The Flyers had some highly skilled players, like centre Rick MacLeish, a fifty-goal scorer in 1972-73, left-winger Bill Barber, now a Hall of Famer, and goalie Bernie Parent, whose play between the pipes inspired a popular Philadelphia bumper sticker that read "Only God saves more than Parent." And they had one of the greatest character players in the game, captain Bobby Clarke, a competent goal-scorer who could terrorize, mesmerize, and neutralize opponents with his fanatical desire to win. "You don't have to be a genius to figure out what we do on the ice," Clarke once said. "We take the shortest route to the puck and arrive in ill humour."

This raucous bunch of rabblerousers was coached by Fred "the Fog" Shero, who was famous for the proverbs and and aphorisms he posted on the dressing room blackboard. The Philadelphia coach kept a selection of books in his office and used them as the sources for most of his daily quotes. Sometimes, he drew upon his own wisdom. A typical Sheroism: "Success requires no explanation. Failure presents no alibis." A revealing Sheroism: "There are things I would do for my players that I wouldn't do for my sons." The Flyers relied on another inspirational gimmick, Kate Smith's rendition of "God Bless America," to get revved up for important home games.

Normally, they played a taped version over the Spectrum public address system just before the opening face-off. Occasionally Kate Smith herself, then in her early sixties and living in Manhattan, made a personal appearance. She charged the Flyers only $5,000 per performance, compared with her normal fee of $25,000, because she received so much favourable publicity right across the United States. "What could be better than being linked with something so wholesome as good, clean sport," she asked rhetorically in one interview. "But it's not just that. I really do love those Flyers."

And they, it seemed, loved her. Over five years, the Flyers compiled a record of thirty-six wins, three losses, and one tie in games before which they heard "God Bless America." On May 19, 1974, on a steamy Sunday afternoon at the Spectrum, the Flyers played the most important game in the history of the franchise. Naturally, they brought in Kate for an added burst of adrenalin.

The Flyers that day were leading the Bruins in the best-of-seven Stanley Cup final three games to two, and were on the brink of becoming the first post-1967 NHL expansion team to capture hockey's ultimate prize. They had arrived at their lofty perch by eliminating two other opponents, the Atlanta Flames and the New York Rangers. They had taken control of the final by virtue of Parent's breathtaking goaltending, Clarke's bulldog tenacity, and by collectively throttling Bobby Orr and Phil Esposito.

"They contained our big line," Orr recalls. "The Esposito Line wasn't scoring like it could score. The Flyers would grind you. They were all over us all the time. They'd have guys like Gary Dornhoefer sitting on your doorstep all night. Bobby Clarke was in all night poking and jabbing. They didn't give us a chance to move. Their plan was to make me work. They were throwing the puck in my corner and making me work my tail off. When they dumped it in my corner, I had to either give it up or they were going to grind me. I didn't pick that up in the series, but that's what they told me later."

The Flyers' strategy completely derailed the most devastating part of Orr's game, his dazzling end-to-end rushes, thereby allowing them to build up a 3–1 series lead. Nevertheless, Orr broke loose in the fifth game, a match marred by the usual Flyer shenanigans: spearing, butt-ending, six fights, and a record forty-three penalties. Orr managed to rise above the sordid spectacle by setting up one goal and scoring a couple in a 5–1 Bruin win.

Kate Smith launched game six with "God Bless America," but her voice was barely audible above the the sustained and deafening roar of 17,007 wild Flyer fans. Boston began with a flourish and outshot Philadelphia 16–8 in the first period. However, the Flyers skated off with a 1–0 lead. Rick MacLeish had deflected Moose Dupont's harmless shot from the blue line past Gilles Gilbert in the Boston net.

With Parent guarding the Flyers' cage, one goal was all the Flyers needed that afternoon. As the final seconds in regulation time ticked away, Bobby Orr fired a long shot at the Philadelphia net. Parent gloved the puck. And the Flyers were champions. Hundreds of rowdy fans leapt over the boards and mobbed the players. Under the circumstances, a formal presentation of the Cup was impossible. Someone handed it to Clarke, who attempted to circle the ice. That, too, was nearly impossible.

As the Flyers headed for their dressing room, the biggest spontaneous celebration since the end of World War II erupted on the streets of Philadelphia. A local audience estimated at 1.5 million had watched the game on television. When it ended at 5:00 p.m., thousands of fans hopped in their cars and headed for downtown. The party lasted until 2:00 a.m. Major roads and streets quickly became clogged with cars full of bellowing, beer-swilling Flyers fans, many of them waving Flyer flags, many of them wearing the Flyer colours, and many wearing nothing at all. For reasons no one was able to fathom, streaking was immensely popular with young men in Philadelphia that night.

So were slogans, such as "We're Number One," and "God Bless America." At one point, five thousand people stood outside a downtown hotel and sang the Flyers' good luck song. As for the poor Bruins, they were literally chased out of town. Three hundred delirious Flyer fans pursued the team's bus as it left the

Spectrum parking lot, pounding on its sides and screaming at the defeated Boston players. "The goddamned people are nuts," one exhausted and exasperated police officer told a local reporter. "They're out of their minds. If I had known this would happen I would have rooted for the Bruins."

The Flyers gave their fans plenty more to cheer about during the 1974-75 season. They finished with 113 points and were tied with the Montreal Canadiens and Buffalo Sabres for first place overall. Philadelphia and Buffalo then advanced to the final, the first time two expansion teams had played off for the Stanley Cup. This was a series that pitted the NHL's best goaltender, Bernie Parent, against the league's top forward line, centre Gilbert Perreault, left-winger Richard Martin, and right-winger René Robert, Buffalo's so-called French Connection.

From the outset, Shero knew that his team had to derail the Perreault line in order to have a chance of winning. He ordered his players to badger, harass, and intimidate Perreault. He used quick line changes to wear out the French Connection, and he relied on delays to rob it of any possible momentum. On their first shift in the opening game, Perreault and his linemates were on the ice for 97 seconds and faced three different lines. On their second shift, which lasted 106 seconds, they again squared off against three lines.

Shero's grind-them-down strategy worked magnificently, just as a similar ploy had pretty well halted Bobby Orr a year earlier. In eleven playoff games against Chicago and Montreal, Perreault and his linemates scored eighteen goals. In six games against Philadelphia, they mustered a mere four. The Buffalo power play connected on just three of thirty-two chances. An offensive powerhouse, with nine players who scored twenty or more goals that seasons, the Sabres won a couple of games at home.

But they folded for good in front of a hometown crowd in the sixth game. The teams played forty minutes of scoreless hockey before the Flyers got a goal from one of their designated sluggers. Bob Kelly, "the Hound" to his teammates, had kept the bench warm for first two periods. He started the third, and became a playoff hero eleven seconds after the puck was dropped. Kelly chased a loose puck behind the Buffalo net but was slammed hard into the boards by Jerry Korab, a six-foot-three, 220-pound behemoth. Clarke then smashed into Korab. The puck spun loose to Kelly, who veered out in front of the Sabre net and slid a backhander by a startled Roger Crozier. Another grinder, Bill Clement, scored to give the Flyers a 2–0 win and their second straight Stanley Cup. "Imagine that," said Kelly afterward. "Me scoring the goal that wins the Cup. If I try that play again a million times it wouldn't go in once."

While the Flyers guzzled beer and champagne in Buffalo, their fans held another gigantic street party in Philadelphia. The revelry lasted until well after midnight, and the following morning legions of the faithful went downtown for the team's second annual victory parade. A squadron of police officers on motorcycles led the procession. They were followed by a mounted police honour guard. The players, their wives, Philadelphia mayor Frank Rizzo, and several local dignitaries rode on two large flatbed trucks. An estimated 2.3 million people lined the parade route, which began in the heart of downtown, near City Hall and proceeded down Broad Street to John F. Kennedy Stadium.

Another hundred thousand people were packed into the stadium, the largest gathering there in almost fifty years. The Flyers arrived after a ten-mile trip that took two and a half hours. They circled the stadium track twice aboard their flat-beds, then clambered on to a huge stage erected for the official ceremony. The mayor proclaimed 1975 "The year of the Flyers II." Shero told the crowd: "This is better than heaven." The players were introduced one by one, and the fans began chanting "Bernie, Bernie, Bernie." A reluctant Parent stepped up to the microphone and said: "Well, we did it again, eh? So all I can say is, I'll see you right here again next May 27."

The Flyers arrived at training camp in the fall of 1975 still determined to make it three straight Cups. However, before the pre-season exhibition schedule was over, the Montreal Canadiens had administered the first blows that would lead to the downfall of the Flyers and prevent them perpetuating their brand of bare-knuckled, roughhouse hockey. Former Canadiens left-winger Murray Wilson says that a pair of back-to-back exhibition games between Montreal and Philadelphia proved to be the turning point for the entire season.

"We always had brawls with Philly, always," Wilson remembers. "That was Philly's style. They intimidated people in those days, and we were heir apparent to their throne. [Coach] Scotty Bowman set the tone for that whole season right in the first two exhibition games because he took some big tough guys we had in the minor leagues: Sean Shanahan, Glenn Goldup, Rick Chartraw, and Pierre Bouchard. We played them in Montreal on Saturday night and in Philly on Sunday, and it was the showdown. They put out their five toughest guys, and Scotty put out his five toughest guys, and our five toughest guys waxed their toughest guys and that was it. We never had another fight when the regular season started. It was like we beat them at their own game."

The Canadiens may have left their calling card during the pre-season, but the Flyers still had lots of fight, and some good hockey, left in them. They led the league in goals scored with 348, and finished with 118 points, five better than the previous season. But they wound up second overall in the eighteen-team league. The Canadiens earned a record 127 points. Five weeks after the regular season ended, the two top teams in the league faced off in what many commentators called a dream series. It was the Flyers versus the Canadiens, champion against chief contender. But there was more than silverware and playoff bonuses at stake here. Nothing less than the future direction of hockey was on the line. This was a battle to determine whether skill or skulduggery would rule the NHL. This 1975-76 final series would come to be seen as the key playoff battle of the entire 1970s.

The Flyers had already realized that they had to forego intimidation and unnecessary penalties or they wouldn't stand a chance against Montreal's speed, finesse, offence, and power-play. They stuck to hockey and kept each game close. Philadelphia led the first game 3–2 with ten minutes to play before Jacques Lemaire tied it. When Steve Shutt scored the winner, there were less than ninety seconds remaining. In the hard-hitting, tight-checking, second game, Montreal fired only nineteen shots at the Philadelphia net but won 2–1.

Back home at the Spectrum, the Flyers played a taped version of "God Bless America" before the third game. But good luck charms were of no use. On his first shift, defenceman Rick Chartraw set the tone for the entire game. Chartraw delivered a thundering bodycheck that sent Flyer defenceman Joe Watson, and much of his team's fighting spirit, crashing to the ice. The scoreboard read Montreal three, Philadelphia two at the end of sixty minutes, but the score in no way conveyed how thoroughly the Canadiens had dominated the defending champions. "They were checking us so closely I could tell the brand of deodorant they were using," said Gary Dornhoefer. Teammate Watson added glumly: "They're so big, so tall. They reach out with their sticks and it's as if they can reach all the way across the rink."

The Canadiens were more than dominant. They were grimly determined to demolish the Flyers and their brand of hockey. "We were up three nothing in the series, and you'd have thought everybody would just be doing cartwheels," Wilson recalls. "But the dressing room was stone silent because we wanted to take it from them in their building in four straight. It became an issue with us. It was never broadcast outside the dressing room. It was closed door. This is what we want to do. Once we got them three nothing there was no way they were going to win the fourth game. It was quiet, quiet, quiet. We hadn't lost focus on what we went there to accomplish.

"We thought: we can change hockey. Thank God, because I don't know whether hockey could have continued the way it was going. They had a western team and we had an eastern, or French Canadian team. They were mostly from the West and had a different style of hockey. They had a big, strong, rough, hockey club where our style was fast with smaller forwards. We had big defencemen with Larry Robinson, Guy Lapointe, Serge Savard, and Chartraw. But our forte was speed. Their game was dump it in, everybody take somebody, and see what's left over. We beat them on the outside. Eddie Van Impe, Tom Bladon, and the Watson boys, they just didn't have the agility. Their forwards didn't have the speed to keep up with us. Usually by the third period of most of the games, they'd just get tired of chasing you.

"I felt sorry for Bobby Clarke," Wilson adds. "We had Dougie Risebrough and Dougie Jarvis as centremen play against poor Clarkie. We'd throw them on for thirty seconds each, and Clarkie would have to try to play a minute against them. By the third period or the fourth game, he was just worn out. There's no way one individual can play against two guys and that's what we used to do all the time."

The Flyers brought in Kate Smith to sing "God Bless America" prior to the fourth game. The Canadiens countered with an equally effective psychological ploy. "We were supposed to be intimidated by her," Wilson says. "This was the great woman who had always been their saviour. Serge Savard presented her with a dozen red roses after she sang, and they said, 'Holy shit, what have they done?' Everything changed a little bit. You could see it in their eyes."

Even though they had been pushed into a corner, the Flyers refused to fold meekly. They made the Canadiens work for their final win of the season. The score was tied 3–3 with less than six minutes to go when Guy Lafleur scored his first of the series. One minute later, Pete Mahovlich put the game out of reach. Afterwards, a subdued Bobby Clarke shook his head in disbelief, and told a reporter: "This team, I thought, would never be beaten four straight."

But in a delirious corner of the desolate Spectrum, the

triumphant Canadiens celebrated at last. "The shrill cries of the beautiful young men are crashing from wall to wall in this Canadiens dressing room," long-time Montreal sportswriter Red Fisher reported. "Boy-men fling their arms around each other and hug each other and pour champagne over visitors and deliver cries of delight while suits are left limp with the wetness of it all."

After stomping on the Broad Street Bullies, as the Flyers were called, the Canadiens received one more challenge in 1975-76, one which they quietly ignored. According to Bobby Hull, a member of the Winnipeg Jets and the biggest star of the World Hockey Association at the time, the Jets approached the Canadiens about a showdown. Winnipeg had won the WHA championship by defeating the Edmonton Oilers four straight, the Calgary Cowboys in five games, and the Houston Aeros in four. Hull said in an interview that Lord Stanley stipulated that holders of the Cup must be open to challenges, and the Jets were merely acting according to the British aristocrat's original terms.

"Montreal played the game the way it was supposed to be played, and we did the same," says Hull. "So after we won, and they won, we sent a challenge to them to play for the Stanley Cup. Our line of myself, Anders Hedberg, and Ulf Nillson could have outplayed the Lafleur Line. Our second line could have outplayed their second line. The only thing we were a little bit shy on was defence. They had Savard and Lapointe and Robinson. Of course, they declined because they had everything to lose. It was kind of hushed up."

Having eliminated thuggery as a winning hockey strategy, the Canadiens then became so powerful that they almost banished surprise and drama from the game. The Canadiens peaked in 1976-77, when they won sixty games and lost a mere eight. They scored a league high of 387 goals and allowed a league low of 171. Wilson recalls losing a game in November and tying the next one, then going until February without another defeat. "It wasn't a question of whether we'd win but by how much," he adds. "We only lost eighteen games in two years."

At the peak of their powers, the Canadiens played against themselves more than their opponents, says former left-winger Bob Gainey, who joined the Minnesota North Stars as head coach in the fall of 1990. "We had different goals. We wanted sixty wins, and we got sixty wins on the last night of the season. We had individual goals, team goals. Everybody had their own things. But as a team we were trying to do something special. It was the competitive make-up of the team. There was a fear of 'don't turn it off because you can't turn it back on when you want it.'"

Those Canadiens were blessed with abundant talent. They had two scoring lines and two defensive lines. They had three all-star calibre defencemen in Serge Savard, Guy Lapointe, and Larry Robinson. They had the best goalie in the game in Ken Dryden. They frequently had half a dozen players, known as the black aces, who sat in the press box but could have started with most opposing teams.

And in Scotty Bowman, they had a clever, Machiavellian coach. "Normally as a player, if you had a relationship with Scotty it wasn't a very good one," says Gainey. "If you didn't have contact with him you were probably doing okay. I did what I had to do. I did it well enough so that I didn't have a relationship with Scotty. He demanded things of you on the ice. Then he called you up if you didn't get them done. He was the arbitrator of what was right and wrong. He was a hard judge."

Bowman worked every possible angle to keep his players sharp or to gain a slight advantage over an opponent. Wilson recalls going out for lunch in Chicago with fellow left-winger Steve Shutt during the 1973 playoffs. Bowman saw them returning to the hotel and called Wilson aside. "Listen, I don't want you two hanging around together because you're playing tonight and he's not," the coach said, apparently fearing that personal feelings might affect Wilson's performance if he became too friendly with Shutt.

At other times Bowman used friendships to his advantage. "One rule Scotty had was you never mingle with the opposition during the season," Wilson says. "You could have your best buddy on another team, but his line was they're trying to make money out of your pocket. But Scotty used friendship when he could. He used to play Doug Jarvis against Boston's Stan Jonathan all the time because they were best buddies. We'd neutralize Jonathan because he wouldn't fight Jarvis. Jarvis wasn't a fighter."

The Bowman-led Canadiens cruised to their second consecutive Stanley Cup after their record season in 1976-77. They eliminated the St. Louis Blues four straight, ousted the New York Islanders in six, and knocked off the Bruins in four. The following season, they again led the league in total points as well as goals scored, and allowed fewer than any other team. Again, they crushed their playoff opponents with grim determination: Detroit in five games, Toronto in four, and Boston in six.

During their entire four-year reign, the Canadiens faltered only once and that was in the spring of 1979 when they encountered Don Cherry's hard-working, lunch-bucket Bruins. Montreal was nine wins and fifteen points better than Boston over the course of the season. But in the Stanley Cup semi-final, any edge they might have had suddenly evaporated, and the Canadiens found themselves fighting for their lives in a seventh game. That game rates as one of the most exciting ever played. It was also one of the most memorable, largely because of the monumental Bruin blunder that became the turning point of the game. With less than four minutes to go in the third period, the Bruins were called for having too many men on the ice. At the time, they held a 4–3 lead.

Gary Darling, a real estate agent in Peterborough, Ontario, was the Bruins' chief scout at the time and attended that now-famous game, played at the Montreal Forum. "I was sitting right at the blue line in the reds watching the extra players on the ice for over thirty seconds," Darling says. "Don Marcotte was shadowing Lafleur, and Lafleur stayed on for a double shift. When Lafleur went off, Marcotte came off. The left-winger from our second line thought it was his turn to go on. He went on as well as the winger from the third line. So it was the two left-wingers going on that caused the problem."

"I think our team was every bit as good as the Canadiens. When you know you had the game in hand and let it slip away like that it's very, very frustrating. After the game, I was down near the dressing room with Harry Sinden and Tom Johnson and some of our scouting staff. It was very traumatic. You work all year for the Stanley Cup, and there's no doubt we would have won the Cup if we'd beat Montreal. It was difficult. I don't think you ever get over it. Once the Stanley Cup playoffs start, that mistake always comes up. Every year. No matter where you are, or who you're with, or whether you're in hockey or out of hockey."

Bruins fans will always remember that semi-final as the series they fumbled and dropped. They will always treat the 1979 Stanley Cup as the one their team should have won because Montreal went on to dismantle the New York Rangers with relative ease. The Canadiens experienced an understandable let-down in the first game of the final and lost 4–1.

They also got off to a shaky start in game two. Bowman decided to start Michel "Bunny" Larocque, who had been the Canadiens' back-up netminder for six seasons. "For some reason, Kenny Dryden wasn't playing well," Mark Napier, a member of the Canadiens that season, recalls. "Bunny had never started a playoff game. At the end of each warm-up, Doug Risebrough would get a puck and fire it into the goalie's glove. Doug went to shoot the puck into Bunny's glove, and shot it and hit him right between the eyes. Bunny went down and hit his head on the ice and was knocked out. So we had to put Kenny in. The first two shots the Rangers took, they scored on him. After those first two, he started playing the way he always played. He was phenomenal."

From there, it was downhill for the Rangers. The Canadiens scored three goals within eight minutes before the first period was over. They added three more in the final forty minutes to complete a 6–2 rout. "We go up 2–0," Ranger left-winger Don Maloney said afterwards, "and the thought hit us that maybe we were going to blow them out, maybe we would sweep. We just relaxed and sat back. The momentum changed so quickly we were never really in it."

The series then switched to Madison Square Garden, "home of the circus in the afternoon and the zoo at night," as one writer put it. The Canadiens cruised to a 4–1 win in game three, but they had to scratch out a 4–3 overtime win in the next game. The key play in the game, according to most observers, was Bob Gainey's third-period goal, which tied the score 3–3. "Gainey charged into the corner for the puck and collided with Ranger defenceman Dave Maloney," Michael Farber of the Montreal *Gazette* wrote. "Both went flying: Maloney to the ice and Gainey toward the net for his shot to the shortside. The goal was a microcosm of the game. The Canadiens gave it their best shot, the Rangers gave it their best shot. The Canadiens' best was better."

Montreal drove the final nail into the Rangers' coffin with a convincing 4–1 win in the fifth game, played in the Montreal Forum. The New Yorkers managed a mere three shots on goal in the second and four in the third. With six minutes to go in the game, and the outcome absolutely clear, the fanatical Forum crowd began celebrating another Stanley Cup. With forty-five seconds to go, they began a final countdown. When the siren sounded to end the game, this particular group of Canadiens had become the second most successful team in the history of the game. Only the five-in-a-row Canadiens of 1956-60 stood above them.

On the surface, the Canadiens were a typical group of victory-crazed athletes that night. They hooted and hollered and embraced one another. The dressing-room floor was quickly littered with champagne corks, and the garbage cans were quickly filled with empty bottles. Yvon Lambert, who had scored the overtime goal that sunk the Bruins eleven days earlier, stood at the door of the dressing room spraying champagne at everyone who entered. Among his targets was Pierre Trudeau, who would feel the sting of defeat twenty-four hours later after Canadians from coast to coast had cast their votes in the country's thirty-first general election. But for all their the revelry and merriment, the Canadiens were mentally fatigued.

"We were pretty well drained by the end of that year," Gainey says. "It was a tough year for a lot of people, starting with Scotty, who felt he'd been passed over for the manager's job. We started to become a little bit spoiled. Players were looking for more for themselves. We had players who had contract problems. That hadn't happened before. There were cracks there. There's no doubt we weren't the same group. We were still winning but some of the reasons changed, the priorities changed. As you go along, the thrill of winning diminishes and eventually becomes replaced with the fear of losing. You're fighting off losses more than you're trying to win. You know things can't go on forever, and you're trying to fight it off as long as you can."

During an off-season rife with upheaval, the cracks in the foundation of the team became breaches. Bowman, still miffed over the appointment of an outsider, Irving Grundman, as managing director, resigned to become general manager and head coach of the Buffalo Sabres. Dryden, only thirty-one years old, retired. So did Jacques Lemaire and Yvan Cournoyer, two holdovers from the 1960s.

By Christmas, the Canadiens' quest for a fifth straight Stanley Cup appeared doomed. Bernie (Boom Boom) Geoffrion, who had been hired to replace Bowman, lasted a mere thirty games behind the Canadiens' bench before quitting in early December. He was replaced by the team's long-time assistant coach Claude Ruel. There were also some humiliating losses on home ice. The lowly Colorado Rockies, winners of just fifteen games the previous season, stunned a Forum crowd by scoring five third-period goals and winning 7–5 one December night. The Vancouver Canucks, then in their tenth NHL season, won their first game ever at the Forum. "It got to the point where I was afraid to go out and get groceries," Larry Robinson says.

The Canadiens redeemed themselves by ending the season with a twenty-one-game unbeaten streak that cheered their fans and unnerved their chief rivals, namely the Philadelphia Flyers, the Buffalo Sabres and the New York Islanders. They promptly ran their unbeaten streak to twenty-four games by eliminating the Hartford Whalers three straight in a best-of-five preliminary round. Then the plot took an unexpected turn.

The Minnesota North Stars, described by one sports columnist as "an amazingly gung-ho bunch of talented kids," strode into the Forum and whipped the Canadiens 3–0 and 4–1. The Canadiens avenged themselves by thrashing the North Stars in each of the next three games. But they faltered in the sixth game in Minnesota and allowed the Stars to tie the series. Three nights later, on April 27, 1980, the Canadiens' reign finally ended when an unheralded journeyman named Al MacAdam batted a rebound by Montreal's startled netminder Denis Herron with less than a minute and a half left in the third period. MacAdam's marker made it 3–2, and silenced a stunned Forum crowd of 17,465.

For many Montrealers, and for legions of Canadiens' fans, the Minnesota victory was the biggest upset in recent memory. Red Fisher no doubt captured the sentiments of the faithful when he declared: "I am astonished that the North Stars were able to maintain their poise and win. They were in a strange and hostile environment. They fell behind early in the game, rallied to lead 2–1, saw their lead disappear in the third period. For a group of youngsters to stay in there and get the winning goal with time running out, that's the beauty of the game."

The day after they were defeated, most of the Canadiens gathered at Henri Richard's downtown brasserie for beers and postmortems. "I've never been on vacation this early," Rick Chartraw told his teammates. "It's the first time I haven't won since I joined the club five years ago. I love winning. Losing is a bummer."

"Look," replied Réjean Houle. "We don't own the Stanley Cup. That belongs to the league."

In relinquishing the Cup, the Canadiens put some surprise and drama back into the playoffs, something that had been missing during their reign. Having won four Cups in a row and six in ten years, they were the most successful professional team on the continent. They rescued the game from its descent into savagery and skulduggery by dethroning the Flyers. They made it a game of speed and skill again, and for a time they played it like no one else.

10

WHEN
DYNASTIES COLLIDE
1980-90

Edmonton, the city where winters are long, summers are short, and sport is king, was savouring its latest athletic triumph and dreaming of the next when the unthinkable happened. This was in early August 1988. The Oilers were Stanley Cup champions for the second consecutive year, and the fourth time in five years. The Eskimos were tied for first in the Canadian Football League's western division, and the triple-A baseball Trappers were two games out of first in the Pacific Coast League.

There were a few clouds on the horizon but they were mainly economic. The oilpatch was facing another tough winter and unemployment was up. Nevertheless, the self-proclaimed "City of Champions" was enjoying summer's embrace. Twenty-five thousand folk music fans had ignored rain and mud to attend a three-day festival in the North Saskatchewan River valley. And theatre-goers were getting ready to binge at the city's annual Fringe Festival, which presented 170 plays on fourteen stages in the space of nine days.

But Edmonton's mid-summer tranquillity was shattered by an event that seemed to the citizenry to be both heinous and incomprehensible: an offence against both common sense and human decency. The offence was the trade that made the Great One, Wayne Gretzky, a Los Angeles King and put $15 million (U.S.) in owner Peter Pocklington's pockets. It was hockey's deal of the century, a transaction as monumental as the one that sent Babe Ruth from the Red Sox to the Yankees in 1920. For days afterwards, Edmontonians bled Oiler blue. They poured out their feelings in letters to the editors and to the hosts of open-line radio shows. They were heartbroken, furious, devastated. They felt betrayed, dismayed, shocked. It was like a death in the family. It was worse than the previous summer's tornado.

The city of champions had been stripped of the greatest hockey player in the world, a young man who had delighted the citizenry for a decade with skills that seemed more divine than human. He had arrived in Edmonton in late 1978, a widely heralded but still unproven eighteen-year-old. He had vaulted from prodigy to celebrity to superstar, from the sports pages to *Time* magazine to Hollywood talk shows. He was to hockey what Mozart was to music, or Picasso to painting: an individual whose talents were so prodigious, whose accomplishments were so extraordinary, that he transcended his craft.

During his remarkable decade in Edmonton, Gretzky set forty-six individual N H L records. He scored 92 goals in a season, earned 214 points in one season, and potted fifty goals in thirty-nine games. He won the Art Ross Trophy as the league's leading scorer seven times, and the Hart Trophy as the league's most valuable player eight times. Personal bests came yearly, routinely, and with apparent ease. The only accomplishment that didn't come easy was the only one that really counts for the great ones, and that's winning the Stanley Cup.

Even for someone as gifted as Gretzky and for a team as talented as the Oilers, the trail to the Stanley Cup proved to be long and arduous, a journey distinguished by a stunning upset over the Montreal Canadiens in 1981 and an embarrassing loss to the Los Angeles Kings in 1982. But for the players and their coaches, there was never any doubt that they would win. The only question was when. After the 1980-81 season, Peter Pocklington gave each player a sheepskin coat as a gift. Inside each coat, there was a label that read "Edmonton Oilers, Stanley Cup champions 198?-8?" Before the Oilers filled in the blanks, however, they were forced to confront the NHL's reigning kings, the New York Islanders, and they suffered one resounding defeat.

Shortly after 7:00 p.m. on May 10, 1983, after the national anthems had been sung, the starting line-ups announced, and the ceremonial first puck dropped, referee Andy Van Hellemond aligned himself at centre-ice at Edmonton's Northlands Coliseum to signal the start of the Stanley Cup finals. New York Islanders centre Bryan Trottier lined up to Van Hellemond's right and hunched over in his predatory face-off stance. Opposite him, Edmonton Oiler centre Ray Cote leaned over and prepared to pounce the moment Van Hellemond dropped the puck.

For the sellout crowd of 17,498, which welcomed the Oilers with thunderous applause, and for hundreds of thousands of hockey fans across western Canada, who were watching on television, this was a magic moment. Glory seemed a mere four victories away, a Stanley Cup championship no longer a dream or a fantasy but a real possibility. Unlike the stodgy, tight-checking Vancouver Canucks, who had been thoroughly thrashed by these same Islanders in the 1982 final, the freewheeling, high-scoring Oilers were expected to win. With a roster that included the magnificent Gretzky, the riveting Paul Coffey, the menacing Mark Messier, the chaotic Glenn Anderson, and the dangerous Jari Kurri, they were picked to become the first western Canadian team in fifty-eight years to capture the coveted trophy, the first since Lester Patrick's Victoria Cougars beat the Montreal Canadiens three games to one in March 1925.

For the men who run pro hockey, from the team owners and league executives to the coaches and general managers and on down to the scouts and trainers, this was the perfect finale to the 1982-83 season, a Stanley Cup showdown between a mature champion and a dazzling contender. The Islanders were experienced, smart, and proud, winners of three straight Stanley Cups. The Oilers were young, exuberant, and arrogant, holders of thirty-two team or individual records. The Islanders had allowed 226 goals during the regular season, fewer than any other team. The Oilers had scored 424 goals, more than any other team in league history. This was a confrontation between a New York team that took itself and its place in hockey history very seriously, and an Edmonton team that frequently failed to take itself or its opponents at all seriously.

The Islanders had arrived in Edmonton for the final, checked into the downtown Westin Hotel, and discovered a city ablaze with Stanley Cup fever and confident of victory. Nearly every storefront in the downtown area was decorated with Oilers' banners or booster signs. A branch of the Bank of Montreal at 101 Street and Jasper Avenue looked like an Oilers' shrine. One Edmontonian told a local newspaper that the Oilers' Stanley Cup celebration would make a Grey Cup victory party look like a backyard barbecue.

Over fourteen thousand Albertans wished the team good luck by contributing their names to Oilergrams, which appeared in the Edmonton *Sun* and the Edmonton *Journal* on the day of game one. That day's *Journal* hardly seemed out of step with the community it served when one of its writers declared on the front page: "There's a fire blazing in the heart of Edmonton and only a champagne bath in the Stanley Cup will put it out."

The fever that infected the entire populace seemed to leave the Oilers themselves a little woozy. "It's Star Wars," said defenceman Kevin Lowe, a normally level-headed young man. "It's like Sugar Ray Leonard against Roberto Duran. We're Sugar Ray, of course. The smoothies, the glamour guys. And the Islanders, they're the hardnosed solid veterans." Amid the hype, winger Dave Lumley tried to make the case that the Oilers had matured since the 1982 playoffs when they had suffered an ignominious first-round defeat at the hands of a much weaker Los Angeles Kings team. "Last year we were so cocky," Lumley said. "The phrase we use this year is: 'Let's quietly annihilate the other team and get out of town.'"

It was enough to make the proud Islanders retch. "We want to beat them more than anything," said New York's big, bearded left-winger Clark Gillies, a Moose Jaw native who was nick-named Jethro. "You know why. Because they think they're the greatest thing since sliced bread." New York's slick, fast-skating centre Bob Bourne, another Saskatchewan native, added: "They think they're so hot. The thing that really bugs us is they don't give us any respect. The Flyers respect us. The Bruins respect us. The Rangers respect us. Edmonton doesn't respect anyone."

These Islanders wanted more than mere respect. They wanted to be remembered as one of the greatest teams ever. They saw themselves standing shoulder to shoulder with the 1976-79 Canadiens, who had won four straight Stanley Cups, and they even dreamed of duplicating the five in a row won by the 1956-60 Canadiens. Before the playoffs started in the spring of 1983, the Islanders had hung a photograph in their dressing room. The photo depicted former Montreal coach Toe Blake standing next to the Cup in 1959 with four fingers raised to signify four consec-utive championships. Underneath the picture, Islander general manager Bill Torrey had written: "History is yours for the mak-ing. Let's put Radar [coach Al Arbour] in this picture."

But when Andy Van Hellemond dropped the puck to launch the 1983 Stanley Cup final, when the hoopla ended and the hockey started, the Oilers appeared to be the team that would make history by winning the Cup for a western Canadian city for the first time in over half a century. After Duane Sutter scored early in the first period to give New York a 1–0 lead, the Oilers attacked with all the ferocity of a pack of pit bulls. They outskated, outhit, and outshot the Islanders. Time after time, they swept out of their own end, across centre-ice, and into the Islander zone looking for the equalizer, never doubting that one goal would lead to a barrage of goals. But with twenty-two seconds to go in the third period, tall, lean Ken Morrow, a defenceman who had scored only five goals in seventy-nine games that season, lofted a seventy-foot shot into Edmonton's empty net to give the Islanders an insurmountable 2–0 lead.

On paper, it looked like a narrow loss. In reality, it was a shattering defeat, and the Oilers never recovered. They had just collided head on with one of the best money players in hockey, the Islanders' portly, bearded goaltender Billy Smith. "The thing I remember about that series was they way Smitty played in the first game," Clark Gillies, now a Long Island stockbroker, says. "You would have expected the players sitting on the bench to be on the edge of their seats saying 'Oh god, another great save.' But we just knew the puck wasn't going to go in the net that night. What normally would have been a very tense situation was ho hum, just another great save."

Smith's miraculous play and obnoxious behaviour rattled the youthful and temperamental Oilers. He drove the Edmonton fans to utter distraction and the Edmonton media to near hysteria. Smith accomplished all this first by stopping the Oilers cold nearly every time they had a chance to score, and second by wielding his goalstick like a scythe.

His first victim was Oiler right-winger Glenn Anderson, who played the game with an unnerving combination of speed and recklessness. Smith hacked Anderson across the left knee in the first period of game one as the Edmonton player rounded the net, an action that drew a minor penalty but was otherwise ignored. The next morning, however, with Anderson limping around the dressing room, his knee heavily bandaged and his ability to play in doubt, Oiler coach Glen Sather exploded. "Anderson was viciously attacked," Sather told a mob of reporters. "Smith deliberately clubbed him. He swings his goalstick like a hatchet. Hopefully, somebody on our team will take care of the problem."

The media pack promptly descended on Smith, who only

inflamed the issue with his provocative response. "If they run me and hurt me, or anybody else on our team, then we have to get even," Smith spat back. "Then it may be Gretzky." The Edmonton *Journal* turned a bit of dressing-room carping and acrimony into an extraordinary front-page story. An italicized, bullet-riddled headline across the top of page on described Smith as "PUBLIC ENEMY NO. 1." The story referred to the Islander goalie as Mr. Obnoxious and Samurai Billy, and went on to describe the Anderson incident as "the latest in a hockey career that reads like a dossier on Jack the Ripper." A Westin Hotel security guard, quoted in the story, seemed to capture Edmonton's loathing of Smith. "That guy is a real creep," said the unnamed guard. "I saw a three-year-old kid come up for an autograph and Smith just brushed him off."

With two minutes to go in the second game, Smith committed the unthinkable. He hacked the Great One himself with a vicious blow across the hip. Gretzky fell, got up, and howled furiously at his attacker while enraged Oiler fans showered the ice with debris. Smith drew a major penalty, but with thirty-six seconds left on the clock, the Oilers had their revenge. Edmonton right-winger Dave Lumley speared Smith in the chest and sent him cartwheeling to the ice. After the game, the Islander goalie admitted he'd taken a dive, and accused Gretzky of doing the same, to ensure that a penalty was called.

The Oilers had not only lost 6–3 and fallen behind 2–0 in the series, they had embarrassed themselves. "Smitty had them in the palm of his hand," recalls Gillies. "He really did. He would laugh about it. He'd say, 'I'm going to get those guys so pissed off they won't be able to see straight.' And he did. He had them so mad they weren't even thinking about scoring goals. Gretzky, Messier, Anderson, all of them. They were thinking, 'How can we get Smith?'"

The series then moved to Nassau County Coliseum on Long Island for game three. The Oilers held their adversaries to a 1–1 tie through forty minutes. But in the final period, the Islanders buried the Oilers with a four-goal outburst. Three nights later, the Oilers expired quickly and meekly, by allowing three goals within ninety-seven seconds in the first period *en route* to a 4–2 defeat. "The image I'll always remember was after the fourth game in Long Island," former Oiler defenceman Randy Gregg says. "Three or four of us were standing in front of a mirror in the dressing room. We were shaving off our Stanley Cup beards and wondering what the heck we could have done to beat that team. They totally dominated us. They took everything away from us."

The most prolific offensive team in NHL history came into the 1983 final averaging 6.25 goals per playoff game. The Oilers mustered just six goals in four games against the Islanders. They were ahead on the scoreboard for a grand total of six minutes, and in game one they were shut out for the first time in 199 matches over a two-year period. Their inspirational leader, the incomparable Gretzky, who had dazzled the hockey world with an unprecedented ninety-two goals and 212 points in 1981-82, was held scoreless.

Where the Oiler game depended on blinding speed and mesmerizing offensive play, the Islanders stressed defence. They controlled their own zone and cleared the front of the net. They forced Gretzky, Messier, Anderson, Kurri, and Edmonton's lesser snipers to shoot from bad angles or from a long way out. And where the Oilers were known for their cheekiness and braggadocio, the Islanders showed Edmonton, their fans, and the entire hockey world that patience, composure, stamina, and discipline also produced champions and nurtured dynasties.

Whether Smith was really a villain, or merely a crafty veteran, hardly matters. He had exposed an emotional flaw in a talented but temperamental young team and ruthlessly exploited it. He was the good, the bad, and the ugly all rolled into one, the player who had made the Oilers and their fans feel the sting of defeat. Smith refused to join his teammates in the traditional centre-ice handshake with the opposition at the end of the series. He did join them as they skated victoriously around the rink with the

Cup held high, the rock tune "We Are the Champions" blasting through the PA system. Then Smith was awarded the Conn Smythe trophy as the best playoff performer. Afterward, he told a "Hockey Night in Canada" interviewer: "There are probably a lot of people in Canada tonight turning over in their beds at the thought of me winning this award. But a lot of reporters in Canada took cheap shots at us and that just provoked us. This fourth Cup is so great because we beat Edmonton."

The Islanders had achieved their place in hockey's pantheon, alongside the 1976-79 Canadiens but still a notch below those 1956-60 Canadiens. They had won their nineteenth straight playoff series, an unparallelled winning streak dating back to April 1979 when they swept aside the Los Angeles Kings three games to one *en route* to their first Stanley Cup. "That's a record that will never be broken," says Duane Sutter, a former Islander who now scouts for the Chicago Blackhawks. "You're not going to see any team come close to that one." They had crushed the Oilers, just as they had dismantled the Vancouver Canucks, the Minnesota North Stars and the Philadelphia Flyers in the three previous finals, with airtight goaltending, formidable defence, and that intangible of immeasureable worth – character.

"We went through some real bitter defeats to get to the point where we weren't going to lose anymore," recalls Gillies. "We lost to Toronto in 1978 in the seventh game, at home, when we were picked to go to the semi-finals or finals. In 1979 we finished first overall and certainly were supposed to go to the finals, and we lost to the Rangers in the semi-final. You've got to learn to hate losing before you learn to win."

Even after serving a painful apprenticeship and reaching the final in 1980, the Islanders had a devil of a time actually getting their hands on the Cup. They built up a lead of three games to one over the Flyers but lost the fifth game at the Spectrum in Philadelphia. Back at the Nassau County Coliseum, the Islanders appeared to be in complete control of game six, then they almost let it slip away.

"We had a 4–2 lead going into the third period," recalls left-winger John Tonelli, who has subsequently played for the Calgary Flames, Los Angeles Kings, and Chicago Black Hawks. "They tied it up, then it went into overtime. If we didn't win, it meant going back to Philly, which was a very tough place to win a hockey game. The winner came at 7:11 of overtime, and I assisted on that goal. Lorne Henning picked up the puck at our blue line and passed it up to me. Bobby Nystrom and I had a two on two and criss-crossed at the Philly blue line. That kind of slowed up their defence, and I broke toward the net. I put it on Nystrom's backhand, and he just directed it into the net. I can still see that puck hitting the back of that net."

Sutter is another former Islander who still remembers that goal and how much that first Cup meant to some of his teammates. "We went somewhere for a Stanley Cup party after the game," he says. "Later that night the Cup disappeared. It wasn't until the next morning that we realized that Bryan Trottier had taken it with him. He told everyone he slept with it that night."

Having won once, the Islanders became commanding champions, hurling aside every opponent they faced over the next three seasons, and only once coming close to elimination. Ironically, that occurred in the opening round of the 1982 playoffs against the vastly inferior Pittsburgh Penguins, who had finished the season forty-three points behind the Islanders. Yet, in a best-of-five playoff, the Penguins stunned the hockey world by pushing the series to the limit. With five minutes to go in the final game, they held a 3–1 lead. But the Islanders scored twice to tie the game and force overtime.

"You can well imagine that the place is going absolutely crazy because we've come back from the brink of elimination," says Gillies. "Then Mike Bullard goes in, dekes one of our defencemen, pulls Smitty completely out of the net. He takes a backhander and hits the post. Tonelli and Nystrom take it back down to the other end, and Tonelli scores. We win it 4–3 in overtime."

The Islanders grew up together as players and they grew old

together, as time is measured in the sport of hockey. In the spring of 1984, as they embarked on the campaign for their fifth straight Cup, there was no disguising the fact that the Islanders were an aging power. Sixteen members of the team had been around for all four Cups, and eleven players were between the ages of twenty-eight and thirty-two. The nucleus of the team, Bryan Trottier, Mike Bossy, Denis Potvin, Nystrom, Gillies, and Bourne, had all been drafted by the Islanders in the 1970s.

Nevertheless, they eliminated their divisional rivals, and advanced to the semi-final against the Montreal Canadiens, the only team ever to win five straight Stanley Cups. Prior to the start of the Montreal-New York semi-final, ex-Canadien Dickie Moore organized a reunion of former players and a dinner to inspire the 1983-84 Canadiens. "We feared the Islanders were going to tie our record," Moore explains. "We were hoping the Canadiens were going to beat them." The Canadiens took the first two games, but the Islanders rebounded to win the next four and snuff Montreal's challenge to their supremacy.

That set up a rematch against the Oilers. In 1983, the Islanders' experience and character had prevailed. One year later, the Oilers' youth, exuberance, and dazzling offence carried the day. It took the Oilers a mere five games to topple the Islanders' dynasty, to stop their self-proclaimed drive-for-five.

When the Islanders skated on to the ice at the Nassau County Coliseum May 10, 1984, to begin their defence of the Stanley Cup, hockey's aging rulers were hurting. "Bossy had tonsillitis, Trottier had a couple of broken ribs, Nystrom was out with a bad knee, Dave Langevin had a separated shoulder, Stefan Persson had a separated shoulder, Smitty had a pulled groin," says Gillies. "Things just didn't go right for us."

This time around, there would be no miraculous comebacks against the ravenous and healthy Oilers. Edmonton won the first game 1–0, which was a huge psychological lift after ten straight losses to the Islanders. "Grant Fuhr played unbelievably in goal for us, and Kevin McClelland scored the goal," Glenn Anderson recalled in an interview following his trade to the Toronto Maple Leafs in the fall of 1991. "All we wanted to do was walk out of there with one win under our belts because we were going back to Edmonton to play three games. We knew we could play well at home. We were fired up, the fans were fired up, and the momentum was in our court. When you get into a series like that, the teams are close, the talent is close. Momentum plays a big part in the game. If you get the momentum going, it's tough for the other guy to knock your car off the roller coaster."

New York thumped the Oilers 6–1 in the second game, making the third match a crucial encounter for both teams. Midway through the second period of game three, with New York leading 2–1, Mark Messier scored what proved to be the pivotal goal of the series. Oiler defenceman Lee Fogolin broke up a three-on-two Islander rush at his own blue line and flipped the puck to Messier at centre-ice. The big left-winger wheeled around and skated in alone on two Islander defenders, the rookie Gord Dineen and the veteran Denis Potvin. After throwing a fake that split the defence, Messier snapped a low, hard wristshot by Smith from thirty feet out. "That was a big goal that really threw the Islanders back," said Anderson. "They just sat back and went, 'Wow, what a play.'"

The Oilers scored two more before the period was over, and another three in the third period, running the score to 7–2 and forcing Islander coach Al Arbour to pull Billy Smith, to the delight of Edmonton fans. Two nights later the Oilers won by an identical score, and in the fifth game they buried the Islanders 5–2. At the sound of the final buzzer, the Northlands crowd unleashed a deafening cacophony of horns, sirens, cheers, and shrieks of pure joy. Fans and photographers mobbed the ice, making it nearly impossible for the blond-haired, blue-eyed, boyish-looking Gretzky to lead the Oilers on a victory skate around the ice. When the Oilers finally made it back to their bench, Gretzky handed the Cup over to Peter Pocklington, who hoisted it over his head, and declared: "This is the biggest high I've had in my forty-two years."

It was a moment of triumph for a proud, sports-crazy city, and the celebrations immediately spread from the arena to the streets. The mayor, Laurence Decore, sipped champagne outside Northlands Coliseum with other fans and said, "This is the best thing that ever happened here." Thousands of fans jammed Jasper Avenue, the city's main street, tying up traffic for several hours and creating a ruckus that could be heard for miles around. Three days after the spontaneous street party, the city held a Stanley Cup parade and reception that drew a hundred thousand fans.

But for all the joy and relief at finally having won, the celebration eventually turned ugly. After the reception at city hall, a mob of unruly and drunken young people took over Jasper Avenue again. They roamed aimlessly for three hours, breaking windows, defacing public property, and shouting "Go Oilers, Go" or "We Want Billy." Firefighters turned their hoses on the revellers but failed to disperse them. Finally, the police moved in with their truncheons, arrested seventy-five people, and ended the fiasco.

The party was over for the fans, but not for the youthful and exuberant Oilers. "We hooted it up pretty good," recalls former winger Pat Hughes, who resides in Ann Arbor, Michigan, and works at the head office of Domino's Pizza. "We left the Cup in a couple of places. One of the trainers, Lyle Kulchiski, it was his job to make sure the Cup got back to where it needed to be when all was said and done. I can remember him telling me that he had to put it back together once."

The Oilers also dragged the official team photographer, Bob Mummery, along for most of what turned out to be a very protracted celebration. "The word would go out where the Cup was going to be that day and everybody would show up," says Mummery, now owner and publisher of the weekly *Tribune* in

Minnedosa, Manitoba. "It ended up in damned near every bar in Edmonton and a few outside Edmonton. Everybody took it to their favourite bar. The Oilers made sure that everybody in the bar got a drink out of it. Every Joe on the street got a chance. It was the thrill of a lifetime for a lot of those people. You know what the Oilers were like. They were different. They broke a lot of new ground. It went on for pretty near two weeks. Those two weeks of my life are lost forever. I can barely remember them."

Having won the Cup once, the Oilers raised their aspirations, as well as the expectations of their fans and the entire hockey world. A team so loaded with talent simply had to win more in order to live up to its potential. The objective was to match the accomplishments of the Islanders, or the Canadiens of the late 1970s. The fate to be avoided was that of the Boston Bruins of the early 1970s. Even with Orr and Esposito as their leaders, those Bruins won only two Cups, and have always been remembered as a team that failed to fulfill its promise.

The Oilers' mission was to become a dynasty, and in the spring of 1985 they took another giant step in that direction. They finished second overall in the league standings, four points behind the Philadelphia Flyers. They then knocked off the Los Angeles Kings, Winnipeg Jets and Chicago Black Hawks to reach the final. Philadelphia, the other survivor of the NHL's playoff marathon, made it to the final with youngest team in the league, and with a rookie coach, Mike Keenan, behind the bench.

But the Flyers stunned the Oilers in the opening game at the Philadelphia Spectrum by winning 4–1. They outshot the Oilers 41–26, and had seventeen good scoring chances to Edmonton's four. Rookie Ron Sutter shadowed Gretzky so effectively that the Great One never even got a shot on goal. Grant Fuhr stopped five breakaways, played sensationally, and kept the game as close as it was.

That night, the Oilers neither looked nor sounded like champions. After the game, Edmonton coach Glen Sather complained about excessively rough ice, unusually bouncy pucks, and abysmal refereeing. Prior to the game, he had insisted that Flyer goalie Pelle Lindbergh remove a water bottle from the top of his net, although other opponents had allowed him to keep it there. "Maybe we want a bucket of chicken on our net," Sather sarcastically told reporters. "Or a bucket of chicken on their net. Maybe hamburgers. I mean, if you have a water bottle out there, let's have lunch."

An intensely competitive individual and an astute coach, Sather would grab almost any issue, even a water bottle, to distract an opponent. Nor did he hesitate to shake up his own troops. For the second game he bumped veteran Mike Krushelnyski off the Gretzky Line and inserted a nineteen-year-old Finn, Esa Tikkanen, who had never played an NHL game. "I've skated twenty minutes with him," Gretzky said to a group of reporters. "As far as hockey goes, you guys probably know more about him than I do." Sather's tinkering worked, however, and the Oilers rebounded for a win that tied the series at one apiece.

The series then shifted to Edmonton, and Sather as the home coach could make the final line change. According to Mark Napier, a member of that Oiler team, Sather used that tactical advantage to the fullest. "Once we got the last line change, we could get Gretzky away from Sutter," says Napier. "He started to get the puck and could freewheel. In the third game, he had three goals in the first ten minutes." The Oilers faltered in the final forty minutes but hung on to win 4–3 and take the lead in the series.

The Flyers still had some fight left in them, but they used most of it in game four. They actually grabbed a 3–1 lead before the Oilers erupted for four straight goals and a 5–3 win. In the fifth game, which proved to be the final sixty minutes of the series, the Oilers simply buried the Flyers with awesome and, at times, mesmerizing offence. Gretzky set up the first two goals of the game, by Kurri and Coffey, with perfectly executed behind-the-back passes. Messier scored a couple on breakaways. The Oilers led 7–1 after two periods and 8–3 when the game was over.

For the second straight year, they were Stanley Cup champions. "We've been in three Stanley Cups in a row," a delighted Gretzky said afterward, "and I said last spring it was going to take a helluva team to take this beautiful trophy away from us."

As for the youthful Flyers, they were dazed and bewildered by the offensive might of the Oilers. "There isn't a whole lot you can do to stop them when they're at the top of their game," conceded Flyer captain Dave Poulin, "particularly Gretzky and Coffey. They killed us. Those two guys are talking without words." Said defenceman Brad Marsh: "They've got some of the greatest players in the world. When you don't have the scorers they do, it takes such an all-out effort to beat them. It's not only physically tiring, it's mentally tiring."

While the Flyers licked their wounds and the Oilers guzzled champagne, thousands of jubilant Edmontonians again took over Jasper Avenue for a spontaneous street party that brought traffic to a standstill for twelve blocks. Police officers stood in pairs every half block or so. But they merely watched as the revellers drank beer, smoked marijuana, tossed firecrackers, and danced on cars. By midnight, the party had run out of gas, and the city was spared the embarrassment of another near riot.

As they savoured their second Cup, most of the Oilers couldn't help but think that another one was theirs for the taking. The core players, Gretzky, Messier, Coffey, Kurri, Anderson, and goalie Grant Fuhr, ranged in age from twenty-two to twenty-five. They had set an amazing twenty-five NHL records during the 1985 playoffs. No wonder, then, that the D-word was on the lips of a few players that night. "There's no reason we can't be a dynasty," said Coffey, who had shattered the old record for playoff points by a defenceman while playing with a tender right foot, a strained back, and a bruised right hip that required painkillers. "We've got the players and the coaching staff. It's up to us. If we're prepared to be dedicated enough, and commit ourselves to the hard work that would be involved, we could be a dynasty."

The following season, the Oiler machine kept rolling and the individual stars kept shining. The team finished first overall with 119 points, Coffey scored forty-eight goals and earned 138 points, both single-season records for a defenceman, and Gretzky broke his old record for total points by compiling 214. The Oilers then dusted off the Vancouver Canucks three straight in the opening round of the playoffs, and turned their attention to Calgary, winner of the other Smythe division preliminary round.

The press immediately dubbed the upcoming series the Battle of Alberta, and predicted it would be an uncivil war between north and south. The players also got into the spirit of things. "The Canucks were the sparring partner before the real thing," the Oilers' bruising defenceman Marty McSorley said. Doug Risebrough summed up the feelings on the Flames' side when he said: "We're going into this for one reason and that's to win, at whatever cost." By talking tough, the players were merely mimicking the normally dignified gentlemen who ran the two teams. Cliff Fletcher, the Flames' general manager at the time, had occasionally referred to the Oilers as "a goon squad" while the Oilers' Sather once described the Flames as "a no class organization."

The dislike between the two teams was almost tangible, and was based on the fact that the Oilers had become accustomed to beating the Flames. Edmonton had lost only two of its previous twenty-four games against Calgary going into the 1986 Smythe Division final. And the battles on ice reflected the historic rivalry between the two ambitious western cities, a rivalry dating to the 1880s, when Calgary got the CPR, and 1905 when Edmonton was made the provincial capital.

But the intensity of the rivalry between the Oilers and Flames surprised even veteran NHL players who were accustomed to the excesses of fanatical followers. Toronto native John Tonelli was traded from the Islanders to the Flames in March 1986 and one month later found himself immersed in a playoff cauldron, the likes of which he had never experienced. "Coming from the

Islander-Ranger rivalry, I just couldn't believe how people in Alberta got into it," he says. "As players, we thought New York–New York was a big rivalry. But the people really take hockey to heart in the province of Alberta. In New York, when hockey is over they can go on to baseball or football. Hockey is number one in Alberta. It's serious business, for the players and the fans."

Just how serious was evident in the spring of 1986. The province was in the midst of a provincial election, yet the uncivil hockey war frequently overshadowed politics on the front pages of Alberta's two largest daily papers, the Edmonton *Journal* and the *Calgary Herald*. "How the mighty have fallen," groaned the *Journal*'s Cam Cole in a page-one story after Calgary won the first game 4–1. "Sluggish, jittery and shockingly short of poise, the Oilers were checked to a frustrated standstill by the Calgary Flames."

Edmonton rebounded for a 6–5 overtime win in the second game, by which time a few of the Oilers began to realize that they had seriously underestimated the ability of the Flames. "Their intensity was never a question for me," said defenceman Kevin Lowe. "But I really didn't think they had the horses to play with us like they are."

The action shifted to the Calgary Saddledome for games three and four. A local radio station exhorted the faithful to turn out in Flames red and, sure enough, the stands were packed with fans wearing red caps, scarves, sweaters, jackets, coats, gloves, and even socks. When the Oilers appeared on the ice, Calgary fans chanted "Whiner, Whiner," a derogatory nickname they had given Wayne Gretzky because of his tendency to question calls by the referee. The hype worked in game three, and the Flames skated off with a 3–2 win, but it backfired in game four when Gretzky tallied five points in a 7–4 Oiler win. The Great One singlehandedly silenced the Calgary crowd with his brilliant performance.

The Edmonton media attempted to whip up the Oiler fans into a frenzy for game five. The *Journal*'s front-page story on game day ran under the headline "GO OILERS, GO." The paper announced that it would be distributing Oiler hats outside the Northlands Coliseum prior to the game in order to create a sea of white. The Oilers-Flames encounter that evening was a classic, full of "relentless skating, fine goaltending, good hitting and scoring chances galore," according to one report. But the Oilers lost 4–1, and the front page headline in the next day's *Journal* told the story: "BACKS TO THE WALL."

A couple of nights later, scalpers outside the Saddledome were getting up to $500 a ticket from fans desperate to see their Flames administer the death blow to the hated Oilers. Inside, fans had hung a sign that read "Champagne for the Flames. Whine for the Oilers." But it was not to be. With twelve minutes to go in the third period, Edmonton's Glenn Anderson broke up a 2–2 tie. "It was an absolute Oiler goal, full of windburn, big names, fancy passing," Cole reported in the *Journal*. "Coffey swooped in on the left side. Gretzky somehow found him with the puck, and Coffey laid a perfect pass in the slot to Anderson, who rifled it between Mike Vernon's legs."

So the teams faced a seventh game, every player's boyhood fantasy. "When you were a kid, every time you picked up a stick and played on the pond it was the seventh game of the playoffs," Gretzky told a reporter as he contemplated the decisive match. "The outcome was never in doubt then. You always won the game in your dreams. This is reality though. This is the real thing."

Through the first forty minutes of play, the big game unfolded just as these things usually do in boyhood fantasies. The score was tied and it was anybody's game to win. Every player had a chance to be a hero. Instead, this game turned one young man, an Edmonton rookie named Steve Smith, who happened to be celebrating his twenty-third birthday that very night, into a goat.

Five minutes had elapsed in the third period when Flames' forward Perry Berezan dumped the puck into the Oilers' end, then headed for the Calgary bench. Smith picked up the puck in the corner and skated behind his own net, pursued by Lanny McDonald. Smith looked for a teammate, spotted Glenn Anderson near the Oiler blue line, and attempted a long, cross-ice pass to him. But Oiler goalie Grant Fuhr was perched near the edge of his crease. The puck hit him on the back of the leg and ricocheted into the net. Berezan, who was given credit for the goal, hadn't even seen the puck go in.

The Flames had the lead, they held on to win, and the Oiler dreams of a dynasty disintegrated. The Oilers and their fans were stunned and shaken by the outcome. The Flames and their fans were overjoyed. The Calgary players hooted and hollered. They sprayed each other with beer. They gave each other high fives. "Everything we do from September to April is compared to and plotted against how Edmonton did," explained defenceman Paul Reinhart. "We can try and fool ourselves and say we're trying to be as good as the Washington Capitals. But that's not what we're trying to do. We're trying to catch Edmonton."

It was an evening when one team's dreams came true, and their fans didn't care how they'd done it. In the first five minutes after the game, Calgarians placed twenty-seven thousand calls to Edmonton, according to a spokesman for Alberta Government Telephones. The circuits were jammed for half an hour. Ten thousand fans flocked to the city's airport, creating a traffic jam five kilometres long. People were lined up thirty deep along a fence outside the terminal building. The downtown was like rush hour. The party lasted until 2:30 a.m., and in the next day's paper the magnitude of what had happened was laid out in black and white. "Stop and think about it," wrote *Herald* columnist Steve Simmons. "The Flames beat the Oilers. Savour it. Cherish it. Remember it. The Flames beat the Oilers. Calgary beat Edmonton."

Calgary went on to beat the St. Louis Blues in an unexpectedly tough semi-final series that went seven games. It was a hard-fought victory but nowhere near as sweet as beating the Oilers.

The Flames then squared off against the Canadiens in the final. However, the city's visions of a Stanley Cup victory were quickly shattered by a Canadiens' team led by two veterans of the 1970s, captain Bob Gainey and defenceman Larry Robinson, a firebrand forward named Claude Lemieux, and a sensational rookie goalie named Patrick Roy. Montreal whipped Calgary in five games, played in the space of eight days, and won its twenty-third Stanley Cup at the Saddledome. As Flames' forward Joel Otto said later: "I woke up one day and the playoffs were over. Everything was a blur."

The 1986 playoffs were an anomaly, a departure from the script, an opportunity for a couple of dark horses to make a run for the money. The following season, the Oilers again established themselves as hockey's pre-eminent team. They finished first overall. Gretzky won the scoring championship, linemate Kurri finished second, and teammate Messier was fourth. The Oilers compiled a record of twelve wins and two losses in eliminating Los Angeles, Winnipeg, and Detroit en route to the Stanley Cup finals. And after winning the first two games of the final at home against the Philadelphia Flyers, the Oilers appeared to be in complete control once again.

In the third game, played at the Philadelphia Spectrum, the Oilers romped to a 3–0 lead early in the second period. That's when things started to go wrong. They were called for too many men on the ice, and the Flyers scored. Philadelphia pumped four more goals by Grant Fuhr to win 5–3. "We were close to being in the grave," admitted scrappy forward Rick Tocchet. "But we've got character. [Assistant coach] Paul Holmgren was on the bench screaming at us. He yelled that we still had another thirty-eight minutes left and you don't roll over in the Stanley Cup playoffs."

In the post-game interviews, the Oilers fretted over the manner in which they had lost. But they dismissed the defeat as a hiccup, and went out and waxed the Flyers 4–1 in the fourth game. Edmonton was a mere win away from its third Stanley Cup in four years, and the city decided that victory was inevitable. Alderman Pat McKenzie announced that a civic rally would be held two days after the final game. "There will be all sorts of entertainment before and after the rally," he promised. "It will be a real celebration."

The Edmonton *Journal* slapped its "GO OILERS, GO!" headline across the top of the front page, and the Edmonton Convention Centre threw its doors open to the public for the game five. A crowd of eighteen hundred showed up to watch it on a big screen, and the City of Champions was ready for a party. The Oilers went ahead 2–0, and then made it 3–1. But again, victory slipped through their fingers. The Flyers came back to win 4–3. "We heard they were planning a parade," snickered Philadelphia's Tocchet afterward. "We used it to our advantage."

The next day a glum group of Oilers boarded an aircraft for the long flight back to Philadelphia and game six. Sather tried to calm his jittery troops. The Flyers' Keenan did his best to get his men primed. Following the morning skate on the day of game six, he barred everyone from the Flyers' dressing room except the players. Keenan then brought out the Stanley Cup and set it on the table. He hoped that his players would look at it, read the names engraved on it, touch it, and draw inspiration from it. Some did just that. A couple of others rolled hockey tape into balls and tried tossing them into the bowl of hockey's most hallowed trophy.

That night the Oilers grabbed a 2–0 lead before the end of the first period, but from that point on Flyers' goaltender Ron Hextall was unbeatable. His teammates clawed their way back into the game with a second-period goal, tied it up thirteen minutes into the third, and scored the winner a little over a minute later. For the third time in the series, the Oilers had gassed a lead, and a chance to bury the Flyers. "This is a little hard to believe," admitted Hextall, a twenty-three-year-old rookie at the time. "If you'd asked me if we could come back that often, three times from at least two goals down, I'd have said you're crazy."

The Flyers arrived in Edmonton looking for one more miracle, and their first Cup since 1975. They opened the scoring before the seventh game was two minutes old. But that was as far as they got. Messier tied the score in the first, Kurri scored the winner in the second, and Anderson added an insurance goal with less than three minutes remaining. Immediately after the game, league president John Ziegler presented the Cup to Gretzky at centre-ice. Gretzky hoisted it aloft, held it there for a few seconds, then handed it to Steve Smith, the goat of the 1986 Calgary series.

"He wanted the younger guys to hold the Cup first and have the same experience he had in '84 after they won it the first time," Smith says. "I grabbed the Cup and turned around immediately and tried to find my family. I picked them out of the crowd right away. Five seconds after I picked up the Cup, a photographer snapped a picture. I've got it hanging on my wall at home right now."

By the time the Oilers had left the ice, with a firm grip on their third Stanley Cup in four years, twenty-five thousand fans had packed Jasper Avenue for another celebration. They climbed lamp poles. They stood on bus shelters. They sang and drank and filled garbage cans with the empties.

While his teammates and his fellow citizens celebrated, Wayne Gretzky sat at his stall in the Oilers' dressing room. He was soaked in champagne, and as unreserved as he ever gets in public. "The greatest high in my life is when I have that Stanley Cup in my hands and I raise it over my head," he said. "This one was the sweetest. This was the biggest game I've ever played. We went through a long summer last year. I knew it would be the greatest summer of my life or the worst. Now I can head for L.A. and watch some basketball."

In 1987, the Oilers reclaimed the crown which they regarded as rightfully theirs. The following season, they earned a place among hockey's all-time élite. With their fourth Cup in five years, they removed all doubts about their ability, their character, their commitment, and their determination, all the elements that go into winning the marathon that the contemporary Stanley Cup tournament has become. They won so convincingly that they seemed destined to rule the hockey world for several seasons to come.

The Oilers romped to the 1988 final with a playoff record of twelve wins and two losses. They eliminated the Jets in five games, the Flames in four, and the Wings in five. They took care of the Bruins with equal ease in the final. The Oilers won the first two games at home and allowed just twenty-six shots on their own net. The Bruins did what professional athletes always do when the situation is hopeless. They talked tough. But after game three in Boston Garden, they were barely even talking.

The Oilers won 6–3 and afterwards half a dozen dispirited Bruins trudged out of the trainers' room one by one to meet the media. Forward Steve Kasper revealed just how bleak things were for the Bruins: "I can't stand here and realistically say we're going to win four straight. What we have to do is win a game and create some doubt in their minds."

In all likelihood, the Bruins would have expired two nights later. But decrepit old Boston Garden saved them. The temperature had risen to twenty-eight degrees Celsius inside the building by the end of the first period. Early in the second, fog began rising from the ice. On five occasions, the referee had to stop the game and order the players to skate around the ice in order to disperse the mist. The teams had managed to play almost seventeen minutes of the second period and tie the score 3–3, when suddenly the lights went out. The blackout, caused by an overloaded switch and a short circuit, lasted half an hour. Because the building had to be evacuated, league president John Ziegler and both teams agreed to replay game four in Edmonton.

The Oilers put the Bruins away on their own ice and made it look easy. But this time around, Edmonton's trail to the Stanley

Cup had been paved with injury and adversity. Kevin Lowe wore a cast through the entire playoffs to protect a cracked left wrist. He also wore a flak jacket to shield three broken ribs on his left side. Gretzky had missed sixteen regular season games due to eye and knee injuries, and had finished second in the scoring race for only the second time up to that point in his NHL career.

Sather had been forced to begin dismembering the previously untouchable nucleus of the club. He had traded Paul Coffey to Pittsburgh the previous November after an acrimonious two-month contract dispute. He had traded goalie Andy Moog to Boston in March after Moog sat out the entire season. A couple of other key players from the 1987 team, Reijo Ruotsalainen and Kent Nilsson, retired and had to be replaced. With all the changes and upheaval, the Oilers had finished second to the Flames that season for the first time.

Mere runners-up after an eighty-game grind, the Oilers were back on top of the world after their playoff rampage. They won eighteen games and lost only two. They were invincible. Everyone who rendered an opinion concluded that they would be the team to beat for the forseeable future. Three Cups in a row seemed inevitable. Sather's rebuilding job looked like a work of genius. Gretzky's performance had been magnificent: forty-three points in eighteen playoff games and his second Conn Smythe trophy as the playoff Most Valuable Player. But the show wasn't over for the man who was the heartbeat of the Oilers. He was scheduled to marry a Hollywood beauty named Janet Jones in mid-July in Edmonton. It would be a sweet summer for the Oilers and their fans.

The Oilers had become an integral part of the city's identity. Edmonton was the City of Champions, a community that took pride in its teams the same way that Vancouver reveled in the splendour of its setting or Calgary in its proximity to the Rocky Mountains. Just as Toronto basked in its size and financial might, or Montreal in its language and culture, Edmonton had a deep emotional attachment to Wayne Gretzky and the Oilers.

Unfortunately, Peter Pocklington owned and controlled both the player and the team. And in the summer of 1988, Pocklington had the opportunity to earn a return on investment that only a Midas could imagine. He had purchased Gretzky in 1978 for $850,000 from Nelson Skalbania, owner of the World Hockey Association's Indianapolis Racers. Now Pocklington had a chance to sell him for $15 million.

Pocklington had devoted his life to making money and had lost most of it in the economic downturn that hit Alberta in the early 1980s. His trust company had gone bust. One of his car dealerships was sold, the other went into receivership. His real estate holdings had plummeted in value. His meat-packing plants were a labour-relations nightmare. Amid all this wreckage, Pocklington's star hockey player gleamed like gold. He couldn't resist selling him.

Wayne Gretzky officially ceased to be an Oiler on Tuesday, August 9, 1988. Many of his former teammates still remember that day clearly and precisely. "I was in Saskatoon, at the University of Saskatchewan, on a fund-raising project," recalls Randy Gregg. "I think two people in the world knew I was in Saskatoon, but I get a phone call in the phys-ed department head's office. It's a media person looking for some comments from Randy Gregg. It was almost eerie that anybody knew I was there.

"Then a friend and I went down to Regina and we stopped at the Regina Golf and Country Club. As we walked in to get a tee-off time, the fella said, 'We've been expecting you. The reporters have been calling to see if they could get a comment.' It showed the magnitude of that trade that they would follow you for something as insignificant as a teammate's comments. It was hard to believe that, under any circumstances, they would trade someone who had done so much for the players, the organization, the city, and the country as Wayne Gretzky. Disbelief is the adjective that comes to mind most often."

And it was disbelief that reigned in Edmonton that day. "I was like everyone else," says former Oiler defenceman Steve Smith.

"Until I saw the press conference with Wayne Gretzky and Bruce McNall I didn't believe it. I was in Edmonton, at home with my family, and I was immediately on the phone to the rest of the guys on the team. There were quite a number of players who stayed in Edmonton for the summer. Edmonton being a small town, we were able to spend a lot of time together. We played golf together. We did a lot of things together. It was a real tight-knit group of guys. We were all close friends."

A friend and teammate was now an opponent. When Gretzky and his former mates had to confront each on the ice, it was a traumatic experience. But the Oilers' loss was everyone else's gain. When the 1989 playoffs began, there was no overwhelming favourite for the first time in fifteen years. The dynasties, first the Canadiens, then the Islanders and finally the Oilers, had been so dominant that they had had a deadening effect on the game. They had taken a lot of the suspense and the unexpected out of the playoffs.

In their first season without Gretzky, the Oilers were defending champions on paper only. They fell to seventh in the overall standings, from third the previous year, and lost in the opening round of the playoffs to Gretzky and the Kings. The chief beneficiary of the Oilers' fall was none other than Calgary. The Flames knocked off the Kings and advanced to the final for a re-match against the Canadiens.

Calgary and Montreal were the two top teams in the league that season, they were equally matched, and the final proved to be one of the most exciting of the decade. The teams split the first two games, which were played at the Olympic Saddledome in Calgary. Montreal then handed the Flames a devastating defeat in the third game. The Flames were clinging to a 3–2 lead going into the final minute of play when Montreal's Mats Naslund tied the game with an unassisted goal. The Habs then won it when Ryan Walter scored in overtime. That should have been the end of the Flames. Yet they rebounded to win the fourth game in Montreal and the fifth game back home. The Flames were poised to win a Stanley Cup at the Forum, something no team had ever done.

Before the sixth game, Calgary coach Terry Crisp made a line-up change that turned out to be an inspired move. He dressed right-winger Lanny McDonald, a sixteen-year veteran and 500-goal scorer who had sat out the previous three games. Early in the second period, McDonald stepped out of the penalty box, took a pass from teammate Hakan Loob, and swooped in on Patrick Roy in the Montreal net. Roy dropped to his knees and McDonald whipped one of his bullet-like wristshots into the top corner on the glove side. He gave the Flames a lead they never relinquished. Calgary's Doug Gilmour added a couple of third-period goals, and the Flames had won their first Stanley Cup.

Amid the post-game bedlam, McDonald recalled how he had scored his first NHL goal at the Forum, and an exuberant rookie named Theoren Fleury declared: "It's the greatest day of my life. I love everybody in Canada." Cliff Fletcher, the only general manager the Flames had ever had, put the victory into perspective. "For sixteen years, we've been saying wait till next year," Fletcher said. "Next year finally arrived."

Back in Calgary, twenty-five thousand fans celebrated on Electric Avenue, a strip of downtown bars and night spots. They were subdued and well behaved, as Stanley Cup crowds go, because of the presence of dozens of police officers. The city police department had warned Calgarians in advance that they would discourage public consumption of alcohol and excessive rowdiness to avoid a repeat of the night in 1986 when the Flames beat the Oilers. The police had also discouraged the public from going to the airport. As a result, there was only a mob of reporters and airport workers on hand to greet the Flames when they arrived home at 4:00 a.m.

Two days later, the city held a parade for its conquering heroes and twenty thousand people showed up on a wet, chilly day. This was another well-behaved crowd that cheered, applauded, and occasionally chanted "Lanny for mayor." One youngster said that winning the Stanley Cup was a bigger thrill than the Stampede, the Olympics, and Christmas combined. A middle-aged fan said he'd ranked it with the Second Coming. And one woman couldn't help but wonder what they were doing in Edmonton that day, a thought that occurred to more than a few Calgarians. "The question is, how are they all taking this in Edmonton?" mused *Calgary Herald* columnist Larry Wood. "Everybody knows the Stanley Cup belongs in Alberta. But Calgary?"

The Cup came to rest in Alberta again in the spring of 1990 when the Oilers won it for fifth time in seven years. Their most recent triumph was a testament to the managerial saavy of Glen Sather, and the competitive spirit of the remaining Oiler originals, the holdovers from the 1984 Cup team, Mark Messier, Jari Kurri, Glenn Anderson, Kevin Lowe, Randy Gregg, and Charlie Huddy. But the Oilers were also a harbinger of the 1990s, a decade that is likely to be dominated by teams that get hot at playoff time, pick up momentum, and become impossible to stop.

The Oilers caught fire in the first round of the playoffs when they eliminated the Winnipeg Jets after being down three games to one. They beat the Kings four straight and the Blackhawks in six. The Bruins were the final victim, and they went down in five games. Messier was unquestionably the team's inspirational leader, Kurri and Anderson chipped in big goals, while Lowe, Gregg, and Huddy provided firm, reliable defence. The veterans blended beautifully, and at the best possible time, with a group of younger players that Sather had acquired in trades; goaltender Bill Ranford and forwards Martin Gelinas, Joe Murphy, Adam Graves, and Petr Klima. Once the Oilers were rolling, they stayed healthy, they got the breaks, and for a few brief weeks they were unstoppable. This, according to many of hockey's brightest minds, is the way the Cup will be won in the nineties.

But as they savoured their fifth championship in seven years, some of the Oilers were haunted by the past and the friend who wasn't there. Sitting in the team's cramped, steamy dressing room in Boston Garden that night, Kevin Lowe said: "Messier and I looked at each other before the game and said, 'This one's for the G-man,' because he's still such a big part of our team." Even Sather, a man hardened by years of trading players, by cutting them loose, and by negotiating contracts, was a little sentimental. "Wayne was the biggest part of this organization for ten years. Part of this Stanley Cup is his. He got these players and this organization to where it is. A lot of guys still feel he's part of this team."

In ten glorious years, Gretzky and his teammates had rewritten the NHL record books and won five Stanley Cups. They grew as a team in the shadow of the Islanders, they put an end to the Islander dynasty, and then they cast their own long shadow over the game. They didn't change hockey, but only because nobody else could play the game with the same artistry and magic. The others didn't have a Gretzky and a supporting cast that included a Coffey, a Messier, an Anderson, a Kurri, and a Fuhr.

The Oilers' reign lasted long enough for most opposition players and coaches and their fans. But it was all too brief for Edmonton, a city that loves winning. For a few sweet seasons, Edmonton's hockey team was the best anywhere, and for a decade the city owned the greatest hockey player in the world. Those days are over, but they'll never be forgotten. Inside the Northlands Coliseum the Stanley Cup banners still hang from the ceiling. Outside the building, there is a bronze sculpture of Gretzky that stands fifteen feet high. The Great One is in his Oiler uniform. His arms are raised and he is holding the Stanley Cup over his head. He has become a silent and permanent reminder of a glorious past.

11

THE CANADIAN GRAIL
1990-92

Two hours before the start of game three of the 1991 Stanley Cup finals, thousands of fans gathered outside the Metropolitan Sports Centre, home of the Minnesota North Stars. It was a warm, muggy Sunday evening in late May, perfect weather for a massive tailgate party. Motorists hammered their horns as they whizzed around the parking lot looking for places to park. Hard rock, blasted from car stereos and portable speakers, reverberated in the air. Young, beer-guzzling men howled and bellowed. Other fans relaxed in lawn chairs. Some played catch with frisbees, baseballs, and footballs. Smoke rose from hundreds of tiny barbecues, and the smell of sizzling meat wafted across the parking lot.

The North Star colours – white, green, and gold – were everywhere, on signs, banners, posters, T-shirts, and the faces of dozens of fans. Five young men in green tank tops had each stitched one large, white letter on their front and back. From the front the letters spelled STARS, from the back SCORE. Three brothers, Tom, Mike, and Joe Wheaton, had painted the team logo, an italicized N nudging a five-point star, on a white sheet and taped it to their Ford Econoline van. It was big enough to cover one side of the vehicle. Scott Means, an eighteen-year-old high school student with chiselled features and the physique of a future linebacker, wore a tight-fitting green hockey helmet and a T-shirt bearing a blunt message: "North Stars. Kicking ass and taking names. Blackhawks, Blues, Oilers." These were the teams Minnesota had eliminated to reach the final.

Amid this partisan pandemonium, there was a tiny but highly visible smattering of black and yellow, the colours of the Pittsburgh Penguins. Nancy Leach, a waitress at a Penguins' hangout in downtown Pittsburgh, and two friends had driven 880 miles to attend game three. They left at 1:30 a.m. Sunday and travelled sixteen hours straight. They planned to leave right after the game and drive back home in time for work Monday afternoon. "Ulf Samuelsson knew we wanted to come, so he set us up with tickets," said Leach. "I love Ulf Samuelsson. You know what Ulf stands for in Pittsburgh? The Ultimate Lethal Force."

Samuelsson, a Swedish defenceman, who's built like a fire hydrant and plays like a pit bull, had arrived in Pittsburgh less than three months earlier as part of a six-player trade with the Hartford Whalers. He had quickly established himself as a fan favourite by alternately pestering and hammering opposing forwards. He was also a crucial factor in Pittsburgh's playoff success. With Samuelsson around, the Penguins were suddenly dangerous at both ends of the rink. Mario Lemieux could undress opposition defenceman and goalies with his deceptive speed, his fluid moves, and his incredible reach. Samuelsson mauled his opponents at every opportunity, at the blue line, in the corners, along the boards. He gave the Penguins a nasty streak that made their flashy offence more menacing than it had been.

On this particular evening, while a parking lot full of fans held a massive tailgate party, the Penguins were about to meet the North Stars for the third time in five nights. Minnesota and Pittsburgh were engaged in the first all-American Stanley Cup final in ten years, the second in sixteen years, and arguably the most unexpected final in several decades. Before the playoffs began, the leading oddsmaker in Las Vegas, Mike Roxborough, had called Pittsburgh a 7–1 longshot to win the Stanley Cup. The odds against Minnesota were a staggering 50–1.

The North Stars and the Penguins had launched their bids for the Stanley Cup two months earlier in the first week of April. They were just two of sixteen teams in the race, and only the most partisan or prescient fans would have picked either of them to make the final. Shortly before the 1991 playoffs began, Toronto-based Gallup Canada Inc. asked a representative sample of Canadians which team was likely to win the Cup. The Calgary Flames and Montreal Canadiens were each picked by 10 per cent, while Edmonton and Los Angeles were favoured by 9 per cent each. A whopping 42 per cent said they couldn't pick a winner. The Penguins and North Stars weren't even rated. Concluded Gallup: "Seldom in recent memory has the playoff season commenced with so little agreement concerning which squad will be the likely victor."

The uncertainty that prevailed at the start of the 1991 playoffs was no accident. The breakup of the Oilers created a vacuum that every team was eager to fill. For the first time in a decade and a half, hockey was a sport without one dominant team towering over everyone else. Many of hockey's brightest executives believe that the 1991 playoffs signalled the start of a new era in the game, an era in which it will become increasingly difficult to keep powerful and successful teams together, largely because of salary demands. Star players are likely to become far more mobile, and success increasingly transitory and elusive.

"I don't think you'll see a dynasty again because of the financial situation," says John Muckler, who coached in Edmonton for nine seasons before joining the Buffalo Sabres in 1991 as director of hockey operations. "Edmonton is proof of that. If they had kept their team together, Gretzky, Coffey, Kurri, Fuhr, Messier, they could still be contending for the Stanley Cup. But salaries dictated that they couldn't keep that team together. You won't see dominant teams any more because they won't be able to carry the players who are successful and demand more money."

Cliff Fletcher, the Leafs' general manager, who is attempting to turn the team into winners after a quarter of a century in the gutter, predicts that escalating salaries will prevent most teams from carrying more than three star players. At the same time, any organization that hopes to contend for the Stanley Cup must be deep in talent, and have capable reserves to call upon in case of injury. "It's an endurance contest now," says Fletcher. "People talk about the great dynasties of the past, prior to 1967. All you had to do then was win one round and you were in the final. Now you have to play for a month and a half and win sixteen games. You've got to have depth, outstanding goaltending, and lady luck on your side."

Even the braintrust of the most hallowed team in hockey, the Montreal Canadiens, has accepted the fact that it is harder to win than it once was. "No longer can you measure success by the number of Cups you win," admits Canadiens' president Ron Corey. "When you look at the tradition of the Montreal Canadiens and the number of Cups they have won, the five in a row in the fifties and the four in a row in the seventies, it's not the same now. That would be unrealistic in the NHL today. Our aim is to have a chance of winning it each year. Our fans demand it. They love a winning team. They are knowledgeable fans. The Montreal Canadiens are in their blood."

It is no exaggeration to say that Ron Corey and the rest of the executives in the Canadiens' front office carry a heavier load than most of their peers around the NHL. They have inherited what might be called the Hab man's burden. They are responsible for perpetuating the franchise's glorious past. The Club de Hockey Canadien is the most successful organization in all of professional sport. The Canadiens won two Cups during the first two decades of their existence. They won four Cups during the next twenty years. Then they soared, winning five in the fifties, five in the sixties, and six in the seventies. A power failure occurred during the eighties when the Canadiens won only one Cup, a dismal performance according to their own extraordinary standards. There was one mitigating factor: the last Cup was their twenty-third. Only the New York Yankees, who have won baseball's World Series twenty-two times, come close to the Canadiens' record for excellence.

The Canadiens have been remarkably successful at renewing themselves. When one group of players began to falter, there was always another group ready to take over. And among each group, there have almost always been a couple of players who could inspire their teammates and dazzle the fans. In the early days, there was Aurèl Joliat and Howie Morenz. Then came Rocket Richard and Boom Boom Geoffrion, Henri Richard and Jean Béliveau, Yvan Cournoyer and Guy Lafleur. But since Lafleur quit the team, suddenly and prematurely in 1985, the Canadiens have not been able to find a game-breaking, heart-stopping leader, a player with speed and finesse, dash and desire. And this, perhaps more than anything else, explains why Montreal suffered a power failure in the eighties.

While the Canadiens have come to epitomize success in sports, the two teams in the 1991 Stanley Cup final had experienced a quarter of a century of failure and futility. The Penguins missed the playoffs seven out of eight seasons prior to 1991, and had never been able to win more than a single round in any playoff. In 1990-91, the Penguins had finally won something, a regular season divisional title. This was a team that was blessed with talented offensive players – Mario Lemieux, Mark Recchi, Kevin Stevens, and Paul Coffey – but said to be lacking the character and drive required to win a grinding, gruelling Stanley Cup tournament.

The North Stars had had only one previous brush with success. In the spring of 1981 they made it to the Stanley Cup final but lost in five games to the New York Islanders. A decade later, after the franchise had come perilously close to folding during the 1989-90 season, the North Stars were still struggling to be competitive and still searching for respectability. They had a new owner, Calgary real estate developer Norm Green, a new manager, Bob Clarke, and a rookie head coach, Bob Gainey. Nevertheless, they finished sixteenth overall in a twenty-one-team league with a record of twenty-seven wins, thirty-nine losses and fourteen ties.

But the North Stars quickly surprised everyone, except perhaps themselves, by staging the biggest upsets of the 1991 playoffs. They eliminated the Chicago Blackhawks, who had finished first overall in the regular season with 104 points, the St. Louis Blues, who had finished second with 103 points, and the Edmonton Oilers, the defending Stanley Cup champions.

For the media, it was the Cinderella syndrome, the miracle in Minny. The North Stars were attempting to become only the third team in NHL history, after the 1938 Black Hawks and the 1949 Leafs, to win the Stanley Cup while finishing below .500 in the regular season. A team that had drawn an average of 7,838 fans through forty regular season home games, and only one sell-out crowd, was playing before a rink full of the noisiest fans on the continent. The accepted wisdom was that Met Centre crowds were worth a goal a game to the North Stars during the 1991 playoffs. As Minnesota veteran Bobby Smith put it: "I don't think a team can really understand what it's like in here until they actually feel it. It's like nothing I've seen in hockey."

When the Stars appeared on the ice at the Met Centre for game three, 15,213 hometown fans immediately rose to their feet. The applause grew in volume until it became a blurred, overpowering roar. It lasted almost ten minutes, drowning out the player introductions and the national anthem, and only began to subside as the teams lined up for the opening faceoff. Then a thermometer-shaped "fan-o-meter" appeared on the electronic scoreboard. The roar of the crowd began rising again, and with it the red bar in the fan-o-meter. According to the meter, the fans had gone from mellow to rowdy to awesome by the time the puck had been dropped.

For the nearly three hours it took to play sixty minutes of hockey, the crowd was constantly up and down. The fans danced, clapped, hollered, screamed, whistled, and stamped their feet. They erupted over the slightest bounce or turn that was favourable to the Stars, a shot on the other team's goal, a save by their own goaltender, a clearing pass, a stiff check. Anything. Even replays on the electronic scoreboard.

The arena management did its part to keep everyone pumped. The PA system bombarded the crowd with hard rock, most often Gary Glitter's "Rock and Roll Part II," a primitive piece of music with one endlessly repeated riff that brought the fans to their feet, punching the air above them, and screaming "Hey!" The electronic scoreboard implored the crowd to cheer louder. The organist filled in with traditional sports cheers, and the NHL's only cheerleaders, four supple young women and two energetic young men called the Electric Stars, kept popping up in different parts of the arena.

Nevertheless, there were a few quiet moments during game three of the 1991 Stanley Cup final. "They weren't as telling as the silences of last December, when from inside the building you could hear snow falling outside," wrote Joe Soucheray, a columnist with the St. Paul *Pioneer Press.* "But they were small moments of perhaps exhaustion for players and fans alike. Those brief silences might have acknowledged a sinking in of a kind. This is a tough job. Winning the Stanley Cup is a long, demanding task."

As impossible as it may have seemed eight weeks earlier, the North Stars were tantalizingly close to winning it all. They won the third game of the final and led the series two games to one. They had survived the playoff grind with hot goaltending from Jon Casey, with a power play that began clicking at a record-breaking rate and by the simple expedient of grabbing the momentum. The North Stars opened all four playoff series on the road, but in each case won the first game and stripped their opponents of home-ice advantage.

It was, overall, a gritty and inspired performance from a team with a few genuine offensive stars like Brian Bellows, Mike Modano, and Dave Gagner, and some promising young players like defencemen Mark Tinordi and Neil Wilkinson. But mostly the North Stars were composed of ageing castoffs, faceless grinders, and competent but unrecognized journeymen.

The castoffs included Bobby Smith, a tall, slender, graceful centre who had started his career in Minnesota, was traded to Montreal in 1983, and shipped back to the North Stars in the summer of 1990 for a fourth-round draft choice. Then there was Brian Propp, a short, barrel-chested left-winger, who was signed as a free agent in July 1990 after playing out his contract with the Bruins. He had been to the final on four previous occasions with Philadelphia and Boston but never won. Among the grinders was left-winger Basil McRae who had spent parts of five seasons in the minors and bounced from Quebec to Toronto to Detroit and back to Quebec before landing in Minnesota. By advancing to the final, he had earned enough bonus money to buy a silver-blue 1990 Mercedes Benz 300 SEL.

But the miracle in Minny, eight weeks of hard work and a life-time of dreaming, began to evaporate in game four of the final. Pittsburgh scored three times in the first three minutes of the game and held on to win 4–3. That tied the series at two games apiece. In the pivotal fifth game at Pittsburgh, the Penguins were ahead 4–0 after fourteen minutes of play and went on to win 6–4. A couple of nights later, they humiliated the North Stars 8–0 in front of their own fans at the Met Centre.

The Penguins eventually roared past the Stars, and ultimately roasted them, largely due to the spectacular performance of Mario Lemieux, the greatest player in hockey today, when he's healthy. Lemieux had missed the first fifty games of the 1990-91 season while recovering from back surgery, and missed game three of the final due to back spasms. Nevertheless, he scored five goals and assisted on seven others in the final. And in three of the four Pittsburgh wins he either scored or set up goals that changed the direction of the game. Lemieux was the top scorer in the playoffs, was named the Most Valuable Player and removed all doubts about his character, his determination and his ability to carry a team.

In the spring of 1992, during the playoffs that capped the NHL's seventy-fifth anniversary season, and that almost didn't finish because of a players' strike, Lemieux reaffirmed his stature as hockey's greatest player. And the Penguins removed all doubts about their capabilities by winning a second straight Stanley Cup. For both Lemieux and his teammates, the championship was a joyous conclusion to a season filled with uncertainty and adversity.

Their former coach, Bob Johnson, a man many of the players regarded as a father figure, died of brain cancer before the season began. He was replaced behind the bench by Scotty Bowman, a formidable and demanding figure, who had led the Canadiens to four straight Stanley Cups during the 1970s. The Penguins also began the season playing for new owners, who were allegedly ready to unload some of the team's high-priced stars in order to cut the payroll. Before the season was over, general manager Craig Patrick had dealt Paul Coffey to the Los Angeles Kings and Mark Recchi to the Philadelphia Flyers in a three-way deal that brought Rick Tocchet and Kjell Samuelsson from Philadelphia to Pittsburgh.

All this turmoil appeared to have mortally weakened the Penguins. They finished fourth in their division and only made the playoffs with a late-season surge. They fell behind the Washington Capitals three games to one in the opening round before rebounding to eliminate the Capitals. They then knocked off the Rangers, who had finished first overall during the regular season. From that point on, the Penguins were unstoppable, even though Lemieux had to sit out five games after Ranger Adam Graves broke a bone in his hand with a vicious slash.

Pittsburgh crushed the Bruins in four games in the semi-final and swept by the Blackhawks in the minimum four games to capture the Cup. The Penguins proved that they are deep enough in talent to dominate for several seasons, provided their star players remain healthy and happy. Jaromir Jagr, a twenty-year-old sophomore from Czechoslovakia, demonstrated that he is one of the games' brightest young stars. Kevin Stevens emerged as one of the game's most potent offensive threats. Tom Barasso provided the quality goaltending a championship team requires. Pittsburgh also has defencemen, like Ulf Samuelsson, who can pound the opposition, and others, like Larry Murphy, who can move the puck.

But Lemieux towers above them all. He played in part of the Boston series and the entire final. He scored sixteen goals and accumulated thirty-four points to lead all playoff scorers, although he dressed for only fifteen games. He scored five game winners, including two in the final. According to Bowman, he was the team's best defensive player in the Chicago series. And he became the second player, after Philadelphia's Bernie Parent in 1974 and 1975, to win the Conn Smythe Trophy in consecutive seasons.

The Penguins have won both their Cups on the road, and on both occasions received tumultuous welcomes from their fans in Pittsburgh. In 1991, they flew home after thrashing the North Stars in game six. When they arrived at Greater Pittsburgh International Airport, forty thousand fans were waiting to greet them. "We didn't get out of Minnesota for about three hours after the game," defenceman Larry Murphy recalls. "I don't know what time we landed, but the fans were there and they were ecstatic. People were yelling and screaming. They were basically on top of you. The terminal was jammed wall to wall. The police had staked off a route for us, but you couldn't really move. You couldn't see anything. You couldn't tell where you were walking to. I remember in the corridor the windows on the stores were steamed right up. The humidity was unbelieveable.

"The trip out of the airport was something. We had three buses, but there were so many cars and people that the buses got split up. It took us over an hour to get out of the airport. People had left their cars everywhere. We had to take a roundabout way into the city because the roads were jammed. It was 5:30 in the morning before we got downtown."

For Murphy and his teammates, the season was finally over when they walked off their buses that morning. For hockey fans across Canada, it had ended the previous evening when they turned off their television sets. For both, it had been a long campaign. The Stanley Cup playoffs have become a marathon that only the toughest and most dedicated athletes survive. They have also become the cultural equivalent of the monsoons, a two-month deluge when Canadians are drenched in hockey.

For the past three seasons, the NHL has staggered its playoff series so that a game is available on television every night. In the spring of 1991, the CBC carried "Hockey Night in Canada" on prime time for thirteen straight nights before the puck chasers took an evening off. They went at it for another thirteen consecutive nights before taking a second breather. Then they skated eleven nights before taking a break, this one three nights in duration. By that time, only Minnesota and Pittsburgh were left standing, and they played every other night.

Perhaps the most visible victim of Canada's version of the monsoons is Peter Mansbridge, the anchor of CBC's "The National," and a man with one of the most recognizable faces in Canadian television. On one of those rare days in May 1991, a day when there were no Stanley Cup playoff games scheduled, Mansbridge sat in his cramped corner office in a CBC building on Jarvis Street in downtown Toronto. He wore a ball cap and a cardigan, blue jeans and running shoes, and had dropped into "The National" newsroom at noon hour to get a feel for the day's events, and how they would shape that evening's newscast. Most days during the Stanley Cup playoffs, when he goes on the air is almost as important as what goes on the air. At the end of each newscast, an apologetic Mansbridge explains to viewers when "The National" will be on the following night. Usually it's before the game in one part of the country, after the game in another.

"The biggest problem is we're never on at the same time," says Mansbridge. "I figure if the people you work with aren't sure when you're on, the audience really doesn't have a clue. People are phoning all the time asking when we're on. But you can't give them a definitive answer because you don't know when the game's going to end. So you hope there's some patience out there for all this. I get a lot of letters from people who are frustrated, and I share their frustration."

However, Mansbridge is enough of a realist and a good sport to take it all in stride. "There's a lot of talk about how we're body-checked around the schedules, but these last few years there's been a grudging acceptance that hockey is worth money to the CBC. I see the economic argument for it at a time when there is a very powerful all-sports network that has had a dramatic effect on audiences for all television. All we hope is that nothing big is going to happen during April and May. If [in 1991] the Gulf War had been on in those two months, instead of January and February, we would have been going nuts. I'm sure there would have been very serious fights within the CBC about who had priority. There were hints of them last year. There was relief in a lot of places in the world that the Gulf War ended as quickly as it did. There was a similar relief within the CBC."

For some Canadians, the annual deluge of televised hockey is infuriating. Periodically, a desperate plea for relief appears in the Letters to the Editors page of one of the country's newspaper. A typical outburst, written by Prince Edward Island resident Kennedy Wells, appeared in the *Globe and Mail* in the spring of 1991. "My wife and I live in a rural part of P.E.I.," Wells wrote. "Cable TV is not available to us. We receive only CBC-TV and CTV.

Reception of both is erratic. At this time of year, my wife is driven nearly mad by the surfeit of hockey on CBC-TV. Even I, who once wrote NHL roundups for The Canadian Press, find it grossly excessive. Allow us some respite."

But given the ratings for playoff hockey, the pleas of the anguished are likely to fall on deaf ears. Between April 3 and May 25, 1991, the CBC carried all or part of forty-nine playoff games on forty-three nights. According to figures compiled by the network and A. C. Nielson Co. of Canada, the average audience per minute for all those games was 1.8 million viewers, up eighty-five thousand from the previous spring. On April 14, 1991, an estimated 7.5 million Canadians, almost one in three, were watching hockey when the CBC carried a Los Angeles-Vancouver game in B.C. and a Calgary-Edmonton game in the rest of the country. Even the fact that two American-based teams made it to the 1991 Stanley Cup final did not dampen the enthusiasm of Canadian sports fans. The six-game playoff between Pittsburgh and Minnesota drew audiences ranging from 1.7 million to 2.3 million viewers.

Apart from their size, the other notable characteristic about hockey audiences is their loyalty. They stick around till the final whistle. The last game of the 1991 Stanley Cup finals attracted 2.3 million viewers per minute even though the outcome was decided early. That game was the top-ranked program of the week, edging out "America's Funniest Home Videos" on CTV by ten thousand viewers.

Despite its enduring popularity with the Canadian public, hockey has probably reached the limits of its growth. What began a century ago as a six-week season and a one, two, or three-game showdown for the Stanley Cup has turned into a six-month season and an eight-week tournament. Contemporary champions must face four opponents and win sixteen games. The playoffs have become a punishing grind, and no player who has gone the distance is likely to forget the experience. "All you did was think hockey for two straight months," says former

Islander Clark Gillies. "The emotional highs and lows are just something that stick in your mind forever; the gut wrenching feeling of not being able to sleep, and hardly being able to eat for two months."

But winning the Cup, and successfully defending it, have never been easy. In those early one-game, sudden death showdowns, or two-game, total-goal series, or best-of-three playoffs, a poor outing almost certainly meant defeat. The margin for error was much narrower than it is today. There was no advance scouting of the opposition, no films available to study an opponent, no plus-minus statistics, no lists of strengths and weaknesses. Defending champions frequently got their first look at a challenger when the players stepped off the train and on to the ice for a practice session. The local paper usually offered the following tidy summary about the opposition: "They looked to be in the pink of condition but not much is known about the strangers."

Even though the contemporary Stanley Cup tournament appears to bear little resemblance to the early Cup battles, a remarkable number of things haven't changed. There has always been heartbreak on the losing side and hysteria on the winning side. Rings were first presented to the winners in 1893, and they were presented periodically over the years until the early 1960s, when such a gesture became an annual practice. Victory parades have been held from time to time since 1902, when the Little Men of Iron returned to Montreal after defeating the Winnipeg Victorias. Fans have always gone to extraordinary efforts lengths to attend Stanley Cup games, whether it was three young men travelling to Winnipeg from "upper Saskatchewan" in 1902, or Nancy Leach and her friends driving 880 miles overnight from Pittsburgh to Minnesota in May 1991.

From the beginning, the players have done some strange things with their coveted Cup. The Silver Seven once booted it on to the frozen Rideau Canal. The 1924 Montreal Canadiens left it in a snowbank after repairing a flat tire on the way to a victory party. Another group of Canadiens forgot it in a photo studio, and it was used as a flower pot. Guy Lafleur left it on his mother's front lawn overnight in Thurso, Quebec. Bryan Trottier and his wife slept with it. And the Edmonton Oilers allowed an exotic dancer to use the Cup during her routine at a local strip club.

Over the decades, the Stanley Cup playoffs have showcased the talents of the game's biggest stars. All the great ones, from Frank McGee to Mario Lemieux, fired up by a potent combination of adrenaline and desire, have used this yearly ritual to soar a little higher than normal and to reaffirm their greatness. The Stanley Cup playoffs have also turned average players, like the Mel Hills and the Modere Bruneteaus of this world, into comets, who appear when nerves are frayed and knuckles are white, when the score is tied and the game up for grabs. They blaze before our eyes, dazzling us for a few moments with great goals or brilliant saves before sliding back into mediocrity. Yet their feats earn these ordinary men a little bit of immortality, a place among the legends of the game.

Other players have earned lasting renown by ignoring cuts, bruises, and serious injuries to compete for the Stanley Cup. It's called playing hurt, and it started in December of 1896 when a fellow named Toat Campbell of the Winnipeg Victorias played the last half of a Cup game with two broken ribs against the advice of the team doctor. Frank McGee played the last two games of a 1905 series with a cracked wrist. Alex Shibicky skated on a cracked ankle for the New York Rangers in the 1940 final and Bobby Baun played with a similar injury in 1962. In 1988, Edmonton Oiler Kevin Lowe played with a broken wrist and two cracked ribs. All of these athletes were merely following the hockey player's creed, as articulated by a swaggering Cyclone Taylor in 1909. "When the Stanley Cup is at stake," the Cyclone boasted, "I can stand any amount of pain."

What is it that makes an athlete go to such lengths to win? Foolhardy machismo, some might say. Sheer lunacy is another possibility. Indeed, hockey players, not downhill skiers, were the original crazy Canucks. But for Lester Patrick, whose career as a player, executive, and student of the game spanned half a century, there was a simple and timeless explanation for the hockey player's mad will to win. "Call them pros, call them mercenaries, but in fact they're just grown-up kids who've learned on the frozen creek or the flooded corner lot that hockey is the greatest thrill in this life."

From the very beginning, the game has been a compelling spectacle, one that has grabbed the emotions and captured the interest of the Maritimes and the West, of French Quebec and English Ontario, of native and newcomer alike. Bruce Hutchison, one of the most eloquent and articulate writers this country ever produced, put it as well as anyone when he wrote in 1950: "Canadians play hockey, talk hockey and dream hockey as naturally as they breathe. Hockey, better than any other thing, expresses Canada. It is, perhaps, our only truly national expression that cuts across language, race, age and distance."

And it is a fact that Canada's game grew up around the simple silver cup that Frederick Arthur Stanley donated in 1893. The Cup was a tremendous catalyst that stimulated competition between leagues, between cities, and between the regions of a far-flung and wildly improbable country. The Stanley Cup has become a cultural phenomenon that has linked Canadians from coast to coast, from decade to decade, and from generation to generation. From the 1890s to the late 1920s, hockey fans gathered around telegraph machines to catch the play-by-plays of big games, particularly Stanley Cup matches. From the early 1930s to the late 1950s, they huddled around their radios. Today, they sit around the television set.

All of this harkens back to an even earlier time when the family or the tribe sat around the fire and when a storyteller or a wise man provided the entertainment. In Canada, the ice surface replaced the fire and the stands replaced the circle. Instead of listening to a story or a fable or a legend, we watched a game, one of our own creation, a game that created heroes and legends, and never more so than when opposing teams players fought for the Stanley Cup.

There is no question that the Stanley Cup, or the pursuit of it, put some sparkle into the hard lives and the bleak towns or our forefathers. And even in these pampered, affluent times, the Stanley Cup shines on like an old and faithful beacon in the minds and hearts of Canadians from coast to coast. For the Stanley Cup occupies a special place in the life of our nation, in the hearts of our children, and in the dreams of anyone who has ever laced on a pair of skates, picked up a hockey stick, and fired a puck. It is, one might say, the Canadian grail.

ACKNOWLEDGEMENTS

In the fifteen months that it took to produce this book, I spent hundreds of hours in libraries reading newspaper accounts of Stanley Cup games, and many more hours at the computer, attempting to do justice to the material. However, the most enjoyable part of the entire project was the time I spent talking to dozens of active and retired NHL players. Their first-hand accounts of Stanley Cup games became an integral part of the book, and I am deeply indebted to those players.

I would like to express my gratitude to three former players, Frank Finnigan, Jim Thompson, and Bob Goldham, who have since passed away. Thanks are also due to Bob Gainey, Randy Gregg, Larry Murphy, and several others who set aside time for interviews and the hectic NHL schedule. I am also grateful to Maurice Richard, Bernie Geoffrion, Murray Wilson, and all the other former Montreal Canadiens who shared their memories with me. And I am equally grateful to Bobby Hull, Bobby Orr, Allan Stanley, and Clark Gillies for their contributions.

Thanks must go to the hockey writers of Canada and the United States who have covered the Stanley Cup for a century. Their colourful and spirited accounts of Cup play have enriched this history. I would like to thank Steve Hopkins, Ric Dolphin, and my brother, Greg, for their invaluable advice. I would also like to acknowledge the help I received from hockey historian James Duplacey, whose quick answers to innumerable queries saved me hours of work. Finally, I want to thank Doug Gibson and Dinah Forbes of McClelland & Stewart for giving me the opportunity to write this book.

INDEX